Specialist Journalism

Combining practical 'how to' skills with reflection on the place of each specialism in the industry, this guide features the skills needed to cover specialist areas, including writing match reports for sport, reviewing the arts and dealing with complex information for science. This book will also discuss how specialist journalists have contributed to the mainstream news agenda, as well as analysing how different issues have been covered in each specialism, such as the credit crunch, global warming, national crime statistics and the celebrity culture in sport. Areas covered include:

- Sport
- Business
- Politics
- Crime
- Environment
- Fashion
- Food
- Music

- Media
- Science
- Health
- Law
- Travel
- War
- Wine

Contributors: Geoff Adams, Julie Bradford, Paul Bradshaw, Tim Hannigan, Paula Hearsum, Steve Jones, Sarah Lonsdale, Ben McConville, Colm Murphy, Mark Nicholls, Andrew Noakes, Richard Orange, Kevin Rafter, Sophie Schünemann, Kate Smith, Nick Spencer, Ben Taylor, Barry Turner, Robert Whitaker.

Barry Turner is Senior Lecturer in Media Law and Public Administration at the University of Lincoln and at The Centre for Broadcasting and Journalism, Nottingham Trent University, UK. Barry is also Senior Lecturer in Science and Environmental Journalism and teaches in Forensic and Biomedical Sciences and in Mental Health Law.

Richard Orange is Managing Director of Orchard News Bureau Ltd, a media consultancy and online publishing business, which specialises in media law, local government and winter sports journalism. He has worked as a general news reporter, sub-editor and political correspondent for newspapers in Bristol, Cheshire, Staffordshire and Lincolnshire. He also worked as a lecturer in journalism, teaching media law, public administration, newswriting and freelancing skills.

Specialist Journalism

Edited by
Barry Turner and Richard Orange

Routledge
Taylor & Francis Group

LONDON AND NEW YORK

First published 2013
by Routledge
2 Park Square, Milton Park, Abingdon, Oxon OX14 4RN

Simultaneously published in the USA and Canada
by Routledge
711 Third Avenue, New York, NY 10017

Routledge is an imprint of the Taylor & Francis Group, an informa business

British Library Cataloguing in Publication Data
A catalogue record for this book is available from the British Library

Library of Congress Cataloging in Publication Data
Specialist journalism / edited by Barry Turner and Richard Orange.
p. cm.
Includes bibliographical references and index.
1. Specialized journalism–Vocational guidance. I. Turner, Barry, 1954–
II. Orange, Richard, 1963–
PN4784.S58S63 2012
070.4'4–dc23
2012021939

ISBN: 978-0-415-58284-1 (hbk)
ISBN: 978-0-415-58285-8 (pbk)
ISBN: 978-0-203-14664-4 (ebk)

Typeset in Baskerville
by Taylor & Francis Books

MIX
Paper from
responsible sources
FSC
www.fsc.org   FSC® C004839

Printed and bound in Great Britain by the MPG Books Group

Contents

List of contributors   vii
Foreword by Phillip Knightley   xi

Introduction   1
RICHARD ORANGE WITH BARRY TURNER

1 Sports reporting   11
   NICK SPENCER

2 Business journalism   20
   COLM MURPHY

3 Political journalism   30
   KEVIN RAFTER

4 Crime reporting   39
   BARRY TURNER

5 International journalism   50
   BEN MCCONVILLE AND KATE SMITH

6 Environmental journalism   59
   SARAH LONSDALE

7 Automotive journalism   69
   ANDREW NOAKES

8 Fashion journalism   79
   JULIE BRADFORD

9 Food journalism   96
   STEVE JONES AND BEN TAYLOR

10 Music journalism   107
    PAULA HEARSUM

11 Media reporting   124
    PAUL BRADSHAW

12 Science journalism   134
    SOPHIE SCHÜNEMANN

13 Medical reporting   147
    ROBERT WHITAKER

14 Legal affairs journalism   160
    RICHARD ORANGE

15 Travel journalism   171
    TIM HANNIGAN

16 War reporting   181
    MARK NICHOLLS

17 Wine journalism   192
    GEOFF ADAMS

    Directory of useful websites   201
    Index   204

List of contributors

Geoff Adams is a published author, journalist and broadcaster. He regularly freelances for various magazines, books, newspapers and the BBC. He is an expert on the subject of wine journalism and is regarded as the foremost expert in the UK on the wines of Greece. His articles have appeared in *Decanter*, *Harpers Wine and Spirits International*, *Drinks International* and *The Journal*, among other magazines. He is also well known in his home city of Lincoln as being the regular wine columnist for *The Lincolnshire Echo*. As well as maintaining a freelance career in journalism, Geoff lectures at the University of Lincoln's School of Journalism, where he is also reading for his Doctorate in Journalism.

Julie Bradford is head of BA (Hons) Fashion Journalism at the University of Sunderland, UK. She worked for 15 years as a journalist for newspapers and for *Agence France-Presse* in the Middle East and Paris. She is currently working on a book, *Fashion Journalism*, for Routledge.

Paul Bradshaw is a visiting professor at City University London, a Course Leader for the MA in Online Journalism at Birmingham City University, and a freelance trainer, speaker and writer. He has a background in magazine editing and editorial website management and has contributed to several books about the internet and journalism.

Tim Hannigan is an author and travel journalist, specialising in South-East Asia and the Indian Subcontinent. He studied journalism at the University of Gloucestershire, UK, before moving to Indonesia where he wrote for various newspapers and magazines, including the *Jakarta Post* and *Jakarta Globe*. His first book, *Murder in the Hindu Kush: George Hayward and the Great Game*, was shortlisted for the Boardman Tasker Prize for Mountain Literature. He continues to write on travel and history for various publications in Asia, the UK and the Middle East, and divides his time between Cornwall and Indonesia.

Paula Hearsum is a Senior Lecturer in Popular Music and Journalism at the University of Brighton, UK. She was previously a music journalist, whose published work includes a biography of the *Manic Street Preachers: Design for Living* (Virgin, 1996). Her current research surrounds the journalistic representation of musicians and death.

Steve Jones and **Ben Taylor** are Principal Lecturers at Nottingham Trent University, UK. They are the co-authors (with Bob Ashley and Joanne Hollows) of *Food and Cultural Studies* (Routledge, 2004) and have written, separately and together, on a wide range of issues concerning food, society and culture.

Sarah Lonsdale is a lecturer in Reporting and Writing at the University of Kent's Centre for Journalism, UK. She has been a journalist for 25 years and worked as a reporter on the *Observer* newspaper before going freelance. She has been writing her weekly 'Be Green' column in the *Sunday Telegraph* since 2006, covering topics including climate change, biodiversity and community environmental action, and for which she has been nominated for and won a number of awards.

Ben McConville is a Principal Lecturer in Journalism at Northumbria University, UK. He is a regular contributor to the Associated Press news agency, former New York correspondent for *The Scotsman* and former International Editor for *Scotland on Sunday*.

Colm Murphy is Head of School of Media, Film and Journalism at University of Ulster in Northern Ireland and a researcher at its Centre for Media Research. He is compiler of *The Sunday Times* Irish Rich List. He established bureau for a real-time financial news service, Emerging Markets plc, in Russia, Turkey, Poland, India, Israel and South Korea. He also helped float the company in the mid-1990s. Prior to this he was business editor of *The Sunday Tribune* in Dublin. He holds a PhD in economic policy to promote high-tech development and has a degree in finance and masters in interactive media.

Mark Nicholls wrote on defence issues for the *Eastern Daily Press*, England's biggest selling regional morning newspaper, for almost ten years. He has reported from eastern Turkey and the activities of RAF Jaguars covering the no-fly zones over northern Iraq, accompanied the Royal Anglian Regiment to Kabul in 2002, and reported on the Iraq War of 2003 as an embedded correspondent with the RAF Tornado squadrons at the Ali Al Salem airbase in northern Kuwait. He returned to Iraq in 2004 to report on the impact of the conflict on Basra one year after the war ended, sailed aboard HMS *Norfolk* in the Persian Gulf as part of seagoing security patrol and surveillance operations and again joined A Company of the 1st Battalion Royal Anglian Regiment in northern Helmand province in 2007, based in the notorious Sangin area.

Andrew Noakes has worked in automotive media for 20 years, as a journalist, editor, photographer and author. In 2006 he became senior lecturer on the Automotive Journalism MA course at Coventry University, UK, at the same time continuing to freelance for a variety of magazines and automotive websites. Andrew has served on the committee of the Guild of Motoring Writers since 2011, and wrote the Guild's guide to entering motoring journalism, *So You Want to be a Motoring Writer*.

Richard Orange is managing director of Orchard News Bureau Ltd, a media consultancy and online publishing business, which specialises in media law, local government and winter sports journalism. He worked as a general news reporter, sub-editor and political correspondent for newspapers in Bristol, Cheshire, Staffordshire and Lincolnshire. He also worked as a lecturer in journalism, teaching media law, public administration, news-writing and freelancing skills. Richard recently took a professional law training course, specialising in employment and commercial law, attends alpine sports events as a writer–photographer, and has written a travel guide to Switzerland.

Kevin Rafter worked for over a decade as a political journalist based at Leinster House in Dublin working in print for the *Irish Times* and *The Sunday Times* and as a radio presenter and television correspondent with RTE, the Irish national broadcaster. During this time he reported on elections in Scotland and Germany as well as from Westminster including Tony Blair's election victory in 1997 and the first mayor contest in London. He now works as a senior lecturer in political communication and journalism at Dublin City University, and is the author/editor of nine books including *Irish Journalism Before Independence: More a Disease than a Profession* (Manchester University Press, 2011).

Sophie Schünemann has a Masters in Science and Environmental Journalism from Lincoln University, UK. Her dissertation focused on the way in which ADHD is portrayed in the media.

Kate Smith is Programme Leader of BA (Hons) Journalism at Edinburgh Napier University, UK, and is a columnist, journalist and award-winning fiction and non-fiction writer.

Nick Spencer is a freelance sports journalist. He covered 1,000-plus football matches in more than 20 countries for the *Yorkshire Post* and *Daily Telegraph* before concentrating on production in old and new media for the *Telegraph*. Nick has spent 2012 writing and working for the official Wimbledon tennis website and as an editor and sports information specialist at the 2012 Olympic and Paralympic Games. He lives in south-west London.

Barry Turner is Senior Lecturer in Media Law and Public Administration at the University of Lincoln and at The Centre for Broadcasting and Journalism, Nottingham Trent University, UK. Barry is also Senior Lecturer in Science and Environmental Journalism and teaches in Forensic and Biomedical Sciences and in Mental Health Law.

Robert Whitaker is the author of four books. His most recent book, *Anatomy of an Epidemic: Magic Bullets, Psychiatric Drugs, and the Astonishing Rise of Mental Illness in America,* won the Investigative Reporters and Editors book award for best investigative journalism in 2010. Prior to writing books, Robert worked as the science and medical reporter at the *Albany Times Union* newspaper in

New York for a number of years. His journalism articles won several national awards, including a George Polk award for medical writing, and a National Association of Science Writers' award for best magazine article. A series he co-wrote for *The Boston Globe* was named a finalist for the Pulitzer Prize in 1998.

Foreword

Phillip Knightley

As a general reporter for most of my career I was always suspicious of specialist journalists. They adopted superior airs, had the mentality of a secret lodge, got annoyed when you tried to prise information from them and protected their contacts like gold dust. Why would any newspaper need them? This book answers my fears and my questions. The modern world is so complex that it is too much to expect journalists to "know it all".

The editor points out that the "jack of all trades" approach is peculiar to the media and that other professions sharing traits with journalism understand and encourage specialisation. With some subjects it is essential. Few medical reporters would attempt to explain to their readers a new medical development without interviewing physicians and researchers in the field. Only when they were confident that they had mastered an understanding of the process and could "translate" it in an interesting manner would they write the story.

I find this convincing and many of the other journalists who have contributed to this book make equally persuasive cases for their chosen specialities. But what about the risks of devoting many years, a professional lifetime in some cases, to single topics? The main risk is that one becomes too intimate with one's sources and too anxious to protect them. This is especially so with some forms of sports reporting. Sports journalists rely heavily on their contacts for the inside information that provides stories. If they offend those contacts they risk being isolated, cut off from the news and gossip.

Take cricket and "sledging", the exchange of insults between the batsman and the fielding side designed to disrupt the batsman's concentration. I have long argued that unless cricket writers tell their readers exactly what has been said, the readers are unable to judge whether the remarks are acceptable or beyond the pale. Cricket writers argue that the good name of cricket depends on everyone following the admonition: "What's said on the field, remains on the field." I suggest that until cricket writers have the courage to break this practice by telling the whole story, they are short-changing their readers and harming their trade.

Similar ethical pitfalls exist for travel, motoring and food specialists. Should travel writers accept holidays, cruises and hotel accommodation from travel companies? Is it all right if they accept but declare the fact that they have to their readers? May motoring writers who need a new car buy one from a manufacturer at a reduced price? Should restaurant critics always pay for their meals? Journalists are human beings with human strengths and failings. We cannot expect them to lead friendless professional lives. But the care they need to exercise, especially those who are specialist journalists, needs a lot of reflection and guidance. This book does its best to provide both.

Introduction

Richard Orange with Barry Turner

In 1758 the great chronicler of his time Dr. Samuel Johnson wrote:

> A news writer is a man without virtue who writes lies at home for his own profit. To these compositions is required neither genius nor knowledge, neither industry nor sprightliness, but contempt of shame and indifference to the truth are absolutely necessary.[1]

What is specialist journalism? Why is it in a reporter's interests to develop expertise in a particular field? How is it done? These are some of the practical questions this book sets out to address. Contributing authors also pose some critical and ethical questions. Is a specialist reporter to be trusted, simply because he or she knows more about the topic than a colleague? Is he or she siding with the public, the advertiser or the people in the hierarchy of the particular field (what the Sir Humphrey Applebys of the world term 'going native')? What does recent history tell us about the relationship between the journalist and his or her quarry, such as the police, the travel industry, or celebrities and sports stars? So this is a practical guide aimed at both journalism students and active reporters eager to carve out a niche in a shifting employment market. It is also a critique of modern specialist journalism.

Of necessity, there is a limit to the number of specialist topics that any single volume may explore with such a diverse choice. Some disciplines would be regarded as essential elements in the editorial portfolio of any self-respecting newspaper from the last two centuries. Dust off an old copy of the *News Chronicle*, *Daily Express* or *Manchester Guardian* and column inches would be filled by an in-house horse racing correspondent, a theatre critic and religious affairs expert *et al*.

From a Fleet Street-centric perspective, niche topics really took off in the print media during the 1980s, with the arrival of the bulky Sunday supplements. In the 1990s the daily broadsheet papers, notably the *Guardian*, placed correspondents' offerings into regular pull-out sections, complemented with a lucrative sprinkling of 'Situations Vacant' advertising. *The Sunday Times* continues to produce its sports, travel and business sections, and the *Guardian* retains its weekly media, education and society supplements, albeit with fewer job adverts. But the real expansion in specialist journalism occurred in the periodicals market. As traditional newspaper circulations continue to decline, the magazine sector has flourished. Thousands of titles adorn shelves, packed with articles, reviews, pictures and features from an army of (mainly) freelance contributors. Media companies that once employed dedicated defence, farming, Court of Appeal and local government correspondents are more likely to carry copy from correspondents acknowledged as authorities on social internet websites, home entertainment technology, consumer protection, human rights, the pharmaceutical business and freedom of information et al.

This book offers a selection of typical specialist vocations likely to be of interest to the aspiring reporter, sprinkled with informative 'A Day in the Life Of' contributions from working journalists. Subjects such as sport, crime, health and politics could each fill the pages of a substantial textbook, but the objective is to provide students and professional writers with a taste of key topics. Sports journalists go through a similar procedure whether they are reporting on football games, rugby matches, cycle events or alpine winter sports races. They need to hear the verdicts of the team coach and leading athletes, the lessons learned and the preparations for the next big game or race. Specialist local government reporters and political journalists working in Parliament secure access to people in the public eye and hold them to account in tandem. General news reporters and health correspondents have no lesser or greater access to hospital patients or nursing staff and travel writers contend with airport security checks, delayed flights, crowds and queues at holiday destinations (along with the rest of us). The authors have drawn out common themes within their disciplines, considered some of the ethical and practical dilemmas facing working journalists and shine a spotlight on positive and negative aspects of the profession.

What is it that defines a 'specialist' reporter from a 'general' reporter? Common sense dictates that specialist skills are derived from either educational study (such as knowledge of the law) or from first-hand experience (for example 'coalface' politics). A reporter is unlikely to be regarded as an expert on a discipline by token of his/her academic qualifications. Is a 'general' reporter (including general sports reporters) in-expert? Surely not. Gavin MacFadyen, director of the Centre for Investigative Journalism,[2] and *Flat Earth News* author Nick Davies[3] have made the same point at media conferences that any journalism requires an element of investigative effort by the reporter. Any self-respecting scribe must look behind the press release hand-out and check the facts, figures, quotes and assertions. Why should it be different for a general news reporter?

Trainees and reporters are expected to cope with the traditional specialist areas such as crime, education, political and business stories. A general news reporter would be ridiculed for declining an instruction to cover an agricultural show on the basis that 'I don't know much about farming', or seek to excuse him/herself from an ecumenical story, or steer clear of reviewing a theatre performance on similar grounds. Newsdesks and editors expect any reporter to be sufficiently trained to cover court cases – from the relatively mundane to a major murder trial – without committing contempt of court or missing out key details of the case. That does not mean they are legal affairs specialists. Alternatively the expectations of the industry veer towards the overly optimistic and unrealistic demand that the reporter should be able to turn his or her hand to anything.

The conventional newspaper approach is that a general news reporter needs to know the essentials about … pretty much everything. 'We want a Jack (or Jill) of all trades; someone who can cover an inquest in the morning, a trade union demonstration at lunchtime, a government ministerial visit to the town in the afternoon, and a golden wedding anniversary at teatime' is the well-worn phrase that many a trainee would have heard from the editor or news editor of the local weekly paper either at the job interview or on the first day of work experience. In journalistic folklore those were the newsroom bosses boasting of an education from 'the school of hard knocks and the university of life'.[4] The risk is that many reporters and news editors have insufficient time to acquire more than a basic grasp of health, business, education, local government, taxation, criminal justice and policing issues, before moving on to regional or national dailies, or provincial and national broadcasters. Knowledge of the subject is reliant on local circumstances and dependant on individual relationships between journalists and their contacts. Specialist reporters will encounter job application problems if they possess an overly-parochial pedigree.

Comparisons with professions sharing traits with journalism suggest that the 'Jack of all trades' approach is peculiar to the media. Solicitors and barristers are required to choose from a series of elective subjects while completing the legal practice or bar courses. Lawyers do not take on a wide portfolio of work, principally because of the risk of exposing themselves to professional negligence actions arising from sub-standard advice or performance. It is precisely to avoid over-stretching resources that legal partnerships specialise and recruit in particular disciplines (criminal representation, property conveyance, wills and trusts, employment or commercial law, medical negligence claims, libel and privacy litigation or exclusive fields such as equestrian, town planning and shipping law et al). Likewise, applicants in the teaching profession are expected to cover a range of topics at primary school but vacancies in secondary, sixth form, further education and university levels invariably call on candidates to demonstrate knowledge, skill and experience in specialist areas.

Vocations closer to journalism (i.e., advertising, marketing and public relations) also tend towards 'niche' markets and client bases because it is in their commercial interests to develop a 'brand' identity and reputation as leaders in a particular field. 'Advertorial' writers may well be expected to turn their hand to a wide variety of assignments but the long-term success of the business depends on the team's ability to build and maintain a strong portfolio. PR and advertising agency websites showcase and emphasise the talents, expertise and achievements of the respective executives and employees, because conventional wisdom is that is what impresses and attracts clients. Not much room for a 'Jack of all trades' recruitment policy here.

The 'consumer' and 'B2B' ends of the journalism market (from national products such as *The Economist*, *Condé Nast Travel*, *Private Eye*, *The Times Higher Education Supplement*, *New Scientist* and *Legal Week* to national and provincial 'leisure' titles such as *Nottinghamshire Life*, *Daily Mail Ski and Snowboard Magazine*, *Garden News* and *Motorcycle News*) provide specialist journalists with job openings that have all but dried up in the newspaper industry. Although competition can be just as fierce, the employment prospects for students on university journalism courses and reporters in the local and regional press and broadcast sector can only improve where candidates demonstrate prior knowledge, skills and expertise in a subject of interest to readers and viewers rather than serve time in the newsroom in expectation of 'learning on the job'.

Fortunately, direct employment is but one avenue open to aspiring reporters, feature writers and correspondents. Freelance journalists have found print and broadcast sectors to be lucrative sources of revenue in the past. However, as income from newspaper sales and advertising declined from the late 1990s and into the last decade so editors found their freelance budgets trimmed and in some cases cut out altogether. Robert Maxwell was one of the first Fleet Street proprietors to engage in a cull of casual freelance labour starting with the sub-editing department.[5] Accountants, chief executives, editors-in-chief and finance directors in weeklies, dailies, commercial radio stations and BBC local radio outlets were not slow to spot that they could axe freelance agencies, pare lineage to the bone and rely instead on a steady supply of material from students anxious to gain a foothold in the business without insisting on standard NUJ[6] rates. Who could blame the media companies, given the burgeoning numbers of undergraduates and postgraduates signing onto journalism, advertising and marketing courses appearing in more major towns and cities?

Again the circumstances appear to favour the freelance journalist pre-equipped with the 'specialist' background, because the knowledgeable and well-connected reporter should be able to get to the relevant facts, to the key people, to de-code the technical data and understand the context and relevance of the story quickly, effectively and efficiently. Take the example of a journalist who found herself parachuted into the local government role on a provincial daily newspaper, a day after a big story concerning a corruption probe[7] broke at a council. She was given the weekend to turn out a news report and a background briefing. The scandal involved technical aspects of local government legislation, legal title to ownership of land, the impact of another council's designation of the land for alternative agricultural and commercial development rights, and previous statements made by councillors in planning meetings. It was more complicated than, for example, a story about an MP claiming expenses for a second home, or claiming expenses for a mortgage that either didn't exist or had already been repaid. After a weekend of ringing around contacts and producing a substantial and informative feature, the reporter confessed that it had felt as though she had 'just had to cram an entire law degree into the space of a couple of days'.[8]

This is where specialist freelance journalists have an advantage, because they can devote more research time to their own stories without the pressure of an immediate deadline and can 'hit the ground running'. While freelance court reporters and sports journalists are largely chasing the clock, the same does not always apply to 'niche' writers. Freelance travel writers, self-employed fashion, music, motoring and science reporters can afford less of the 'ambulance chaser' *modus operandi*. Health, crime, politics and business topics are more likely to be a mix of the two extremes. The features desk can rely on the freelance motoring correspondent to produce authoritative, entertaining and well researched copy.

However, a key problem for freelance journalists is one of resources. Their in-house counterparts have greater scope to handle major investigations, regardless of whether the journalist has any detailed grounding in the topic. The steps that the *Daily Telegraph* took before it went public with its MPs expenses probe (never mind the cost of acquiring the computer discs from the whistleblowers) shows the value of pooling resources and spending days if not weeks on inquiries, including the most time-consuming background checks. Two of the investigators, Robert Winnett and Gordon Rayner, recount in *No Expenses Spared*[9] how colleague Holly Watt was tasked to trawl through MPs' residential and second home claims and cross check details with the HM Land Registry records. It was diligent but 'tedious' work which more than paid off when Watt identified ex-MP Elliott Morley's repeated claims for a mortgage that had already been re-paid to the lender. The newspaper was also able to deploy its specialist crime correspondent Richard Edwards to 'sound out' his contacts at Scotland Yard about the likely reaction to the revelations before the story ran.

We need to distinguish 'specialist journalism' from experience derived from day-to-day investigations. A general news reporter may develop in-depth, technical and valuable knowledge whilst engaged on a particular story (as the above example shows). It is commonplace in the provincial press for business reporters to assist on election night, for the political correspondent to act as Sunday shift duty reporter, for the education specialist to cover courts, inquests and employment tribunals, or for the football writer to carry a digital camera in case they witness a newsworthy incident. Moreover in-house journalists hold down a 'brief' only at the behest of the incumbent editor, and re-deployments are commonplace at the local and provincial level.

This book places specialist topics in neat compartments, but an in-house reporter will be expected to work on a variety of subjects during his or her employment stint at a national, regional, periodical or broadcast outlet. A media 'specialism' is more than a running total of scoops and lucrative contacts, or the product of a learned newsgathering and fact-checking technique. Without detracting from the achievements of the *Telegraph* expenses team, one does not become an expert on the rules governing property ownership and trust funds by familiarising oneself with the Land Registry system. A 'specialist' needs a wider appreciation of the law, of commercial practices and with criminal investigation procedures before he or she can join all of the dots. Case law (i.e., the Reynolds defence[10]) requires a journalist to be pragmatic, methodical, fair and open-minded when it comes to investigating a potential crime or wrongdoing. The manner in which the reporter scrutinises paperwork, evidence and invites a response from the subject of the story (as exemplified by Watts' approaches to Morley[11]) is critical where there is an intention to claim publication in the public interest. A 'trial and error' approach of 'learning on the job' is reckless and career threatening.

Freelance specialists are at an advantage where there is pressure on editorial management to re-shuffle internal responsibilities either to make room for a newcomer or to cover for staff holidays or for a departing journalist. Sir Humphrey Appleby's boss in *Yes Minister*, cabinet secretary Sir Arnold Robinson, quipped that prime ministers relish reshuffles because they keep everyone on their toes (the subtext being that the civil service mandarins encourage reshuffles to make it more difficult for ministers to get to grips with their Whitehall departments). Power goes with permanence and rotation is castration, as Sir Arnold put it.[12] In-house specialist correspondents can be re-deployed at an editor's whim, not necessarily out of desire but sometimes out of departmental necessity.

To the extent that freelance specialists have a market for their wares, they are their own bosses. This is not to acknowledge that many freelance journalists lost their jobs and livelihoods during the last 20 years, because regional and national newspapers and broadcasters slashed agency budgets. As Nick Davies and his team of Cardiff School of Journalism researchers observed: 'National newsdesks cut back on commissioning stories from the agencies and froze the prices of those they did commission. The agencies started to shed jobs and then close.'[13] *Flat Earth News* identified a series of major criminal trials, including some which exposed police corruption, in the 1990s which went unreported. But all this indicates is that it is economically unviable to run an old-style big-town agency employing half a dozen reporters. It does not mean that individual journalists are unable to make a living – or at least to supplement a main career – by supplying newspapers, magazines, websites and broadcasters with 'niche' market stories.

Where there is a healthy, professional relationship and a newsroom sufficiently staffed to absorb personnel changes then specialist reporters have scope to flex their muscles and sometimes at a personal cost, as BBC political stalwart and former Independent editor Andrew Marr testifies in his narrative *My Trade*. Marr recalls a productive story-wise friendship with ex-Tory minister John Patten and his family until things went wrong.

> As education secretary his policies were unraveling. Instead of writing supportively I joined the critical pack. It seemed to me the correct objective judgement of his performance, and therefore a kind of journalistic duty. It seemed to him a personal betrayal and he never forgave me. The cynical but professional answer is to have a range of good sources with more always under cultivation.[14]

Nowadays not all principal sources need to be human. The *Guardian* reported world wide web pioneer Sir Tim Berners-Lee, at a data.gov.uk launch in 2010, as claiming that 'data driven journalism is the future'. 'Journalists need to be data-savvy' he told delegates.

> It used to be that you would get stories by chatting to people in bars, and it still might be that you'll do it that way some times. But now it's also going to be about poring over data and equipping yourself with the tools to analyse it and picking out what's interesting. And keeping it in perspective, helping people out by really seeing where it all fits together, and what's going on in the country.[15]

The London-based Centre for Investigative Journalism runs regular 'data mining' and 'forensic accountancy' workshops aimed at encouraging students and free-lances to unearth exclusives buried within financial spreadsheets and governmental records. In the USA, similar training 'webinars' are staged by the Reynolds Centre for Business Journalism.[16] Experts[17] on 'Computer Assisted Reporting' from both sides of the Atlantic regularly demonstrate software packages to aspiring and working journalists, using programs from Excel to ArcMap to transform raw statistics into graphic and compelling images, diagrams and league tables. Maps identifying hotspots and trends relating to everything from knife crime and unemployment, to housing and health problems leap out at the reader. Where it would take considerable effort to explain from interviews and in words alone that a particular city neighbourhood had sustained higher than expected damage from a hurricane, a 'data expert' could tell and sell the story at the touch of a button. While city buildings in the affluent districts withstood the storm, the graphic image alerts the sharp-eyed journalist to the fact that more homes in poorer neighbourhoods more distant from the strongest winds collapsed. The case for an official investigation into potential corruption and cost-cutting by construction firms and poor supervision by government inspectors gathers strength.

Human nature being what it is, editors should be mindful that specialist reporters holding down a 'brief' for a lengthy period are vulnerable to forging too 'cosy' a relationship with organisations and senior figures within the respective hierarchies. Journalists tasked to hold public officials, politicians, corporate bosses, senior sports administrators, police and health executives to account tread a difficult path between keeping sources and contacts at 'arms length' on one hand, but close enough to maintain confidentiality and mutual respect on the other. More often than not it goes wrong. Take the example of a crime reporter on a regional newspaper incautious enough to allow a force press officer overhear him telling a fellow journalist that 'if the Chief Constable decides he is going to deny saying something, then there is not much I can do about that as it is my word against his'.[18] There must be a proper degree of trust between the reporter and the editor, where a verbatim shorthand note survives a sustained complaint from the local force.

Unfortunately some provincial editors do not do enough to remind journalists where their loyalties should lie. Too many media executives rub shoulders with the 'high and mighty'. If reporters suspect or know that senior MPs or councillors, industrialists, 'top brass' police officers and landowners socialise with their editors, the pressure to 'go native' is irresistible. Specialist reporters will attract criticism and hostility precisely because they are so well connected. Editors need to develop a thick skin and expect sustained sniping at their football writers, local council correspondents and crime reporters. So anything less than 100 per cent support from the editor is destructive, because it undermines the professional relationship of mutual confidence between employer and employee. It is no different to the respect and trust that should exist between editor, reporter and in-house media lawyer. Likewise the editor must be 100 per cent assured that the reporter's loyalties lie squarely with the media company, and indirectly with the readership or audience.

Peter Finlay Dunne is credited with the famous quotation (often parroted by editors) that it is the job of the newspaper (and therefore the editorial staff) to 'afflict the comfortable and comfort the afflicted'. It has entered media folklore. But appearances are deceptive and another well-worn newsroom phrase is 'never let the facts get in the way of telling a good story'. Dunne's original unabridged quote is: 'Th' newspaper does ivrything f'r us. It runs th' polis force an' th' banks, command th' milishy, controls th' ligislachure, baptizes th' young, marries th' foolish, comforts th' afflicted, afflicts th' comfortable, buries th' dead an' roasts thim aftherward.' Dunne was concerned about the unbridled abuse of power of the press. The irony is that his critique has been re-edited to justify and celebrate media intrusion.

So it is also important to consider the issue of the specialist journalist's credibility. Alongside the risk that the journalist will get so close to the subject matter that he or she will 'go native' is the prospect that the specialist will turn out to be a parrot rather than a watchdog. Parrots are a by-product of the 'churnalism' phenomenon identified by Nick Davies[19]. Let's be clear that this is not a handbook for journalists who see it as their job to 'parrot' statements made by sources, press officers and spokespersons. It is a guide for students and journalists aspiring to make their mark as experts in a chosen field; for writers who take the trouble to look beyond the bland and transient event, distinguish between PR-fed hype and substance, trivia and gravitas, and who possess more than a 24-hour rolling news interest in an issue of legitimate public interest. This is what distinguishes a specialist newshound from an autocue reader, a 'hit and run' story merchant, or a 'Jack of all trades' hack.

Of the specialisms covered in this book, perhaps health journalism poses the weightiest ethical and commercial dilemmas. Readers suffering from illnesses and medical conditions, and their relatives, are prone to take information from the media at face value and are liable to become desperate in their search for answers and a solution. The current convention in the media is that journalists must provide 'balanced' coverage of any given topic. It should be the job of the specialist reporter to seek out the 'truth'. But many reporters (especially in the broadcast sector) go little further than locating sources and spokespersons willing to express contrary viewpoints on any issue. Health journalists bear a responsibility to society at large for ensuring that what they write is not only in the wider public interest, but also sensitive to the personal interests of individual sufferers. Credibility is not necessarily built on objectivity. There are occasions where the reporter must be subjective and sufficiently self-disciplined not to slip into 'parrot mode'. As *MedPage Today* executive editor Peggy Peck has argued: 'I do fault journalists who think balanced reporting means giving voice to charlatans and quacks; journalists who lionize crackpots.'[20] Three journalism students[21] at Lincoln, tasked to unearth examples of 'parrot' and 'watchdog' reporting in the media, identified instances where specialist health correspondents had either produced directly contradictory articles, or relied on PR briefings in preference to professional journal articles, or had taken defective statistical data at face value. One example concerned the benefits and risks of an oily fish diet. A *Daily Mail* story in April 2007 claimed that scientists 'believe' (sic) that eating oily fish could increase the risk of childhood diabetes due to seaborne chemical contaminates[22] but in September the same reporter wrote that an oily fish diet from the oceans could prevent childhood diabetes[23] (with no acknowledgement or explanation of the veracity of the journalist's earlier article). Similarly *Metro* ran a report in January 2010 that doctors feared a rise in cases of rickets could be due to children spending too much time indoors playing video games and suffering Vitamin D deficiencies.[24] But as the Lincoln researchers noted the *British Medical Journal* article concerned did not make any such claim. The line had been picked up from a press release issued by a body keen to promote the research results for its own commercial reasons. A third example concerned a *Daily Mail* article published in April 2011,[25] which claimed a third of women under 30 were unable to remember their own mobile phone numbers because of 'information overload'. As the student researcher noted, the findings were based on an un-scientifically and under-representative population survey sample, but the article did not alert the reader to that point.

Perhaps these are products of the tabloid maxim 'never let the facts get in the way of a good story'. Undoubtedly freelance and staff specialist reporters are constrained by newsdesks and sub-editors, whose own prejudices and 'Jack/Jill of all trade' shortcomings lead them to trivialise serious topics and to revise articles to fit a fashionable, populist and sensationalist agenda. The good news is that newspapers which 'dumb down' and at the same time undermine the credibility of specialist correspondents no longer dominate the media employment scene. Talented and experienced journalists with expertise in mainstream topics should look at the flourishing periodicals marketplace for work, freelance commissions and rewards. Media students with knowledge and skills (whether technical or traditional) have advantages over other job-hunters, and the authors of the following chapters provide valuable insights into what awaits those successful applicants.

Journalism today extends well beyond the imaginings of Samuel Johnson. Not only do we have many more platforms on which journalism can be disseminated, extending the profession well beyond the handful of elites of earlier days but journalism is truly a sociological and political influence impacting on the lives of many, even those who may not be avid readers or listeners of the news, rather than simply story telling. Modern journalism has become so complex that some might argue it is a very different creature from the days of its origins. The subject has evolved from what began as a political platform for dissent into part of the political process itself, not always for the good.

Modern journalism has an academic division with many universities now offering journalism courses and the development of journalism training into journalism education is probably the best indicator of the need for specialism. Andrew Marr in his autobiograhy described journalism as a trade and romantic journalists still like to employ this description of their vocation. Modern journalism much more resembles a profession than a trade and the two influences of academic courses and the need for specialism underpin that redefinition of the job.

Stories of the downfall of journalism fill editorial commentary, popular books and biographies and, sadly, university classrooms. The demise of the local paper may be well advanced and the dumbing down of the broadcast news an observable fact but specialist journalism is not only alive and kicking it is a major growth area. The traditional hack may now be an endangered species and even extinct in some habitats but the journalist lives on in the specialist. Today's reporter needs to be a specialist, an expert in a field.

Dr. Johnson would no doubt be amazed if he could see the world of the journalist today, not just because of the arsenal of technology they can employ in their day-to-day work but in the vast range of expertise possessed by the individuals themselves. Saying that, we can be sure that behind all the technical wizardry and the degrees in microbiology and MBAs in business he would still recognise the journalist.

Notes

1 From the *Idler,* printed in *Paynes Universal Chronicle,* 11 November 1758.
2 Centre for Investigative Journalism, City University, London, www.tcij.org.
3 Davies, N., *Flat Earth News*, Chatto and Windus 2008.
4 'New York Globe' daily news editor Jim Gannon, played by Clark Gable, *Teacher's Pet,* Paramount Pictures, 1957.
5 Author in conversation with former *Mirror* sub-editor Michael Cowton, June 2010.
6 National Union of Journalists.
7 Story originally published by Orchard News Bureau, November 2001; R. v. Speechley, Sheffield Crown Court, April 2004; R. v. Speechley [2004] EWCA Crim 3067, November 2004.
8 In conversation with the author, November 2001.
9 Winnett, R. and Rayner, G., *No Expenses Spared,* Bantam Press, pp. 219–31.
10 Reynolds v. Times Newspapers [1999] 3 WLR 1010.
11 Winnett and Rayner, *No Expenses Spared,* pp. 225–27.
12 Lynn, J. and Jay, A., *The Complete Yes Minister,* BBC Books, 1989, p. 279.
13 Davies, N., *Flat Earth News*, p. 66.
14 Marr, A., *My Trade,* Macmillan, 2004, p. 184.
15 www.guardian.co.uk/media/2010/nov/22/data-analysis-tim-berners-lee.
16 Walter Cronkite School of Journalism, Arizona State University, Phoenix AZ.
17 David Donald, Center for Public Integrity, Washington DC; Tommy Kaas, Danish International Center for Analytical Reporting; Jennifer LaFleur, ProPublica; Cynthia O'Murchu, *Financial Times,* et al.
18 In conversation with the author, June 2004.
19 Davies, N., *Flat Earth News.*
20 Peck, P., *MedPage Today,* 7 January 2011.
21 Michael Hodges, Jonathan Creswell and Michael Mumford, April 2011.
22 www.dailymail.co.uk/health/article-447997/Could-eating-oily-fish-increase-risk-diabetes.html.
23 www.dailymail.co.uk/health/article-483926/Oily-fish-cuts-risk-child-diabetes.html.
24 www.metro.co.uk/news/810028-video-gaming-leads-to-surge-in-rickets.
25 www.dailymail.co.uk/femail/article-1381294/Goldfish-Memory-Syndrome-A-women-remember-phone-number.html#comments.

1 Sports reporting

Nick Spencer

Introduction

There has never been more top-quality sport played around the world. Weary international cricketers typically play 14 Test matches a year and innumerable one-day internationals. Like nature, football abhors a vacuum and fills the calendar accordingly with matches of questionable significance. The injury toll in rugby union rises inexorably. At too many major tournaments, the complaint is that by the time the final comes around the protagonists are exhausted.

Should this huge expansion in the quantity of sport be good news for journalists, who share much of the hard work but without the spectacular financial rewards? Travelling to matches is vastly expensive but unless the reporter is there to convey the 'why' and the 'how' as well as the 'what', then it is legitimate to ask what precisely is the point of sports journalism.

As newspapers retrench on an unprecedented scale and shed jobs in jaw-dropping numbers, one theory is that sports writers – like film reviewers, for example – might be expendable; that well-informed fans and opinionated bloggers could be drafted in to fill the void, and at minimal cost.

It is a theory that is wrong on so many levels. Anyone who has spent time in cyberspace will be aware of the ignorance, spite and misinformation abroad. To subvert the famous dictum of the legendary *Manchester Guardian* editor, CP Scott, about facts being sacred but comment being free, the internet has made facts a little less sacred and comment rather more free.

There remains no substitute for speed, accuracy, wit and informed comment, however, and it is the challenge for journalists and their employers to be able to find a platform to provide it. After all, cyberspace should be as much about shedding light as generating heat.

However, this quest must inevitably take place against a background of severely contracting media budgets and, increasingly, the would-be journalist would be well advised to think laterally about how to remain relevant when staff jobs are becoming rarer by the day and short-term contracts and poorly paid freelance work the norm.

We are in the age of the portfolio career, but all is not lost. However, at a time when even the most anodyne tweet by England and Manchester United striker

Wayne Rooney is regarded as newsworthy, what price the more erudite views of the non-international sportsman or woman?

The grip of sport

Sport has the capacity to unite populations in the way few major events can aspire to. When Novak Djokovic finally beat Rafael Nadal, at 1.30am, in the final of the 2012 Australian Open on a sweltering January night in Melbourne, almost ten per cent of the Australian population was still watching on television at the end of their six-hour marathon. In America a week later, the Super Bowl attracted a record US TV audience, for any programme ever shown in that country, of 111.3 million. These were true water-cooler moments, by any definition.

However, while this was fantastic news for Australia's Channel 7, which broadcast a truly epic tennis match, it did not prove a great boon for Melbourne's *Age* newspaper, whose deadlines were long past by the time the match was won. What is good for TV is not necessarily good for newspapers, although that, in turn, could send readers to their website. If it all sounds faintly cannibalistic, it does illustrate a fundamental problem for media organisations.

In an Olympic year, when 20,000 journalists descended on London to cover the 2012 Games – and as many again failed to get accreditation – it does not pay to be unduly pessimistic about the future of sports journalism. After all, there were only 17,000 athletes at the Games. But while professional sport at the highest level often appears to be awash with money, some of the statistics about the composition of the media are alarming. According to recent figures, there are only 40,000 journalists in Great Britain, but 8,000 journalism students. Suddenly, the odds on getting a professional contract as a sportsman don't look so bad after all. However, as any successful sports coach would testify, it does not pay to be defeatist and there are certain core skills and key strategies which should enable the talented and knowledgeable would-be journalist to fashion a career.

Finding your voice

The aspiring sports journalist might have imbibed every fact about his or her favourite sport almost from the cradle, but mere knowledge is not enough. Competition is intense and 'match reporting' (generally the most obviously appealing aspect of the job at the outset) represents only a fraction of the work involved. Sport never sleeps, which means chasing news stories and answering mobile phone calls at all hours from anxious desks wanting news lines which are running elsewhere to be chased up. This can be thrilling, but equally it can be exhausting and frustrating. The ubiquity of technology has meant that the 'dream job' can seem a bit of a nightmare at times.

As in so many walks of life, contacts are key. Although the distinctions are becoming increasingly blurred, it might be worth considering whether you favour what might be described as either the tabloid or the broadsheet approach. It is all too obvious when a newsman lacks writing skills, or a fine writer is struggling to stand up a story. Versatility is a supreme asset but it is vital that you find your voice.

Consider, for a moment, what makes the journalists you admire most standout from the crowd. It will vary: some are calm and witty, others iconoclastic and opinionated, but the best are always distinctive and able to convey their message concisely and simply.

There is no substitute for speed and accuracy but if you can be laugh-out-loud funny to order you can virtually name your price. There is a sporting shorthand which is common currency but it is vital to avoid the clichés that make you sound like everybody else.

Not all five-set tennis matches are epics, even if it is difficult to think of an alternative way of describing Djokovic's victory over Nadal; 'fortuitous' is not a useful alternative to 'lucky'; rows are 'defused', not 'diffused'.

These might seem obvious points but there is a surprising amount of illiteracy and unintentional humour in the copy of even the most famous reporters: 'From my hotel room overlooking Mount Everest' is a personal favourite that failed to make it past an amused sub-editor, while another wrote, in all seriousness, of Arsenal manager Arsene Wenger 'tearing up one of his own unwritten rules'.

This effort, from a senior football reporter, was spiked by a sub editor:

> It has been a dramatic fall from grace for Robbie Keane, who was a deadline day signing for Harry Redknapp in the January 2009 window, returning to the club he left the previous summer, joining Liverpool for more than £20 million, in a £15 million deal after being guaranteed the captaincy.

Clarity is all and this example fails on most counts. You could doubtless do better, and if not then perhaps the written word is not for you.

Technology has opened up an array of alternative ways of delivering journalism and it is difficult to imagine that future generations can know too much about the potential of the iPad or Photoshop. Above all, learn to touch type. If you can watch a match with both eyes while still typing 40-odd accurate words a minute, you will be – you might be astonished to learn – in a tiny minority among sports reporters.

An alternative approach

What do Kazan, Maribor, Gwangju, Granada, Taipei, Almaty have in common? They are the cities chosen to host the World Student Games, winter and summer, in 2013/15/17. At the time of writing, there are 55,000 building workers in Sochi, the Black Sea resort that will host the winter Olympics in 2014. The same year, Incheon in South Korea will host the Asian Games. While many traditional media outlets are contracting, there is a substantial band of people who make a good living travelling the world and bringing their expertise to bear on these specialist events, using the personal capital they have accrued over many years.

Brazil, which hosts the football World Cup in 2014 and the Olympics two years later, will generate countless stories over the next few years which will be of interest to media organisations all over the world who perhaps do not have the appetite or resources to send their own man or woman. Although the rates of pay they offer might not be great, there will be a huge appetite for stories and features from an alert journalist who can mine this rich seam. There is no substitute for being where the story is and several far-sighted sports journalists have already spotted a gap in the market and are poised to make journalistic hay.

Alternatively, you could do worse than follow the example of Simon Kuper who, as a young man, travelled to 22 countries to research a book which became *Football Against The Enemy*. His thesis was that each country's style of play reflected the character of its inhabitants. What might otherwise have been a glorified gap year turned out to be a successful book and a ticket to a successful career.

What if your favourite sport is not a staple, like football, rugby or cricket? You might know all there is to know about skiing or be a world authority on curling, but those who set the news agenda might remain oblivious.

However, anyone who saw the South Korean contingent of journalists at the Olympic archery warm-up event at Lord's cricket ground in 2011 will appreciate that tastes vary around the world and magazines, websites and sports' governing bodies are there to cater for them.

The club or competition website might be a better avenue to get you closer to the action and connect you directly to your reader or listener.

Journalistically, would you be compromising your integrity by being, say, the person who interviews Manchester City captain Vincent Kompany for a live post-match interview with fans on Twitter and Facebook – to be streamed on YouTube – as opposed to a TV, radio or newspaper reporter? Granted, you might have a freer hand as an outsider, but you could hardly be closer to the action than being part of the 'team', whether that is an individual club or sport's governing body.

If you happen to be on good terms with a prominent squash player, gymnast, or anyone with a good tale to tell, don't discount the possibility of ghost writing their story. Fans of so-called minority sports are often desperate for decent coverage and the internet has opened up enormous possibilities for selling books directly and actually turning a profit.

An alternative strategy is to go into production and hone the efforts of others. However, one caveat is that newspapers, in particular, are cutting down on the backroom staff. Where once, vast armies of fierce, pedantic (almost invariably) men checked and weighed every word, a theory has grown up that whatever is submitted by the man in the field should be of sufficient quality to go straight on to the internet and, with minimal editing, into the newspaper.

Alas, this is wishful thinking on a grand scale and the number of legal actions, never mind the typographical and grammatical errors, illustrates that this is not a good way to proceed. Readers do notice, whatever the number crunchers might think.

Then there are magazines, websites, tweets, videos. Technology means it is relatively easy and cheap to put something out there yourself – the trick is finding an audience in an overcrowded cyber world.

The good news is that social media means it is not unusual for someone relatively young and inexperienced, but with something pertinent to say, to acquire tens of thousands of followers for their blogs or twittering. The most financially savvy might get a sponsor and make a living out of it and soon have traditional news outlets beating a path to their door. Hey presto, there is your own distinctive, digital cuttings library, although in February 2012 a co-founder of Twitter, Chris Stone, urged its 500 million users to get off the micro-blogging website, because it is 'unhealthy', and do something else instead. Perhaps there is more to life than 140 characters after all.

An industry in crisis?

In recent years, the United States has seen a number of major metropolitan daily newspapers close. In Great Britain, executives at the *Guardian* have talked openly about a time when there is no newspaper, just an online presence. Internet technology threatens to do to newspapers what is has done to the music industry, with the added irony of papers apparently being hastened into oblivion by their own websites.

Until relatively recently, the career structure for young journalists was quite predictable and logical. A weekly or local daily newspaper to start, or perhaps a local radio station, where, besides the rather mundane assignments, one would acquire the rudiments of libel laws, shorthand, microphone technique or photography.

Graduate schemes do still exist, of course, and should be pursued ruthlessly but it is now more of a free for all and the concept of the journalistic apprenticeship has largely been lost. Most graduates head for the big cities and have to be prepared to work for little or nothing at first to show their commitment. This is not unique to journalism but it can mean that the acquisition of basic journalistic skills is skated over. Repackaging internet reports is no substitute for slogging around the parish learning interview techniques.

Local and regional coverage is an obvious casualty of the blanket coverage of the most prestigious events. Newspapers used to strive to be part of the fabric of sport, whether that was lower league football, county or state cricket or club hockey. Unfortunately, for the wonderful variety that sport could provide, that has largely been eclipsed by the supremacy of international sport, Champions League football and the like.

The dilemma for newspapers now is whether the reader is going to want to read an in-depth report on the match he or she watched on the television the previous night. Perhaps they will skip the match report and head straight for the colour piece or the quotes from the key participants.

Too many media outlets – written and broadcast – are obsessed with running quotes pieces just because a manager or player has opened his mouth, but the preoccupation with not being seen to 'miss a story' may just indicate an underlying fear of having to accept a diminished role behind the broadcasters and websites.

What type of coverage works best?

It is hardly contentious to say that newspapers' most influential days are behind them. In a 2012 study on trends in media consumption in Great Britain, only

38 per cent of respondents gleaned their news from paid-for printed newspapers. More people used a free website in an average week than bought a newspaper. At the same time, Eurosport's director of new media, Arnaud Maillard, said that the company sees itself as a media rather than a TV brand. Twenty-five per cent of Eurosport's internet traffic now comes from mobile devices. Users who were in the habit of visiting the site every day, now log on every hour.

Speed is of the essence but even in an industry in flux, where few outcomes are certain, there will surely still be plenty of opportunities for the journalist with something intelligent to say. So how to learn your trade and to stand out in a competitive market place with diminishing opportunities to shine? It is no easy task, after all, to turn in a lively 90-second radio report or 500 beautifully crafted words on a goalless draw in the Scottish First Division. It might be easier said than done but, as a simple rule of thumb, find your angle, don't follow the pack, and have the courage of your convictions.

In my early reporting days I was told that the reader was interested in what a newspaper's correspondent had to say about a particular match. If there is an obvious angle or controversy, follow it, but the number of overheated post-match controversies is wearying for everyone.

Aim high, but above all, know your stuff. It is very difficult to blag it, as one head of sport revealed on being told that Tiger Woods had missed the cut in a particular golf tournament. 'What's the cut?', he could not stop himself saying.

Be a generalist but don't be afraid to be an expert. Modern sports are so all consuming that it makes it very difficult to dip in and out. Don't forget that they, too, are trying to survive in a fiercely competitive market place. In recent years, rugby league in Europe reinvented itself as a summer game. The annual NFL match at Wembley is a model other sports have sought to imitate, although the Premier League in England had to abandon plans to play a '39th game' in all corners of the world to exploit the competition's phenomenal global reach. The 39th proved a step too far.

An alternative strategy

The key word for online journalism is an unattractive one in more than one sense: 'monetising'. While the internet is unparalleled in its ability to deliver work to a target audience in the blink of an eye, it is worth considering that if your words are being consumed for free the chances are that there might not be a great deal in it for you.

However, if conventional journalism looks a risky proposition, there are countless less conventional opportunities to consider.

Sky's five-year partnership with British Cycling is a fascinating example of a media outlet broadening its reach with a stated aim of encouraging a million more people to cycle regularly. As well as sponsoring a professional road-racing team, the TV company is supporting a series of mass participation Sky Ride events – opening up city centres for traffic-free cycling days. They estimate that 375,000 people have become regular cyclists as a result.

Sport means events, some of the biggest events in the world and it attracts sponsors, caterers and creates jobs. They might not be conventional journalism jobs but plenty of people have found that there is no substitute for just being around. It's the way to meet people, to network and if you are available, persistent and enthusiastic there will undoubtedly be jobs to do, even around the periphery. It is then but a short step to the press tent or media village.

Is it good to specialise?

There are so many ways for the fan to consume sport and it varies from country to country. Specialist sports papers like *L'Equipe* and *Gazzetta dello Sport* have flourished in France and Italy while the concept never took hold in Great Britain.

Tennis is an interesting example of a relatively small professional sport with a vast global reach. It also strikes me as fiendishly difficult to commentate on or write about. At a time when Novak Djokovic, Rafael Nadal, Roger Federer and Andy Murray are dominating as no quartet has ever done, there is a very limited cast list on either side of the net at most of the top men's matches. Cricket, or any team game, gives you a far greater dramatis personae. And how do you condense a four-hour match into 800 words? It's a very good exercise.

Without Andy Murray, it is doubtful whether some British newspapers would bother with a tennis correspondent, given the lack of success of his compatriots.

It's a small world, journalistically speaking, so when a vacancy arises on a website, magazine or, just occasionally, at a newspaper, there are relatively few people to have impressed to earn a recommendation. Experience shows that knowledge of the game and a little persistent networking can land you a pretty good job.

Contacts

For English football, 1992 was year zero. The introduction of Sky TV's millions – now billions – transformed the game. With it, clubs were able to afford the cream of international talent but it also altered irrevocably the nature of the relationship between club and local reporter.

Twenty years ago, reporters chatted to players and established relationships with them. Then the clubs began to move their training grounds further out of town with security to match. The casual, invaluable relationship with players was broken.

The days when Ron Atkinson told reporters, on his first day as Manchester United manager, 'You're welcome to my home number, gentlemen, but please remember not to ring me during *The Sweeney*' are long gone and reporters have had to reinvent their relationships with the stars and, increasingly, their agents. Access all areas is a thing of the past.

In 2011, a reporter so incensed Atkinson's successor, Sir Alex Ferguson, with a relatively innocuous question about Ryan Giggs before the Champions League final against Barcelona that Ferguson was overheard saying: 'We'll get him. We'll ban him on Friday.'

Relationships are anything but cosy, but how could it be otherwise, given the exponential growth in media coverage of sport?

The journalist is in a tricky position. It is a struggle to emerge through the scrum to forge a personal relationship with a coach or player, who are kept at arm's length, or further, from the media. A few minutes in a 'mixed zone', where reporters are entitled to ask a handful of questions after a match, is no substitute for a one-on-one conversation.

Then there are agents, who might find a journalist very useful for telling the world how in demand his client is from other clubs. The clubs, meanwhile, are more and more keen to have copy approval for interviews – and occasionally try to control the flow of photographs from big events, or even replace photographers altogether with their own placemen – and the players have their image rights to worry about.

As players have become more remote, journalists have been left with a huge problem. Fortunately, the advent of Twitter has lent a helping hand. It is a news event every time Wayne Rooney takes to Twitter, no matter how many spelling mistakes he makes. He recently opined: 'If ref sees that kick from suarez and books him for it it should be red' and everyone followed up the story. It is not journalism in any conventional sense and the thought occurs that most people who are interested in Rooney's utterances could obtain it directly without the inconvenience of buying a newspaper.

It would be wrong to generalise too much about access. Cameras in dressing rooms after a match are the norm in American sport and the Italian media expects, and is granted routinely, an hour or more to chat to players on an almost daily basis at their football clubs' training ground.

And inevitably it is a chat, because no sportsman could endure an hour's forensic cross-examination several times a week.

Reporters need access, so what happens when unpleasantries are exchanged on the pitch, such as sledging in cricket? It is a particular problem for the local/regional reporter who has to deal with just one club and the same players week in, week out.

Does he report without fear or favour and risk severing the very links on which his job relies? It is an age-old dilemma but the best rule of thumb is to run a 'sensationalist' test.

Anyone who has played sport will understand that there are flare-ups that can be settled with a handshake at the end of the game. But if boundaries of decency, racism or sexism are crossed, then the reporter has a duty to report them because, ultimately, it is in the interests not just of his audience but of sport as well. He just might need a tin hat for his next few visits to his local team.

The march of the ex-player

Punditry is one of the few growth areas in sports journalism and, unsurprisingly, it is a market cornered almost exclusively by ex-players. Given the choice, would readers prefer to hear from the former international or the ex-fan in the stand?

The answer might not always be as clear-cut as it seems. Michael Atherton is as fine and perceptive a writer now as he was redoubtable opening batsman for England. His *Times* colleague, Matthew Syed, from the far less celebrated world of table tennis, is perceptive enough to know what makes sportsmen of every hue tick and has an aptitude for writing about it.

At Staffordshire University in England, former footballer Lawrie Madden runs journalism courses which attract dozens of current and retired sportsman who fancy a second career in the media. Happily, for the aspiring journalist without 100 international caps to his name, Atherton and Syed are two exceptional cases and a lot of money is spent on star names to negligible effect.

One of the solecisms newspapers perpetrate on their readers is that their star columnists actually write the pieces themselves. There are worthy exceptions but most are the result of a hurried 10–15-minute conversation with a reporter who then has to conjure 800-odd words of journalistic gold out of what can be some pretty base metal opinions. And too often it shows.

Star columnists also have a habit of costing a lot of money; of being too close to the game they recently left to be anything other than anodyne; or controversialists in search of a profile. So all is not lost – the young journalist's analysis, insight and greater fluency could still win the day, but if you can get capped by your country it certainly won't hurt!

Follow the money?

We are in the era of the mega-brand. The biggest clubs leave no corner of the globe unexploited and forge links with everyone from clothes companies to vineyards. As well as their websites, they have their own TV stations, which can be watched all over the world.

It can all seem rather daunting, or cynical, depending on your point of view. If you have a financial head on your shoulders, there is unlimited material to work on. The politics of sport, from the International Olympic Committee down, is a mine of intrigue and stories.

It is just possible though that, to you, sport is more local, more to do with volunteers, coaching, participation – 10km runs and the like. It is certainly a valid point of view and you should focus on what interests you most.

It is simple really. Be the best you can; be confident of your voice and your opinions and not what other people might want you to say. Go where the work is. Be prepared (though not too prepared) to work for nothing, but try to avoid being exploited.

It can still be a wonderful job. If there is one thing better than being able to say 'I was there' then it is surely being in the privileged position of being able to tell millions of others what it was like to be there.

2 Business journalism

Colm Murphy

Follow the money. That is the maxim of all good investigative journalism. Following the money too are some of the world's smartest people alongside some of the most corrupt. So too is the average person trying to secure or retain their job, buy a house, sell a house, make a pension provision and make good investments for their family's future. It is the daily drama of all these people chasing money that is what makes business and financial journalism so fascinating.

Financial journalism has been propelled around the world on to the front pages in recent years with the banking crisis and recession that followed in Europe and America. The collapse of leading investment banks like Bear Sterns, Lehman Brothers and rescue of others by governments between 2008 and 2009 were unprecedented events. For financial journalists it was their equivalent of covering a war.

But the credit crunch also raised serious questions about financial journalism – how stories are researched, sources used, how they are written and its role in creating the credit bubble internationally (Porter, 1998; Schechter, 2009; Tett, 2009). It was the same 80 years ago after the Wall Street crash of 1929 and the depression that followed.

Many journalists then like Alexander Noyes, the financial editor of *The New York Times*, warned of that crash too, just like they did the 2008 one, but other reporters seemed to lose their critical faculties. Many reported without scrutiny what they were told by the financial institutions, governments and venture capitalists in the years preceding the crash. Many argue this all helped to fuel the credit bubble (Porter, 1998; Schechter, 2009; Tett, 2009).

But from its embryonic days in the late fifteenth century, financial journalism has always been questioned for its independence. Ever since the Fugger family, the German merchants who dominated European business in the fifteenth and sixteenth century, published newsletters in 1568 informing customers of events that might impact European economies, questions have been raised about the objectivity of business reporting. Business reporting proper began as an addition to stock market prices which began to be published in the 1750s in so-called price currents, publications comparing the prices of goods in different towns. By 1835 the *New York Herald* published a dedicated business page covering Wall Street, the emerging financial capital of America. On the other side of the Atlantic, Scottish hat maker

James Wilson in 1843 founded *The Economist* newspaper in England to fight the Corn Laws and promote free trade. Today it sells over 1.3 million copies a week worldwide and its website has also double that in unique users. A few years later, in 1851, Julius Reuter, a German emigrant to London, starts using carrier pigeons and telegraphs to send stock prices. It was the foundation of Reuters, today the world's largest business news agency and part of the Thomson Reuters group with over 55,000 employees in over 100 countries.

Parallel with the growth of business news came that of public relations – companies or organisations trying to represent themselves to the public. In 1887 the American company General Electric hired a publicity agent to promote its businesses. Public relations have become intertwined ever since with business journalism.

So too did financial journalism's independence come under scrutiny again. Even when the Wall Street crash came in 1929, many business publications played down the impact of the market drop and remained quite reverential to the chieftains of industry. It later came out into hearings in the 1930s on what caused the crash that in the 1920s several reporters at *The Wall Street Journal* accepted bribes from investors to write good comments about certain stocks.

After the depression other positive change began to happen too in the nature of financial reporting. In 1936, the first personal finance column started in the *New York Post* creating a new genre in financial journalism that is still developing today internationally. In the 1950s other change too began to happen in financial reporting. Its location in newspapers began to move from a spot hidden behind the classified advertisement, it became more direct and less reverential to the captains of commerce. Reflecting this in 1950 *BusinessWeek* in America published its first executive pay story indicating a more analytical and questioning approach. Its rival *Forbes* magazine also created a new type of investigative style business feature story that was more questioning and blunt.

This more aggressive style began to be adopted into British business journalism, which typically has taken its innovations from America. Particularly influential amongst business journalists in Britain are *Forbes*, *BusinessWeek* and *Fortune* who have the resources and access to have their business writers spend months on a 1,600-word feature and also excel in photography and graphics to illustrate their stories. But it was not until the 1980s that the output of financial journalism in the UK expanded rapidly in tandem with the liberalisation of the British financial markets by the then Prime Minister Margaret Thatcher. She tried to expand home ownership by opening up the mortgage market, widening pension provision and bringing share ownership to the masses by selling off nationalised industries like BT and British Gas. The interest in money this awakened led to a plethora of personal finance and property supplements to tap into the middle classes' rising aspirations. Business coverage also expanded on TV and radio to meet this new appetite. But there soon became anger too at the million pound pay for executives that the nationalisation and deregulation had led to.

In unison with the growing British business media, the public relations industry grew rapidly in the 1980s and 1990s. Many journalists left for better salaries, opportunities and working conditions on the so-called dark side (McCrystal, 2008). But traditional reporting beats, such as the industrial correspondent, declined in importance – as did the influence of trade unions. The dot.com boom of the early noughties brought new excitement for business journalists. They watched young entrepreneurs – including some of their own former colleagues – make millions. Reporters like Greg Hatfield and Martin Lewis formed specialist websites.

Many business journalists temporarily lost their usual cynical attitude as the mega deals were done on each side of the Atlantic before the so-called dot.com bubble burst all over their pages in April 2001. The period did, however, see the successful launch of FT.com and WSJ.com, making business journalism one of the few areas online where subscription could be charged, thus safeguarding its future. The bust also led to a more questioning attitude amongst financial journalists. The first expose about Enron, for example, was published in March 2001 in America's *Fortune* magazine, which led eventually to the company filing for bankruptcy over its accountancy policies but re-awakened interest in investigative business journalism (Doyle, 2006).

But reporting such a story is not easy for a journalist. The people who sue most often for defamation tend to be business people and their companies. While instruction in media law is good on most journalism courses and organisations, generally training in business and financial journalism is not. There are three masters courses in the UK in business journalism at City University, London, and two in Scotland at University of Stirling and Glasgow Caledonian University. These are fairly recent additions. In America, there is a longer tradition of formal training for business journalists with well-established degrees at New York University, Columbia University (New York) and a business journalism centre in Arizona State University. But many business editors prefer if their reporters train and start as news reporters as it helps them to develop a strong news value and clear writing for the general public.

The father of economic and business reporting, the late NBC economic correspondent Irving R. Levine, was a general correspondent first. He explained his technique that made him legendary for being able to explain complex stories to the American public: 'How does this economic news affect the man in the street? In simple words you must explain this. That is your story' (Levine, 1998).

But interpreting statistics and figures are something that a lot of journalists and journalism students dislike. A 2002 survey in America of journalist educators concluded that business journalists, as a group, were lacking sophisticated knowledge of the complex issues and concepts they cover. This is mirrored in surveys of journalism graduates who, after new media and design, listed business as the area which they would have liked more tuition.

But still the main route into the profession is people starting off working as freelance or on a placement as general reporters and then going onto a business desk or trade magazine. This kind of work comes through informal contacts made during a placement from college. The starting salary for a trainee reporter on a regional paper can be as low as £12,000, a National Union of Journalists survey in 2008 showed, but can be a little higher for business journalists.

Once you gain experience there is a wide variation generally between salaries in business journalism. The large news agencies and national newspapers pay the highest salaries. Some of the more established business-to-business publications can also pay well too. Some will pay above the average £24,500 salary for general journalists as there is a smaller supply of business journalists. Those with over ten years' experience can expect to start at over £22,000 to about £40,000. Business reporters or editors with a track record of breaking stories in their sector will often be able to negotiate their salaries, which range from £50,000 to £85,000 or more. It can, however, take a number of years and a lot of hard work to establish such a reputation. Business newsrooms are generally open plan and noisy. Increasingly, however, much work for business publications is done by self-employed business journalists working from home. For some this is a lifestyle choice, but for many it is forced upon them by the lack of staff jobs. Many business journalists can expect to spend at least part of their career as freelance (self-employed).

Most business journalists spend most of their day on the phone, e-mailing or on their PC or mobile device. Given deadline pressures, many will only get out of the office a few times in the week to cover events or meet key people within their sector who are known as contacts. Most business journalists will also specialise in a particular sector, for example in communication companies, but will still be able to cover business generally as well.

On the bigger titles where there is more competition for stories they will often work long hours, often up to 60 hours a week. However, for most business journalists the hours they work are generally less unsocial and less unpredictable than those in general news reporting. Their day is generally more aligned to business hours. But social and work life can get intertwined given the long hours and events to attend. Great flexibility is required within the working week when stories are breaking or to meet deadlines. There is also strong competition against rival publications to get the best stories so the job can be quite stressful but very interesting too.

The largest proportion of business reporting jobs, over 40 per cent according to several surveys, are concentrated in London and the south east of England as it is an international centre for business media. This is due to London being a world centre for finance, its former role as head of an empire, the global importance of the English language in business and the fact it is in the middle of world time zones. This means that specialist business news agencies like Reuters, Dow Jones and Bloomberg can control their 24-hour, seven-day operations around the globe from London. The business reporting day for these agencies starts with Asia and Australia and finishes the other side of the world on America's west coast.

Reuters is the largest in the UK. Its main customers are traders, analysts and other professionals around the world who require up to the millisecond financial news and prices. Its main rival is New York-based Bloomberg, established in 1981 by Michael Bloomberg, Mayor of New York, after he was fired from New York investment bank Salomon Brothers where he had risen to a senior partner.

It has the world's largest private computer network as it does not trust the reliability of the internet. It employs 11,000 people in 72 countries and runs multilingual business TV, radio and online services. Its main offices are in New York, London, Tokyo, Sao Paulo, Dubai, Hong Kong, Singapore and Frankfurt.

The third is New York-based Dow Jones, which operates in 58 countries and in a dozen languages. It was bought in 2007 by News Corporation, as part of its purchase of *The Wall Street Journal* and its accompanying WSJ.com website. These three agencies compete fiercely to provide effectively real-time important news 24 hours a day, seven days a week across the globe. A millisecond delay can cost their clients, who manage millions of pounds on behalf of others, huge money. This is because many clients across the globe have their trading systems programmed to automatically respond to news or fluctuations in prices that are fed into them by these agencies.

These agencies like new recruits to have language skills and some business knowledge and journalistic experience. They recruit trainees mostly through paid internships advertised annually on their websites but will also recruit business specialists directly. They will usually have a business news exam for applicants to complete before shortlisting and competition is usually intense even for placements.

Despite business people using the internet almost every day, far more than the average person, they also still read more newspapers, magazines than those in other professions. Business people watch less television but listen to more radio (British Business Survey, 2008).

The most widely read financial news by business people is *The Sunday Times* business section which 29 per cent read regularly (British Business Survey, 2008). See the accompanying case study of its business editor. It is followed by the *Mail on Sunday* (26 per cent), the *Daily Mail* (21.2 per cent) and *The Times* (21 per cent) in terms of the percentage of business people who read them. There is then a fairly even spread of business readers amongst the other titles. The main ones being the daily edition of the *Telegraph* (12 per cent), the *Guardian* (11 per cent), the *Sunday Telegraph* (10.8 per cent), the *Observer* (9.4 per cent) and the *Evening Standard* (8.6 per cent) (British Business Survey, 2008).

The London-based *Financial Times* is the largest selling specialist business print publication in the UK and has 500 journalists. About 11 per cent of business people read it regularly. Its distinctive pink salmon pages date from 1893, four years after its foundation, when it was cheaper than white paper. Its owners also wanted it to stand out on the newsstand. It is printed in 22 sites internationally including New York and has sister papers around the world in India, France and Russia as well as its online services. Its parent company, Pearson, the London stock market quoted educational services company, also owns half *The Economist* magazine.

The larger of the 14,000 newspapers in the UK like the *Birmingham Post*, *Belfast Telegraph* and *Scotsman*, each have business editors and reporters. They normally take their national and international business news from the Press Association, the national news agency for Britain and Ireland, which also has a large business desk. Their own reporters complement this by generally concentrating on business stories in their circulation area.

In terms of business readership national business publications like *The Economist* (10 per cent), *Private Eye* (9.8 per cent) and *Business Life*, the on-board magazine with British Airways which 8.4 per cent of business people read regularly, are significant publications. The percentage of business people within the audience for any media product is very important in attracting advertisers. Not only do they tend to be high spenders themselves, but also they generally control budgets in their workplace, giving them the type of high spending power advertisers seek.

There are also several thousand specialist weekly, monthly and annual magazines, known as business-to-business publications which are a very important part of British business. The most popular of these weekly magazines are *Management Today* with 7.4 per cent of business readers viewing it followed by *Computer Weekly* (6.4 per cent), *New Scientist* (6.1 per cent), *Marketing* (3.7 per cent), *Accountancy Age* (3.7 per cent) *Marketing Week* (3.6 per cent) and *IT Week* (2.8 per cent) (British Business Survey, 2008).

In terms of fortnightly magazines, *Accountancy* is the most popular with 6.1 per cent of business people reading it regularly. It is followed by *People Management* (4.6 per cent), *Public* (3.4 per cent), *Director* (3.1 per cent), *Human Resources* (3 per cent), *Money Management* (2.9 per cent), *Financial News* (2.7 per cent), *Investor's Chronicle* (2.1 per cent), *Campaign* (1.5 per cent) and *Media Week* (1.1 per cent).

Some of the UK's best business reporters have started off on these and similar publications as they are an excellent entry and training point for those wanting to become a business journalist. Professionals from doctors to the corner shop owner need specialist information to keep up to date with trends in their sector from new laws, products and industry gossip. England is a world centre for this with groups like Reed Business Information, the largest business-to-business publisher in Europe, based there. It has over 100 brands, ranging from *New Scientist* to *Farmweek*, and is also involved in web products, exhibitions, conferences and industry awards.

Other major players in this sector include Emap, which produces everything from *Broadcast* magazine to *Heating & Ventilation News*. Haymarket Media Group, Incisive, GDS Publishing, Cavendish are amongst others in this sector. While these publications are largely subscription based, the fall in advertising coupled with its migration to the internet and new rival services online is creating a challenge for these publishers. To counteract this, they are attempting to transform themselves into multimedia content produces in their own specialist niche as well as providing more market intelligence as opposed to industry news. These are low profile publications but many command huge followings within the industry they serve.

At the other end of the spectrum is the BBC's Robert Preston. He is probably Britain's best-known business correspondent. He works across BBC radio, television and online and has his own blog.

The BBC also leads in terms of radio which is one of the main sources of business news in the UK through the business segments on drive-time radio as they commute to work (British Business Survey, 2008). But having an audience of over ten million people means that what they say can have significant repercussions for the economy. There was, for example, controversy over Preston's breaking of the story in 2007 that Northern Rock had problems raising finance. This and subsequent stories led to queues outside the bank, the first for 150 years in Britain.

Preston and the 4,000 other journalistic staff at the BBC have to adhere to strict rules on objectivity and accuracy, which they did in covering the story. Similar general rules apply for most professional media organisations in Britain as well as codes drawn-up by the National Union of Journalists, the largest journalist union, the Press Complaints Commission, the self-regulator for the print industry, and Ofcom, the communications licensing authority.

As well as these general rules there are additional rules for business journalists in the UK because of their potential to enrich themselves or others through either the stories they write or the information they possess. This is known as insider dealing. There have been detected cases from *The Wall Street Journal* to the *Daily Mirror* of business journalists using their knowledge to financially benefit themselves through share dealing. They have led to convictions of journalists. This was based on recommending a particular share for purchase. Two former *Daily Mirror* share tip columnists, James Hipwell and Anil Bhoyrul, were convicted in 2005 for buying shares before they tipped them in their popular City Slickers column which they knew would increase their price.

Today, however, most media organisations require those reporting on stocks to disclose to management any securities held by them or their close family. They are usually forbidden from short-term trading.

All business journalists must comply with the Investment Recommendation (Media) Regulations 2005, which is policed by the Financial Services Authority and comes from a European Union directive. In addition, the print media in the UK is governed by Clause 13 of the Press Complaints Commission Editors' Code and Practice. It prohibits journalists writing about shares in which they or their close family have a significant interest without internal disclosure. It also regulates journalists giving recommendations to buy shares known as tips. Ofcom, BBC, Reuters, Bloomberg, Dow Jones and most other media organisations strictly regulate their journalists' involvement in share dealings.

But a more common ethical issue for business journalism is the acceptance of hospitality or gifts from companies or organisations they write about. Large companies, financial institutions and public relations companies each year target thousands of pounds from marketing budgets particularly at business journalists. In the past it has included British Airways flying business journalists to a World Cup and tickets for Twickenham, Ascot and Wimbledon. Most media organisations have strict codes on what hospitality and gifts can be accepted and disclosures have to be made. *The Sunday Times*, for example, bans most hospitality and gifts.

Increasingly, too, public relations operators are becoming smarter at filling the void left by business desk understaffing due to cutbacks. Technology too means that the traditional press release is been augmented with online video, blogs and social media content bypassing the role of the financial journalist as gatekeeper of information. While at the same time reporters are under pressure to produce instant business news coverage to feed websites. They have less time to stand back and analyse. There is also little cash to spare for business investigations.

There are also increasing amounts of information available online from business people and experts through blogs and websites. There is a rapid shift of business news online while those in business still like magazines for longer articles. The BBC website is the most popular one for business people with over half using it very regularly (British Business Survey, 2008). It is followed by Google News (17.6 per cent), Yahoo News (11.4 per cent), MSN News (9.6 per cent) and Telegraph.co.uk (4.6 per cent). Largely subscription websites and their accompanying digital editions for mobile devices, FT.com and Timesonline.co.uk are also popular for their specialist business coverage and analysis. About 12 per cent of business people have used with their own blog (British Business Survey, 2008) or services like Twitter. Sites like LinkedIn have become popular social networks for business people.

But the strength that business journalists have is their independence, accuracy and objectivity and the trust they have with their audience. It is not by accident that the most popular business content on the web comes from sources like the BBC and the FT, who have spent decades building trust with their audiences.

But despite the huge daily output of business journalism large amounts of what goes on in the financial world goes unreported. For example deficiencies in many company pension funds, for which hundreds of thousands of people will rely on for their retirement, go unreported as companies only need publish an actuarial examination on them once every three years. Big takeovers go through and only the drama of them is reported. There is little analysis as to their long-term repercussions for jobs, communities or regional economies.

But the future is not all dim. Technology has opened up access to customers and employees and could democratise business journalism. Print business editors have been setting-up their own business news online sites. For instance in 2007 David Parkin, the former *Yorkshire Post* business editor, established the regional online business site theBusinessDesk.com. Others are following with more specialist business sites to provide independent coverage.

In the information age, with economic uncertainty the greatest for a generation, the value of trustworthy, quality business news and rigorous analysis is paramount. The daily avalanche of information means readers are searching for trusted, independent and accurate navigators.

But, however it evolves, the need for well-informed, well-educated, curious and persistent independent financial journalists has never been greater.

Case study – business journalism – Dominic O'Connell, *The Sunday Times* Business Editor

Dominic O'Connell, *The Sunday Times* Business Editor, is one of the UK's most influential financial journalists.

The newspaper has three million readers making his section the UK's most read business supplement. It often sets the agenda for the week's business coverage.

O'Connell says: 'The great and good of British business see us as their in-house paper. We have good access to chief executives because they read the section. Our style is aggressive and fun. We like to report excesses, bonuses and luxuries.'

Like many financial journalists O'Connell has no formal business qualifications. Instead he uses the techniques he learnt when starting out in newspapers in New Zealand covering councils and crime. This involves systematically meeting the key players in his designated reporting area and developing their trust and then hoping the stories follow.

He and his team of nine reporters spend Tuesday to Saturday meeting and phoning chief executives, bankers and others. Each reporter has to produce several exclusive stories each week in their designated business area, for example, airline companies. They also have to help research and write the section's 1,600-word features which generally give the inside story of the week's main business issue.

When meetings with contacts are included, O'Connell and his team often work over 60-hour weeks. The pressure is particularly intense leading up to the deadline for features on Thursday evening and Saturday afternoon for business news.

In addition to writing his business column and several stories each week, O'Connell also works with a design editor, associate business editor and three business sub-editors to produce his section. John Witherow, the newspaper's editor, will sometimes reject his completed pages if he thinks the stories are not strong enough forcing O'Connell to start over.

Despite this pressure, O'Connell laments that other newspapers have decreased the resources devoted to their Sunday business sections. O'Connell says: 'Business is where the money is. So it is where you find the interesting people who matter. It involves politics, drama, people and technology.'

O'Connell took-up the position in January 2010 after joining the section ten years previously, having worked for a rival and before that trade magazines. John Waples, his predecessor, had left to become UK managing director of FD, a City public relations company. This is a route taken by many experienced business journalists due to the significantly higher salaries and shorter hours available in other areas of finance and communications.

Bibliography

British Business Survey (2008) *British Business Survey*. Ipsos Media CT [Internet]. Available from: www.bbs-survey.com [Accessed on 27 September 2010].

Doyle, G. (2006) 'Financial News Journalism: a post-Enron analysis of approaches towards economic and financial news production in the UK', *Journalism – Theory Practice and Criticism*, Vol. 7, issue 4, p. 433. SAGE Publications, England.

Levine, I. R. (1998) Interview with author, Dublin 1998.

McCrystal, D. (2008) 'It's more fun on the "Dark Side"', *British Journalism Review*, Vol. 19, Issue 2, p. 17. SAGE Publications, England.

Porter, D. (1998) 'City Editors and the Modern Investing public: establishing the integrity of the new financial journalism in late nineteenth-century London', *Media History*, Vol. 4, issue, p. 49.

Schechter, D. (2009) 'Credit Crisis: how did we miss it?' *British Journalism Review*, Vol. 20, issue 1, p. 19. SAGE Publications, England.

Tett, G. (2009) 'Icebergs and Ideologies: how information flows fuelled the financial crisis', *Anthropology News*, John Wiley & Sons Inc, USA.

Useful websites

Advice and listing of useful websites about UK journalism: www.prospects.ac.uk/indus tries_media_contacts.htm [Accessed on 27 September 2010].

Free online tutorials on business journalism from the Donald W. Reynolds National Center for Business Journalism at Arizona State University: http://businessjournalism.org/ [Accessed on 27 September 2010].

History of mainly American business journalism compiled by the School of Journalism and Mass Communication at the University of North Carolina at Chapel Hill: www.bizjourna lismhistory.org [Accessed on 28 September 2010].

Reuters free extremely useful staff handbook on everything you need to know about financial journalism: http://handbook.reuters.com/index.php/Main_Page [Accessed on 27 September 2010].

3 Political journalism

Kevin Rafter

Introduction

Winston Churchill would not go to bed until the first editions of the daily newspapers were delivered to 10 Downing Street in the early hours of the morning. Today few politicians – from the lowly backbencher at Westminster to the holders of high governmental office – can afford to ignore the print and broadcast media. In a moment of stark honesty Tony Blair, as he prepared to leave Downing Street in 2007, admitted that, 'we paid inordinate attention in the early days of New Labour to courting, assuaging, and persuading the media' (Blair, 2007). Politicians may argue that they have the ability to set the news agenda but, in truth, they have little direct control over how the issues on that agenda are covered by the media. There is, as such, an interdependency in the relationship between politicians and journalists, and in few arenas is still as evident than at the Houses of Parliament at Westminster.

In an era of almost unlimited access to political and parliamentary information it is worth recalling that reporting of the proceedings at Westminster was subject to legal restriction until 1771. Until near the end of the eighteenth century journalists and printers faced imprisonment for publishing the contents of parliamentary debates while one MP, who published a collection of his own speeches, was actually sent to the Tower as punishment. The relaxation of the secrecy on the reporting of parliamentary debates came after a long campaign for reform and increasing breaches of the publication prohibition. In subsequent decades newspapers such as *The Times* and the *Daily Telegraph* reproduced lengthy verbatim accounts of parliamentary debates. Charles Dickens remains one of the best-known gallery reporters.

From the mid-1800s onwards the practice of covering parliament changed as a more commercial orientation in the newspaper business saw political stories having to battle for space alongside other news stories. The arrival of broadcasting brought further change during the twentieth century. The BBC's public service ethos influenced its coverage of parliament and politics first on radio and subsequently on television. Broadcasters worked to rules of impartiality and balance which the partisan print media did not have to consider. A deferential attitude to politicians existed well into the 1950s but this was challenged with the arrival of commercial television Radio broadcasts of political leaders were a feature of the airwaves from the 1920s but the television cameras were only allowed into the Houses of Parliament for the first time in 1988. In more recent years, alongside the televising of proceedings, the role of the Internet has had a significant impact of how journalists cover the workings of parliament and political life.

In the corridors of power MPs and political correspondents continue to rub shoulder to shoulder but as is discussed in this chapter their interactions in the Lobby and at private briefing sessions increasingly have to adapt to the wider changes in the contemporary media world. Section one of this chapter provides background to the Westminster lobby system and the briefing systems between government and a select group of political journalists. Section two discusses the role of the Prime Minister's Official Spokesman and the changing nature of this position in contemporary political life. Section three outlines the challenges faced by those who work at Westminster and the dangers inherent in close working relationships.

The Lobby and the briefing system

The Parliamentary Press Gallery represents the interests of journalists working in the Houses of Parliament. Membership is restricted to journalists who are formally accredited to work at Westminster as representatives of their specific media outlet. As the number of media organisations covering politics has expanded so too has membership of the Parliament Press Gallery. Today over 300 journalists are accredited to work at Westminster. Within the wider Press Gallery a subsidiary group known as the Lobby represents political correspondents. The Lobby operates as an independent body and has its own committee and rules. It is named after the physical area within the Houses of Parliament where journalists and politicians conduct off-the-record briefings. This system has been in place since the end of the nineteenth century when following an attack on the Houses of Parliament access to the corridors of power was restricted. The Sergent at Arms at Westminster continues to keep the list of accredited journalists who are issued with coveted identification passes – marked with the letter 'L' in the case of Lobby reporters – which provide access to the parliamentary complex.

This formalised communications system has survived for well over a century although membership of the Lobby has expanded in more recent times while some of its secrecy rules have been lessened. Technology has impacted on the use of the lobby area as mobile phones and email mean it is now possible for journalists to work successfully with far less direct face-to-face contact with their political sources. As one Labour MP explained:

> When I first came here […] it would be rare for that lobby not to include some journalists, and sometimes it could be as many as ten or a dozen or twenty. Now, the only people you see in the lobby are the fellas in the fancy breeches after the place […] I think it's the advent of 24 hour news.
>
> (Davis, 2010: 136)

The modern public relations apparatus emerged in the twentieth century and was first in evidence with the establishment of a press office in the Foreign Office in 1919 (Curran, 2002: 36). Over subsequent decades – but particularly in the 1980s and 1990s – the governmental publicity machine and news management systems expanded significantly, in part, to deal with an expansion of news outlets and the transformation in the nature of news delivery. When Margaret Thatcher came to power in 1979 the government was only really concerned with about a dozen newspapers and a handful of key radio and television programmes. Over the following decade the media sector expanded dramatically – Channel 4 first broadcast in November 1982, Sky News launched in 1989. These new outlets were matched by an increased number of programmes across all channels including, for example, *Newsnight*, which first broadcast in January 1982. Not only was there now more media for political stories but also technological developments in the communications sector meant news delivery became faster and more immediate which in turn placed greater demands on politicians to respond to events.

The exclusive nature of Lobby reporting was emphasised by the right of its members to attend daily private briefings given by government representatives. Throughout the last century the core of the relationship between 10 Downing Street and the Lobby has been this system of twice daily briefings. They were held in private usually off-the-record with attribution to 'government sources' or occasionally with agreement to 'a government spokesman'. The spokesperson was rarely identified by name. The cardinal rule of the Lobby was never to identify an informant without specific permission. The briefings provided the opportunity to ask questions and to tease out issues related to ongoing controversies.

The briefing system was the source of some criticism. First, the ethos of secrecy underpinning the information flow between the two sides created an environment in which rumour rather than fact could drive political news. Second, the exclusion of specialist correspondents undoubtedly assisted the government when their area of expertise was the main news item of the day. Third, the absence of cameras was very much to the advantage of the government representative. Ross made the telling observation that, 'Spin-doctors are learning that by their body, by the way they emphasise or downplay words and phrases, they can influence how the newspapers report something. You cannot do that when cameras lenses and microphones are fixed on you' (Ross, 2009).

During the 1980s the Westminster Lobby system was embroiled in controversy when Bernard Ingham the spokesperson for Margaret Thatcher was accused of using private briefings to undermine ministers of the Conservative Party government. The newly established *Independent* opted not to join the Lobby and subsequently the *Guardian* and the *Scotsman* withdrew. All three newspapers returned to the Lobby after election of John Major as Prime Minister in 1992 with a promise to allow previously unattributable lobby briefing to be credited to 'Downing Street sources'. The election of the New Labour government in 1997 brought further reform. Alastair Campbell ended the 70-year-old Westminster system of secret unattributable briefings for a selective group of journalists. Campbell effectively dismantled the closed shop that was lobby reporting. Some briefings were put 'on-the-record' – transcripts with summaries of the daily briefings have been available online since 2000 – while access was granted to specialist and foreign correspondents. Moreover, monthly televised prime ministerial media conferences were held. While Campbell's approach as Blair's spokesperson (discussed below) generated controversy one of the impacts of reforms from this period was to increase transparency and accountability – while lessening the importance of the Lobby itself.

The emergence of the Internet – and the use of social media as a political communication resource – has further facilitated more direct engagement between politicians and their supporters and members of the public. While the mainstream media remains vital for communicating with the wider public the Internet has reduced the dependency of politicians and their officials on Lobby members. The Internet has not just opened up new means for politicians to communicate with the wider public – beyond interactions with the Lobby – but has also created new sources of political news beyond the established newspapers and broadcasters. Several political blogs have established high readerships including those written by Iain Dale (www.iaindale.com) and Guido Fawkes (www.order-order.com). These online offerings have also become a form of news competition for the Lobby. The revelation that one of Gordon Brown's media advisors was planning to use the Internet to published untrue rumours about Labour Party opponents first emerged in the political blogosphere.

The Prime Minister's Official Spokesman

There has been a long tradition of Prime Ministers employing media strategists. Lloyd George relied upon the services of a press advisor to influence his relationship with the newspapers during World War I although the increasing importance of media relations was really only clearly signalled with the recruitment of the first chief press secretary in 1930. George Steward was given the title of 'chief press liaison officer of His Majesty's government'. Today, his successor in 10 Downing Street has the title, 'Prime Minister's Official Spokesman'. The holder of the position has been described as the prime minister's spokesperson and main media advisor as well as the coordinator of government information (Seymour Ure, 2003: 125). Media management strategies pursued by the Prime Minister's media advisor involve attempting to drive the news agenda, create favourable headlines and a positive narrative while destroying a bad one and fire fighting unfavourable stories (Heffernan, 2006: 587).

Bernard Ingham for Margaret Thatcher and Alistair Campbell for Tony Blair remain two of the most dominant press secretaries to have worked at 10 Downing Street. They each had a combative relationship with the parliamentary lobby journalists. Contentious queries to Ingham about the business of government were frequently met with the words, 'bunkum and balderdash' while Campbell favoured 'complete crap, C-R-A-P' or 'G-A-R-B-A-G-E' (White, 1994: 95). Following his departure from Downing Street Ingham wrote about his twice-daily encounters with the Lobby journalists:

At 11am members of the Lobby saunter over to No. 10 from their office in the Palace of Westminster for the first briefing of the day in the Chief Press Secretary's Office. My deputy and I sat in extremely comfortable arm chairs on either side of the grand fireplace with a set of tongues on the hearth. My press officers sat with their backs to the windows looking out into Downing Street. The Lobby used the settee and the black plastic chairs stacked against the wall for their convenience. I would tell them what the Prime Minister was doing that day and what Government news events, announcements or publications to expect and then I would place myself at their disposal. They would ask anything they liked and I would answer as I wished. We would each form our own conclusions.

(Ingham, 1994: 557)

Ingham's influence was, in fact, far more substantial than that of a mere provider of information to Lobby correspondents. He was a significant political player in his own right and used his influential position to drive the media agenda of the Thatcher administration. In this regard, the role of spokesman for the Prime Minister – and in effect the senior government spokesman – departed from the traditional civil service neutrality towards politics to being an active participant in the media–political process. Campbell's role was also significantly wider than his job specification. He had an input into policy formation and was one of Blair's closest political advisors. It has been argued that Campbell's 'position at the heart of Whitehall signified the centrality of political communications within the New Labour project' (Heffernan, 2006: 584). The New Labour approach to communications was certainly more proactive than anything witnessed previously. There was far greater central control and coordination with much more emphasis on proactively setting the news agenda coupled with a rapid and robust response unit. From his pivotal position in 10 Downing Street Campbell oversaw this entire communication system and, such was, used his influential reach across all areas of governmental activity. It is little wonder then that one political commentator very early in his term as Blair's spokesperson described him as the 'real deputy prime minister' (Oborne, 1999: 2).

Campbell was aggressive in his promotion – and protection – of his political master. He had no difficulty displaying contempt for individual journalists. Oborne in an unofficial biography claimed that, 'he dislikes political journalists with an intensity bordering on hatred' (Oborne, 1999: 7). In the end, however, his zeal for the New Labour cause – and his overwhelming desire to protect Blair – were his undoing. His successors during the remainder of the Labour term in office – under both Blair and Brown – had far less influence and were significantly less controversial. The New Labour communications system came under the spotlight following the Iraq dossier crisis and the Kelly affair. Campbell had, however, been a source of negative comment throughout his period as Blair's media champion with ongoing criticism of an unhealthy attention to style over substance, and also a blurring of the lines between what was the party political interest and what was the business of government. The example of Campbell in the aftermath of the Iraq dossier controversy – and more recently Andy Coulson in the *News of the World* hacking scandal – illustrates how the media strategist effectively becomes a political liability when they become the story. While Tony Blair may have felt his media strategist was 'irreplaceable' once he had become the news story it was a case of 'he can't stay on. He's a marked man' (Mandelson, 2010: 363).

Relationships

There is a necessary interdependence underpinning the relationship between journalists and politicians. Journalists need stories while politicians need exposure. The politician can provide the journalist with news while the journalist, in turn, can provide the political with access to the public. The key for political journalists is to develop contacts with elected representatives and their advisors. Patience is required as cultivating contacts takes time and these contacts are ultimately built on a sense of mutual trust that is not easily acquired. One of the challenges, however, is to ensure that these coordinal relations are not confused with friendship. Journalists have to be able to maintain contacts while, when required, providing the public with critical commentary about government decisions. This type of reportage is not always welcomed by politicians seeking positive headlines for their actions. Balancing the interdependency in the relationship is essential as astutely explained by Jane Patterson, the chief political reporter with Radio New Zealand:

> That's when your professionalism has to kick in and you have to make it clear to those MPs that you're doing your job as they are doing theirs ... you do have to maintain a bit of distance, otherwise you are not going to be effective.
>
> (Ross, 2010: 275)

Achieving this distance is not always an easy undertaking. One political journalist – Kevin Maguire – has written about the 'pull' factor at Westminster which turns reporters into 'insiders': 'Westminster works on nudges, winks and a quiet word here and there ... They pull you in and make you part of the club' (Barnett and Gaber, 2001: 125). Critics of the Lobby system see this close working environment at Westminster as gradually muting political journalism – and that coupled with the secrecy of non-attribution at briefings – places Lobby reporters in a situation of being 'co-opted as honorary MPs' (Cockerell *et al.*, 1984: 36). More recently, Bob Franklin from Cardiff University has led the charge about the effectiveness of the Westminster Lobby in holding the government to account amid the dangers of journalists establishing close relations and thereby merely acting as conduits for information. In this view, political and parliamentary journalists have 'metamorphosed from an active and critical observer of political affairs into a passive purveyor of government messages' (Franklin, 1994: 87).

The failure of Lobby journalists to expose the MPs' expenses scandal has been used most recently to illustrate the problems inherent in the media contact system at Westminster. One former chairperson of the Parliamentary Press Gallery said the fact that Lobby reporters missed the expenses scandal was 'an indictment of the lobby system itself' (Hencke, 2009). Ivor Gaber went further in arguing that the expenses scandal – and the publications of the expenses revelations in the *Daily Telegraph* – will 'be seen as the moment when the Westminster lobby, if it didn't actually die, did reach a terminal moment in its continuing slide into irrelevance and decline' (Gaber, 2010). The calls for reform – and a change in how politics is reported – have come from many quarters. 'It's a closed shop. A club. A bizarre Petri dish of rivalry, personal enmity and the occasional fistfight. It needs major reform,' said the former New Labour minister for digital engagement Tom Watson during the height of the expenses scandal crisis in the summer of 2009 (Watson, 2009).

The movement of journalists into the political communication arena has undoubtedly complicated this already complex situation. The number of poachers turned gamekeeper – Campbell and Coulson are prime examples – leads to a myriad of overlapping professional and personal relationships between journalists and politicians. The so-called 'spin doctor' is not a recent arrival on the political scene but the sheer number of political PR operators and their professionalism has brought an additional layer of complexity to the nexus between politics and the media in the contemporary era. In this regard, however, former *Guardian* Political Editor Michael White has offered some words of caution:

> In a half-functioning democracy you can, as it were, spin some of the media all of the time, all of the media some of the time, but not all of the media all of the time. And the evidence suggests that voters wisely mistrust both sides.
>
> (White, 1994: 104)

The media's influence may not be as strong as many would like to believe but in framing stories journalists do play a powerful agenda-setting role. Journalists are important participants in the political process in their own right. Their work has an impact upon – and influences – political debate. Critics claim the substance of political information has lessened with an emphasis on framing and interpreting debate over providing facts and explanations. Several studies have pointed to increased mistrust and cynicism at the heart of political-media relations not just in the United Kingdom but also in other western democracies (Brants *et al.*, 2010: 36–37). A healthy scepticism towards those in power is an essential component of how political journalists work. But politicians increasingly complain that scepticism has been replaced by cynicism and that the media's portrayal of politics has enhanced public cynicism and has impacted negatively on the democratic process. In this argument, the media has moved from a socially responsible role in its coverage of politics to approaching politics as a sport and as a form of entertainment. Tony Blair famously spoke about the media acting like 'a feral beast, just tearing people and reputations to bits. But no-one dares miss out' (Blair, 2007). The complaints naturally come from both sides. Politicians see a trivialisation of politics. Journalists point to excessive spin.

Conclusion

The MPs' expenses scandal in 2009 reverberated beyond calls for reform of the business of politicians at Westminster. The role of political journalists – and the failure of Lobby reporters to expose such wrongdoing – called into question the institutionalised arrangements under which the media operates at Westminster. The danger of being part of an 'insider club' – underpinned by culture of close relations with politicians and their advisors – is not unique to British politics. Similar concerns have been expressed elsewhere (see Rafter, 2009 and Ross, 2010). This nascent debate about the relevance of lobby reporting, however, has coincided with wider changes in the world of journalism which means that the historical exclusivity of the Parliamentary Press Gallery is vanishing. Political journalism is now practised outside the walls of the Houses of Parliament. Political stories emerge online; they are also pursued by specialist journalists working in the newsrooms of their own media outlets. Yet, notwithstanding the reforms instigated under the Campbell regime the Lobby has itself been slow to respond to these external changes. For example, calls to admit television cameras to lobby briefings have been ignored – in part, perhaps, because opening up the briefing system would at once shatter its mystique and sunder the apparent elite position of the holders of Lobby passes. But for the Lobby – as elsewhere in the media world – standing still is no longer an option. The debate about the role of the Lobby – and the reporting of politics in the UK – is set against a wider debate about the role of the media and its interactions with the political system alongside the fallout from the *News of the World* hacking controversy in 2011.

References

Barnett, S. and Gaber, I. 2001. *Westminster Tales: The Twenty-first Century Crisis in Political Journalism*. London: Continuum.

Blair, T. 2007. *Reuters Speech on Public Life*. 12 June 2007. See http://news.bbc.co.uk/2/hi/uk_news/politics/6744581.stm (Accessed: 12 December 2010).

Brants, Kees, Claes de Vreese, Judith Moller and Philip van Praag. 2010. 'The Real Spiral of Cynicism? Symbiosis and Mistrust between Politicians and Journalists'. *International Journal of Press Politics* 15(1): 25–40.

Cockerell, M., Hennessy, P. and Walker, D. 1984. *Sources Close to the Prime Minister: Inside the Hidden World of the News Manipulators*. London: Macmillan.

Curran, James. 2002. *Media and Power*. London: Routledge.

Davis, A. 2010. 'Politics, Journalism and New Media: Virtual Iron Cages in the New Culture of Capitalism'. In Fenton, N. (ed.) *New Media, Old News: Journalism and Democracy in the Digital Age*. London: Sage.

Franklin, B. 1994. *Packaging Politics*. London: Edward Arnold.

Gaber, I. 2010. 'The Slow Death of the Westminster Lobby: Collateral Damage from the MPs' Expenses Scandal'. London School of Economics.

Heffernan, Richard. 2006. 'The Prime Minister and the News Media: Political Communication as a Leadership Resource'. *Parliamentary Affairs*, 59(4): 582–98.

Hencke, D. 2009. 'Westminster's Lobby is Too Clubby'. *Guardian Blog*, 7 September 2009. See www.guardian.co.uk/media/organgrinder/2009/sep/07/david-hencke-westminster-lobby (Accessed: 11 December 2010).

Ingham, B. 1994. 'The Lobby System: Lubricant or Spanner?' *Parliamentary Affairs*, 47: 549–65.

Mandelson, P. 2010. *The Third Man: Life at the Heart of New Labour*. London: Harper Collins.

Oborne, P. 1999. *Alastair Campbell: New Labour and the Rise of the Media Class*. London: Aurum Press.

Rafter, K. 2009. 'Run Out of the Gallery: The Changing Nature of Irish Political Journalism'. *Irish Communications Review*, 11.

Ross, F. 2009. 'Where the Cameras Can't Go'. *New Statesman*. 18 October.

Ross, Karen. 2010. 'Dance Macabre: Politicians, Journalists, and the Complicated Rumba of Relationships'. *International Journal of Press Politics* 15(3): 272–94.

Seymour Ure, C. 2003. *Prime Ministers and the Media: Issues of Power and Control*. Oxford: Blackwell.

Watson, T. 2009. 'Crack open the lobby cartel, rip up the rules and let a new era of accountability begin'. *Independent on Sunday*, 21 June.

White, M. 1994. 'Monarchs of Spin Valley'. Glover, S. (ed.) *The Penguin Book of Journalism: Secrets of the Press*. London: Penguin.

4 Crime reporting

Barry Turner

Reporting crime

The subject of crime features large in our media. As a specialism it is one of the oldest of them all and ranks alongside political reporting as having been there since the start. Crime has a special fascination for all and it is hardly surprising that people have always sought out stories of evil and of the derring-do of the crime fighter. Criminals and their behaviour touch on some of the most basic of human instincts and feelings and can leave us disturbed, disgusted, thrilled, amused and frightened, sometimes all at the same time. Crime is the subject of myth and we encounter it every day, in most cases vicariously as consumers of news or entertainment rather than as victims or perpetrators but crime is never far from our thoughts.

The media fascination with crime starts right at the beginning of the modern press. As we will examine later in this essay the modern police and the modern media grew up together out of necessity and the crime writers of the eighteenth century, were they able to see it, would probably be surprised as how little has changed in the way we report crime today. Starting from this historical perspective we will now take a look at what makes the crime reporter tick and how our news media informs and very often misinforms us about crime in our society.

Even before the foundation of the modern press, indeed even before the printing press brought journalism as a craft to life, crime was reported. The Bedfordshire coroner's rolls note that on 28 April 1272 an incident took place in Dunton.[1] The report describes the arrival of vagabonds in town. The vagabonds are up to no good and the report goes on to describe them as eventually falling out among themselves and one killing another, for which he is subsequently hanged. The story is interesting in that while it is not journalism as we would know it many of the facts described are the very thing that grabs the reader's attention in our modern newspapers. The vagabonds were outsiders, men of no tithing. Placing criminals in a deviant group outside the norm is still the basis of our crime stories today and a journalist will always seek to categorise a law breaker this way even though the majority of law breakers are surprisingly conventional are often part of the in group rather than of a deviant sub-class.

What is conventional about this very early crime report is the way that the criminals are described right up to the point of getting their just deserts. The fascination with crime involves the crime itself and the punishment that followed in equal measure. Between the mid-seventeenth and eighteenth centuries this had become the stock in trade of the crime writer. Reciting the dastardly villainy of criminals and their well-deserved fate, usually on the scaffold, was not just an early form of specialist reporting but had become almost an art form.

What then is the formula of the modern crime story? This has been extensively covered by sociologists and criminologists for the last four decades at least. The most common observations are those of the moral panic as described by Stanley Cohen in 1972[2] and the news values model of crime reporting as described by Steve Chibnall in 1977 and Yvonne Jewkes in 2004 (see later). While Cohen is credited with the invention of the term 'moral panics', the concept has always existed in societies where criminality and deviance are present. Since criminality and deviance to some degree are present in all societies we can assume that moral panic is a universal concept.

Our media likes to think of itself as a watchdog of the public interest and of a guardian of public decency. Criminality is therefore an obvious target of its attention and a firm platform for expressing what is believed to be a traditional, common sense interpretation of the world. Why then is it widely understood that crime reporting in reality is distorted to a point where it does not represent anything like a true picture of what is going on? Study after study of crime tells us that the crimes that most people worry about are in fact rare. Murders, rapes, serious violent crime and robbery represent only a small proportion of reported crime[3] with the majority of crime by far being of a less serious nature.

It is not the purpose of this chapter to discuss the statistics of crime in detail. The statistics themselves can at times be misleading and in spite of the fact that as individuals we are statistically unlikely to be victims of serious crime that is no consolation to those that have been. In *Folk Devils and Moral Panics* (1972: 9), Cohen describes the concept as '[a] condition, episode, person or group of persons emerges to become defined as a threat to societal values and interests'. Moral panics then represent a threat to society rather than to the individuals in it. Cohen's description is interesting in the use of the word 'emerges'. We have an image of this threat spontaneously generating within our society as if it were some kind of infection or contamination. It fully represents the way our media report on crime and we can see it repeatedly portrayed in the history of crime reporting.

In the decade Cohen coined the term Moral Panic the media in the UK began using a new word to describe a certain type of street crime. Mugging, a slang term imported from the United States to describe a type of street robbery started to appear in the tabloid press in the early 1970s. The press eagerly reported what at the time was an emerging 'new' crime wave. These robberies were portrayed not only as novel, always a news value, but as alien and the target of the moral panic was in the main young black men. A ferocious campaign by the press put pressure on the police to fight this 'new' crime wave and the judiciary to impose ever-harsher sentences. Little if no emphasis was placed on the actual circumstances of the robberies except to focus on black youths robbing white people.[4] The social consequences of this press campaign caused misery and social disorder well out of proportion to the actual threat caused by the muggers themselves with a targeting of black youths culminating in the infamous 'sus' laws of the 1970s.[5]

Was mugging a new crime wave? No, street robberies have occurred ever since there were streets and the press has always had a fascination for them in spite of this type of crime representing only six per cent of recorded crime in Britain. We can go back to the 1860s and compare the muggings of the 1970s with another media invented crime wave. Over 100 years before Cohen coined the neat term moral panic and panic was sweeping the cities of Britain. This panic like the one of the 1970s was conjured up by the press and led to an unjustified attack on police competence and hasty and ill-considered legislation.

A 'new' type of attack on the respectable citizens of the metropolis was being described as garrotting. The method employed involved two assailants, one of whom approached the victim from behind and placed a ligature around their neck. The second assailant would then approach from the front and rifle through the pockets of the disabled victim. The term 'garrotting' was used in spite of there being little evidence that the robbers actually sought to kill their victim and the majority of course lived to tell the tale, but the type of robbery had all the necessary elements to make it a huge story, all of the elements that would be over 100 years later described by criminologists as news values. As the story began to spread not only in the scandal sheets of the time but in the respectable press, elaborate theories began to emerge. As if it was not enough that street robbers represented a threat to civilised society, a foreign element was added. In *The Victorian Underworld* (1970) Kellow Chesney describes the garrotting scare in detail and discusses one of the central news values that made the scare such a widespread panic in the Victorian press. The victims were frequently described as 'respectable' people. This gave the reader something to identify with: respectable readers of newspapers identified themselves with these respectable victims of the garrotter. The brutal but exotic nature of the attack was associated with the thuggee cult in India and occasionally demobbed and destitute soldiers were blamed as perpetrators of these attacks with suggestions that they had learned this sinister trade while on foreign postings.[6]

Steve Chibnall identified what he described as professional imperatives in crime reporting,[7] these being immediacy, dramatisation, personalisation, simplification, titillation, conventionalism, structured access and novelty. It was clear from the nineteenth-century newspapers that these imperatives were at play very early in the reporting of crime. The garrotting scare as identified by Chesney earlier in 1970 provided at least some of these. The 'respectable' nature of the victims was easy to personalise in respect of the readers. Violent robberies were naturally dramatic. Blaming out groups, especially if they could be identified with foreign and sinister cults, offered simple explanations for the phenomena. Chibnall's 'professional imperatives' are still influential in criminological studies but in 2004 Yvonne Jewkes described a set of newsworthiness criteria arguing that media audiences have become more sophisticated.[8] Jewkes describes 12 'news values' that determine the structure and content of crime stories. The first of these she describes as threshold, which requires the events or circumstances of the crime to have importance or dramatic effect. Naturally this threshold will eliminate common and minor crimes from having any news value except at a local level. Minor examples of so-called anti-social behaviour may appear in local newspapers but are unlikely to be in the national news except in terms of political debate.[9]

Jewkes describes the next news value as predictability referring to the use of crime statistics and reports to allow the media to plan ahead when considering covering types of crime stories. The third category is simplification. This is a very old category in terms of crime reporting and we have already seen it in the Victorian press. The model relies on reducing crimes to a minimum number of themes and is the principal target of criminologists. An example of simplification is relating two issues such a drugs and crime. The illegality of the possession and supply of narcotics makes them naturally the territory of the criminal, consequently the media will focus on drugs as the cause of crime on 'sink estates'. Actual causes of crime will, of course, be much more complex and the intertwining of drugs and crime are actually symptoms of more complex social dysfunction than causes in themselves. Sadly, our media do not have the capacity to examine complexity in crime.

Like simplification Jewkes goes on to describe individualism as a news value in crime reporting. Again this relies on the simplest explanation for criminality. Political and social dysfunction will be avoided or at the very least reduced to conflicting positions of individuals or political parties. Individual definitions of crime and individual responses are reduced to policy differences where the Home Secretary for instance will take one position and the Shadow Home Secretary another. This is a feature of news reporting that permeates the whole of the media where balance is often a substitute for substance in a news story.

The most prominent of the news values described by Jewkes is risk and the most exaggerated elements of news stories on crime misrepresent the risk of an individual being the victim of crime. This again can be seen in the newspapers of the eighteenth and nineteenth century and is a very long established tradition. The reader and viewer are given a view of crime as random, mindless and unpredictable. The streets are seen as places where out of the blue an unsuspecting and presumably 'respectable' member of the public can be the victim of a mindless attack. This is probably the most insidious of the news values and has created a moral panic beyond those originally described by Cohen. The National Crime Statistics[10] are a vast data set and well beyond this chapter's capacity to examine in detail; however, we can say that in 2011 4,150,097 crimes of all types were recorded in the UK, the vast majority of which would be considered low-level crime related to property. Even allowing for an adjustment for unreported crimes there would appear to be less than a one in ten chance of being a victim of crime.

As well as the relatively low risk of being a victim of crime the majority of crimes are not committed randomly but are planned and targeted. Many of the victims of crime are not representative of the 'respectable' reader. Certain population groups are higher risk than others but in the main it is far less likely that a member of the public will become a victim than our press would lead us to believe.

Sex is another misrepresented element in crime reporting and has led to more distorted perceptions of criminality in society. This is undoubtedly deeply rooted in society's attitudes to sex in general and certainly fits in with the peculiar duality of the press with its moral prudishness on the one hand and its prurient titillation on the other. Returning yet again to the newspapers of the nineteenth century, sex crimes gave the journalist the opportunity to describe in detail sexual deviance that could not ordinarily be discussed in polite society. Placing sex in a criminal scenario allowed a 'surgical or pathological' façade and gave the press an opportunity to engage in a kind of voyeurism. A classic example of this was seen in the scandal perpetrated by the great Victorian journalist WT Stead when he set up the purchase of a 13-year-old girl to demonstrate the ease by which children could be bought for sex.[11]

Jewkes in her news values introduced the concept of celebrity and criminality. This was a relatively new concept that had not been the focus of attention in earlier news values models and it has led to some fascinating sociological and legal debate. The celebrity as criminal gave new impetus to the press as a lecturer on morality. The celebrity has a far lower threshold of deviance than the ordinary member of the public and journalistic opprobrium is lavishly applied where any celebrity shows deviance. On 3 June 2007 the strapline from the *Sun* read 'TODAY The Sun blows the lid on the sleazy drug-fuelled world that held Kate Moss in a vice-like grip for TEN YEARS'. In a typical tabloid frenzy and hack language the paper described the supermodel Kate Moss as a depraved and degenerate individual who actually snorted coke from a 'dirty' floor. The justification for this type of hysteria is that Kate Moss was not only a supermodel but also a role model. The singer George Michael was similarly a target for the hyped-up disgust displayed in the media in spite of it being rather difficult to justify that as holding him to account as a role model.

Proximity is yet another of the categories of news values that Jewkes identified in crime stories. This proximity category is subdivided into both geographical and cultural elements. Like threshold this relates the criminality to different levels of reporting, which may be local, regional or national. As well as the geographical proximity the cultural one can create a moral panic in a socio-economic population group. The comparison between the cases of Madeleine McCann and Shannon Matthews graphically illustrates cultural proximity. The coverage of the disappearance of the middle-class respectable girl Madeleine McCann was unprecedented in intensity and starkly contrasted with that of Shannon Matthews, a girl from a dysfunctional lower-class background. The press is often fixated with a very Victorian concept of criminal classes and will frequently associate socio-economic groups such as the unemployed and council estate dweller with 'criminal types'.

Violence has always been integral to crime reporting for the most obvious of reasons. Violence offers both spectacle and drama and is the essence not only of crime reporting but of fictional crime drama. Graphic imagery was identified by Jewkes as a separate category but for the purposes of this definition can be rolled up with violence. A category of crime reporting that is now standard fare on

TV is the 'fly on the wall' documentary. This often uses CCTV footage of violence and even on occasion shows the use of force by police officers.

Children represent the penultimate category in Jewkes' analysis and once again this is a reworking of a very old news value. The involvement of children in crime is always considered to be of high newsworthiness. Children as victims and as perpetrators grab headlines and both stories have a very long history. In considering children as victims of crime certain models always come into play, some of which are based on well tested social theory while others are based more on prejudice and distorted press morality.

The modern press has a morbid fixation on paedophilia and sex attacks on children. This is of course the modern moral panic writ large. It is not the intention of this author to in any way deprecate the seriousness of sexual assaults on children or the profound individual and societal damage that this kind of crime is capable of causing. However, it is observable that such media coverage has profoundly affected the behaviour and attitudes towards children in a number of ways. Lurid press stories of ritual child abuse, of roving paedophiles representing a threat to all of our children have created a fear among many parents out of all proportion to the actual threat.[12]

Children as perpetrators of crime create to some extent an even greater moral panic and a study conducted by the children's charity Barnado's discovered some astonishing attitudes toward children displayed in the media. According to the poll 49 per cent of adults think children pose an increasing danger to society and 54 per cent say children are 'beginning to behave like animals'. The authors of the survey referred to children being described in the press as 'animal', 'feral' and 'vermin' and as perpetrators of unparalleled acts of barbarity. Forty-three per cent of adults believed 'something must be done to protect us from children'; 35 per cent agreed with the proposition that 'nowadays it feels like the streets are infested with children'; 45 per cent said people 'refer to children as feral because they behave that way'; and 49 per cent disagreed with the statement that 'children who get into trouble are often misunderstood and in need of professional help'.

The charity said the latest official crime survey found that adults think young people commit up to half of all crimes, when in fact they were responsible for only 12 per cent.

The language used in the modern press to describe juvenile offenders matches the most lurid and sensationalist reporting of the nineteenth century and supports the final element of Jewkes' news values. Conservative ideology is at the heart of the majority of the popular press. This is moral rather than political conservatism and is reflected in demands for higher sentencing or popular punitiveness. The conservative press pander to the populist belief that harsher punishments act as deterrence to crime in spite of decades of research to the contrary. The press parrot constantly the need for greater police powers, more prisons and tougher criminal justice. Rehabilitation is not a feature of press reports on criminal justice except where they can demonstrate it to have failed. It would perhaps help if they for once took a look at the history of criminal justice to note that some of the worst periods for criminal activity were during the Victorian period and that the death penalty, corporal punishment, hard labour and transportation for life had little impact on the commission of crime. Linking this philosophy to the penultimate category of children we can see the basis for the naming and shaming campaign often directed at juveniles by the press. The anachronistic morality of the press supports a view that naming children and juveniles is in the public interest. It is noteworthy that Parliament does not agree and since 1933 we have had a law designed to give juveniles anonymity as a means to possible rehabilitation.[13]

Chibnall and Jewkes as well as other criminological researchers have correctly identified the structure of crime reporting. In their studies they have demonstrated the weaknesses in structuring news stories around a populist model. The quality of reporting in this area is in the main low and the prognosis for improvement poor. Like many other areas of modern journalism in crime reporting the old joke 'don't let the truth get in the way of a good story' is alive and well after at least three centuries.

The police and the press

The relationship between the police and the press has a very long history. The British tradition of a civil police service was born out of this relationship and contrasts clearly with the police systems of our near neighbours in Europe. It is clear from examining the shared history of our police service with that of our media that the long history has shaped the type of policing Britain enjoys and that our free press also owes much to cooperation between what can rightly be described as public services.

The modern police in Britain can be traced to the foundation of the Bow Street Runners in the mid-eighteenth century. Although not a police force in the sense of today's police this organisation was set up to tackle the massive social problems caused by crime in eighteenth-century London and evidence exists to demonstrate that despite the very small number of officers it had some success.

When established, Britain (unlike most of its continental neighbours) did not have any state-controlled organisation with a policing or crime fighting function. Policing was largely a problem for the parish and parish constables were responsible for keeping order and securing criminals for trial. The state-controlled police forces of our European neighbours were in the main concerned with the security of the state, or more accurately those running the state. They were more like secret police organisations with very little civil function and as such did not advertise their existence by forming relationships with the nascent news media in their respective countries.

Britain too had its share of secret police spooks with a similar role of securing the interests of the ruling parties and they too kept themselves hidden from public view. The concept of a civil police force formed ostensibly to keep the peace among the general public and fight crime was unknown. At the beginning the public and parliamentarians strongly resisted the formation of a police force for London. A great deal of suspicion was to be found at all levels of society of the real reasons for such a force's existence and many believed that it was and many considered it a threat to civil liberties enjoyed in Britain.

It is here, right at the beginning of modern policing, that the relationship between the police and the press was established. The press were in fact co-opted into the argument for a modern police force and used its already considerable influence to convince people of the need for such a force.

The Bow Street Runners were the brainchild of Henry and John Fielding, magistrates at Bow Street Court. The Fielding brothers were highly adept at publicity and had combined their judicial roles with being active political pamphleteers and journalists. Henry Fielding was a successful author and playwright too and a commentator on social dysfunction within society. By skilful manipulation of the press the Fieldings convinced a very sceptical Parliament to finance this venture and with only six officers for the entire policing of London the modern police was born. This manipulation had in many cases been in the form of reporting on the very high levels of street crime and the lack of any effective organisation to deal with it. Interestingly the methods used show signs of manipulating moral panics and much of our crime journalism today still shows very many of these traits.

It can certainly be argued that this was the beginning of the now complex relationship between the police and the press, it could even be ventured that this very early relationship demonstrates the absolute necessity for this special relationship to exist. The Bow Street Runners evolved slowly into a visible police force uniformed and on patrol following the death of Henry Fielding. John Fielding introduced the first routine patrols setting the scene for beat policemen and placed these officers in recognisable uniforms to give the public confidence in the force's presence and fight against crime.

While many would argue that the Bow Street Runners were not police in the sense we know it there is no doubt that the Metropolitan Police when formed in 1829 was a direct descendant of this first civil police organisation and like its predecessor from the very beginning established a close, even symbiotic, relationship with the press.

A modern civil police force needs this relationship. Both organisations rely on similar functions, traditions and ethics. Both organisations are in the business of looking for information and processing it for the public good, albeit in different ways. Both organisations rely on transparency and ethical conduct because both claim to be acting on behalf of society. The press has a social responsibility to assist in the fight against crime and the capture of criminals. The press claims as its greatest credential that it acts in the public interest and there can be few issues in the public interest more important than public safety and the protection of life, limb and property.

In the main the relationship between press and police is a positive one and has undoubtedly led to the apprehension of criminals who would otherwise have escaped justice. The success of *Crimewatch* first broadcast on 7 June 1984 is well recognised by the police even though they were very sceptical about involvement and at first some forces refused to take part. In its 25-year history the programme has been responsible for the apprehension of 57 murderers, 53 rapists and 18 paedophiles[14] and one in three of the cases featured in the programme result in an arrest and one in five a conviction. The programme idea came from Germany originally where *Aktenzeichen Ungelöst XY*[15] first aired in the 1970s. It has since been copied as a programme format worldwide.

The relationship has had is downs as well as ups. The news media can as well as strongly assisting the police in the apprehension of criminals act as a serious hindrance to both investigation and prosecution of crimes. In 1994 a research study was carried out on the effect of news reporting on criminal investigations.[16] This report examined the notorious West case where serial killers Fred and Rosemary West had been investigated for a series of horrific murders of young women. The case was inevitably going to be a huge media story involving, as it did, the news values most prominent in crime reporting: sex, violence, threshold, proximity, etc. The Gloucestershire Police were overwhelmed by the media attention and as a rural force unaccustomed to mass murder investigations found the management of the press to be their most onerous responsibility. Many serious and dangerous practices were undertaken by unscrupulous reporters. Journalists were discovered to be covertly following off-duty officers to eavesdrop on their conversations, setting up their own lines of enquiry including setting up a telephone hotline. The media published what they believed to be the best lines of enquiry, interviewing witnesses sometimes before the police had had time to interview them and using the infamous practice of chequebook journalism to buy access to witnesses, victims and members of the West family. Journalists were even caught at the crime scene, endangering the evidence sought by police. The interference with the investigation eventually resulted in Rosemary West's solicitor arguing that she could not get a fair trial and any journalism student burdened with learning media law knows the dangers of unbridled reporting on criminal proceedings.[17]

There is now a crisis in this relationship which is undermining public confidence in both organisations. Many are now questioning the relationship and even suggesting that more distance should be put between the media and the police. This represents a failure to understand the relationship and is ironically in large part a failure of the media itself to understand it. In the long and complex history of the relationship between the press and the police the 'marriage' has often had its ups and downs. There is often ambivalence between the two partners and this is occasionally a love–hate relationship. Errors of judgement on both sides have resulted in many difficult periods frequently accompanied with cries for a distancing of the parties from each other.

This is an error in judgement based on a fundamental misunderstanding of the functions of both organisations. Neither a civil police service nor a free press can exist without each other. A police service attempting to operate without a collaborative press would be seriously handicapped and would almost certainly have to function more like a secret police force and less in the public interest. A press without access to the functions of the state would not be able to inform the public and any distancing of these two essential elements of our society would leave us all worse off. The relationship between the press and the police has like many other relationships had its ups and downs, some of them very troublesome indeed, but close examination of the circumstances of these troubles always reveals individual lack of judgement to be responsible, not the relationship itself. It is the ethical conduct of individuals that are to blame not some institutionalised corruption.

Both police officers and journalists have at the very root of their professional ethics the concept of acting in the public interest. All professions purporting to act in the public interest have individuals within them who break the rules and ignore the ethics. It is curious that it is almost traditional when this happens for there to be a cry for tightening the regulations or breaking down the ties between organisations that could not function autonomously without them.

The current crisis in the media is far from over and it will almost certainly leave deep scars. Public confidence is low in the ethics and integrity of the press, the police and those who govern us and it is probably normal that there are cries that 'something needs to be done'. What does not need to be done is the introduction of bureaucratic and stultifying regulations affecting the essential working relationship between the press and the police. A free press and a civil police service are the essential components of a democratic society; if history teaches us anything then we should look back to the Bow Street Runners. No one would have argued that in the mid-eighteenth century they did not need a force to fight against crime. What alarmed the population and Parliament then was not the presence of officers on the beat but a sinister 'regulator' acting behind the scenes and manipulating the police against public interests and civil liberties.

Over regulation has never prevented crime and no amount of regulation would have prevented the current crisis. The current strain on relationships between the press, the police and politicians is a result of criminal behaviour of a group of individuals not a failure of regulation. A vigorous prosecution of those individuals and a forthright condemnation in the press of those convicted will do far more for improving public confidence than any introduction of new regulations ever could.

Notes

1 Geremek, B. (1990) 'The Marginal Man', *The Medieval World: A History of European Society*, Jacques Le Goff (ed.) London: Collins and Brown. Originally published as *L'Uomo Medievale* (1987) Laterza, G. and Spa, F. Roma-Bari.

2 Cohen, S. (1972) *Folk Devils and Moral Panics*. London and New York: McGibbon and Kee Ltd.

3 Reported crime in this context means the crime reported to the police and not the crime reported in the media.

4 In fact according to a Metropolitan Police Report in 1987, 54 per cent of victims were also young black men.

5 A reinterpretation of the 1824 Vagrancy Act whereby anyone suspected of being a potential felon could be considered such and stopped and searched at will by police. The powers were disproportionately aimed at young black men.

6 Chesney, K. (1970) *The Victorian Underworld*. London: Temple Smith.

7 Chibnall, S. (1977) *Law-and-Order News: An Analysis of Crime Reporting in the British Press*. London: Tavistock.

8 Jewkes, Y. (2004) *Media and Crime*. London: Sage.

9 The term 'anti-social behaviour' was adopted as a political slogan and incorporated into the Crime and Disorder Act 1998. Much of the behaviour described is low-level criminality and the introduction of the legislation was part of a political philosophy under the heading of 'tough on crime, tough on the causes of crime'.

10 www.ons.gov.uk/ons/rel/crime-stats/crime-statistics/year-ending-december-2011/index. html.

11 *The Maiden Tribute of Modern Babylon,* a series of highly controversial newspaper articles on child prostitution. *Pall Mall Gazette,* July 1885. Stead was jailed for three months for abducting the child.

12 Biehal, N., Mitchell, F. and Wade, J. (2003) *Lost From View: Missing Persons in the UK.* Bristol: The Policy Press. Seventy per cent of children and young people reported missing had done so by choice. This included those who stayed away from home without permission, without intending to leave for good. Furthermore, four per cent of the young people had 'drifted' away, ten per cent were unintentionally missing, and eight per cent had been forced to leave, which included both parental abduction.

13 Children and Young Persons Act 1933 ss.39, 49.

14 Source: www.bbc.co.uk/crimewatch/aboutcrimewatch/25_anniversary.shtml.

15 'File XY Unsolved'.

16 Berry, G., Izat, J., Mawby, R.C. and Walley, L. (1995) *The Management and Organisation of Serious Crime Investigations.* Stafford: Staffordshire University. Report to the Home Office Police Operations Against Crime (POAC) programme.

17 The Contempt of Court Act 1981 makes it an offence to publish any information that might interfere with the administration of justice and prejudice the right to a fair trial.

5 International journalism

Ben McConville and Kate Smith

Introduction

Winston Churchill said the UK and US are 'divided by a common language', but does this hold true of the US–UK journalism market? This chapter examines the journalistic practice of operating as an international journalist and the different news values and newsgathering between the US and the UK. It also makes a comparison of traditional journalism and Journalism 2.0 to gain insights into current practice. It will also look at both reporting about the UK for a pre-dominantly American audience and reporting as a foreign correspondent back to the UK.

The dominant cultural hegemony in international journalism has been the Anglo-American model, formed by the Big Four news agencies, The Associated Press, Reuters, UPI and AFP, and their largest market, the US. Chalaby argues that the Anglo-American model is borne out of discursive practices such as interviewing, newsgathering and fact checking (1996). The historical development of the Anglo-American model of journalism assumes that practice and practitioners on both sides of the Atlantic are a homogenous group, socially, culturally and professionally. Working practices such as writing, newsgathering, news values, accuracy, fact checking, the significance of official sources and the weighting of official quotes and information vary significantly on both sides of the Atlantic. How much do differences in reporting practices vary in reporting standards between the UK and US? Our case study draws on experience of international journalism to look at what drives some stories to resonate across the Atlantic.

In observing the globalisation of news Boyd-Barrett (1998) pointed out that the number of players in global journalism had diversified over the previous 90 years as traditional news outlets such as TV, radio and newspapers thrived, though the locations or interests represented had not diversified. He also noted that the global news agencies had gained greater autonomy in that period and that this is a desirable condition for the agencies. Although the growth of the Internet since 1998 has tested the dominance of the Anglo-American model of journalism, it still prevails and the major global news agencies formulate operations around the US and the UK with common western political and economic values. The fragmented, fractured and individualistic nature of the Internet means that a serious challenge to the Anglo-American model has been slow to materialise. This might be down to the market dominance of the AP and Reuters, particularly in terms of TV output, which is expensive to make and distribute. This distribution is also top-down and arranged and organised by a small number of gatekeepers with common socio-economic beliefs and world views. Golding and Elliot point out that TV news provides an ideological distinctive world view that reinforces skepticism of 'divergent, dissident or deviant beliefs' (1979: 210). Multimedia forms of distribution are predicted to replace TV in the long run (Paterson in Boyd-Barrett, 1998), and although the Internet has so far failed to achieve this with TV news, it has made significant inroads into text-based journalism.

International reporting

International reporting is primarily carried out by news agencies and foreign correspondents. Flows of information around the world have altered significantly since Boyd-Barrett's assessment of 'the Big Four' (1980). The hegemonic position of the Anglo-American model is being challenged, however, by consumers who are able to access information from myriad sources. This creates challenges around issues of veracity, accuracy and speed. The immediacy of the dissemination of international news through live televised events, 24-hour rolling news and social media has elevated the need to be first.

A foreign correspondent is stationed in another country and lives in that country. The value of the foreign correspondent is that he or she is expected to contextualise and interpret the news from the foreign country to the home country. They are expected to give their opinion and perspective on the country. They use opinion and reportage as well as fact-based reporting of events.

Singer describes fluidity across borders in terms of journalism, not just as the fluidity of form and content, but the fluidity of consumption (2008). Form has moved from the static and vertical media of newspapers, radio and television bulletins. By vertical we mean the top-down nature of news, with journalists acting as gatekeepers. Rogers (1994) interprets Lewin's classic study of decision making by 'Mr Gates', a wire editor in a small Midwestern newspaper (1951) as a decision-maker who filters copy using subjective criteria, explicitly on the basis of personal prejudices. Now there is horizontal journalism, meaning open-ended news dissemination and consumption through the Internet and to a lesser extent 24-hour rolling news. The means of dissemination are no longer held by the few gatekeepers, but by the many, through social network sites such as Twitter, Facebook and YouTube. The power of Journalism 2.0 comes from the inter-activity of the news plus User Generated Content. This can include UGC from eyewitnesses in areas to which journalists have no access or are not yet present at the scene, such as the death of Iranian activist Neda Agha-Soltan, the 7/7 terrorist attacks on London and the Asian tsunami of 2005. The lines between journalists and consumers appear to have blurred. Content is now updated instantly and endlessly. News is constructed before the consumer's eye, with consumers adding to the process through forums and comments. Mistakes are fixed and pasted over with the journalistic artefact becoming a constant work in progress. The WikiLeaks website was able to publish thousands of documents relating to the US military's conduct in Iraq against the wishes of the US government. It was able to do this by publishing outside of US jurisdiction. Here Journalism 2.0 comes into its own as its practitioners are able to defy authority, but it does also raise questions about accountability and ethics.

With the production of news visible, the meaning of the news is constructed collaboratively with the consumer. Also, with retweets and copy posted under various bylines and not just the journalist-originator of the story, news is increasingly produced collaboratively. As Singer points out: 'When everyone can publish information instantly and disseminate it globally, everyone is a publisher – but not necessarily a journalist' (2008: 153). Before Web 2.0 and live rolling news content was stable and fixed, established journalists worked to static deadlines and consumers waited for a top-down delivery on news. Singer points out that content is now unstable, changing and expanding. Not only is it unstable, it is also open to interpretation, comment, re-use and editing. This has significant implications for US agency journalism which nominally operates on the Kovach and Rosenstiel's ideal of journalists and journalism as an objective source of news (2007). This interactive recycling and re-use of copy and ideas can transform journalism from an objective artefact such as the notion of telling how it is to an output that is more an opinionated piece, reproduced across the world and outside the control of the journalist-originator of the article or content.

This has a number of implications for the international journalist. At its most basic level the work is being used without consent and without payment and so others may be profiteering from the original work. Also, the interpretation and contextualisation may be so different as to change the meaning of the original work. This may be acceptable to a degree, but the framing of the work could turn it into something defamatory or a piece that incites the reader to extreme views or actions.

International audiences

With this fluidity of production comes a fluidity of consumption. The relationship between the journalist and their publics is changing. As Metykova (2009) points out audience is an abstract and debateable term that does not necessarily denote social collectivity. With interactivity via online forums, comment boxes and email breaking down the barriers between the journalist and consumer, and audiences becoming participators in the news, rather than merely recipients of information, these changes, Metykova argues, are due to more than just technological advances, but also societal structures and processes. Dialogue is now instant, but there are issues with the quality and meaning of the exchanges between audiences and journalists. Some go so far as to announce 'the death of audience' (Rosen, 2006) in as much as new media platforms such as blogs remove the idea of an audience that is merely a receptor of ideas and elevate the blogger on a par with journalists. Citizen journalism in the form of blogs and wikis allows millions of amateurs to constantly update work online. As Singer asks: 'Are bloggers producing "mass communication" or "interpersonal" communication or a hybrid?' (2008: 152). That might depend on the audience for the blog, as some of the more successful bloggers have niche audiences. Other high-profile bloggers, such as Perez Hilton and Arianna Huffington of *The Huffington Post*, perhaps no longer fall into the category of blogger, as they are in fact editors of larger news organisations.

Audiences on either side of the Atlantic can now easily access information and works of journalism from around the world via the Internet. A UK reader seeking information on an American Presidential election could rightly click on to the *Washington Post* and read a first-hand account, complete with local knowledge and understanding. Likewise the British General Election could be viewed by selecting '*The Times* of London'. However, domestic journalists still write and produce in such a way as to assume a large amount of social, cultural and political knowledge on the part of the consumer. Domestic journalists write and produce primarily for domestic audiences (Metykova, 2009). Journalists still write to an audience held in their line of sight. *New York Times* journalists make assumptions of their readers' social class, education and values as much as geographical location and the same applies for the UK. As a result, there is still a vital role for the international journalist or foreign correspondent to play. The function of the traditional foreign correspondent was not solely to describe events in a foreign land. The best journalists give meaning to events and are able to interpret the social, political, cultural and commercial significance of the narrative. By making meaning, they give value to what is being said. For international journalists the interpretation of events is essential in order to give value as a work of journalism. The line of sight for an international journalist is a global audience, with the domestic context and assumptions removed.

This is also a role that a citizen journalist cannot fill. Blogs, Twitter and other forms of citizen journalism or social media are by their nature often about the personal experience and may be even more localised than that of a domestic journalist on a national newspaper. While technology has allowed the blogger to potentially enjoy a readership in the billions, few, if any, will achieve these numbers. Contrast this with the AP which supplies content to more than 8,000 media outlets around the world and claims a potential one billion readers or consumers for its output. This interpersonal, or individual, form of communication does not fit into traditional models of mass communication, but according to Singer (2008: 152) perhaps fits into a uses and gratifications framework as audiences are selecting content to fit their desires, interests and needs.

The challenge for journalists of the future will be how to produce unique copy that the consumer will not find elsewhere online as news consumers are able to access source material, foreign news outlets and interpretations via RSS feeds and retweets in a way which enable them to bypass the bloggers.

Accuracy, speed, veracity and gatekeeping

Accuracy and speed cannot be uncoupled in journalistic practice. It is a reporting convention that both are essential. Another impact of microblogging on international journalism has been to encourage speed over accuracy, particularly in breaking stories. To be the first to say that the Chilean miners in 2010 were rescued is one thing, but in more complicated stories, such as a conflict, to ensure that you give meaning to events is an imperative. Accuracy is being sacrificed at the altar of speed by the demands and needs of the technology. The drive and the desire for alacrity, coupled with the new conventions of short, sharp bursts of information reinforce the need for speed at any cost.

British news agencies in particular have always prized speed as a virtue. There is a business imperative to be there first, to reveal information first and to get unique information and quotes. Competition among London news agencies in the late 1980s and 1990s was intense as smaller independent agencies such as National News Agency encroached on the Press Association's monopoly of courts and tribunals such as the Old Bailey and the High Court. Journalists would battle to reach the only pay phone in a court house to file copy for the last edition of the evening newspapers or to get the best lines out first. Now that fight to be first is down to seconds.

As a result, news is being rushed out in bite-sized chunks with little editing, gatekeeping or thought. It is delivered via secondary agencies of dissemination such as social networking sites such as Twitter and other aggregators that recycle news. This has added to the need for speed in journalistic practice. At the same time bloggers 'copy and paste' works almost always without permission and often with the original byline removed, to give their opinion on the work without having to research, interview or even understand the issues, contexts or line of sight of the journalist. This is sometimes passed off as their own journalism and their opinion is often characterised by the use of the first person, not only as a writing style, but also heavily weighted in the content and context of the work. This practice is legitimised by the New Journalism style of Hunter S. Thompson, where objectivity is lost. This banal journalism is, for many bloggers, personalised exhibitionism, where self-selected works are used to make a point about how the blogger feels about issues. Banal journalism is about the self and the constant need to reference news, ideas and dissemination of the news in terms of the self, whilst illicitly reproducing news.

Banal journalism

Billig (1995) described banal nationalism in terms of mundane everyday expressions of national identity and characterised by its ubiquity. 'The metonymic image of banal nationalism is not a flag which is consciously waved with fervent passion; it is the flag hanging unnoticed on the public building,' Billig (1995: 39–41). Billig points out that such symbolism is effective because its constant presence has a subliminal effect on those who receive it: the nation. Its very ubiquity leaves it unquestioned.

Similarly, banal journalism, by its very ubiquity, is left unquestioned. On an international scale, it could be argued the effect of this proliferation of illegitimate reversioning leaves international journalism superficial and anonymised, removed from the established or traditional practises of accuracy, veracity and gatekeeping, all sacrificed at the altar of speed. McLuhan's prophecy of the medium being the message has become apparent (1964). Its constant presence has a subliminal effect on those who receive it.

There is a constant buzz of updates and straightforward information which engages the audience in news. However, a constant stream of headlines and breaking news alerts can only give a superficial understanding of the issues and news of the day. Rolling news channels now tend to use breaking news alerts in a way that has devalued the notion of breaking news from the days when traditional media would break from programming to make a major announcement, such as the death of a public figure. While more research is needed on this phenomenon, it is clear that the term 'breaking news' no longer carries the weight it once did.

Without the filter of discursive practices such as gatekeeping, research and interviews, banal journalism is news/opinion which is not created by established journalists. One question here is whether or not artefact without the gatekeeping function is journalism at all.

The substance of banal journalism is characterised more often than not by second-hand reporting which does not go further than the descriptive phase of journalism and is often bereft of interpretation or meaning-making. Meanwhile, bloggers use material 'lifted' from others to create outputs with opinions and comments carried alongside the copied piece of journalism. There has been little or no input into the original piece. There are plenty of professional journalists who blog as an addition to journalistic outputs. This is not necessarily banal journalism as it usually serves as an opinion function, as a diary or an opportunity to contextualise complicated and difficult stories. These journalists are largely the exception as they blog as part of their employment and the blog is one output of original work. Their blogging is characterised as an extension of their journalism.

What should be the response of professional journalists in the UK and US to the rise of this banal journalism? As Singer points out (2008) against the onslaught of bloggers, US journalists must adhere to the ethical guidelines of their professional culture, namely commitment to truth, independence and accountability.

The working international journalist is still left facing the daily challenge of newsgathering, of balancing accuracy and speed. The major global agencies still value accuracy over speed, US journalism in particular practices the need for accuracy and veracity. The international journalists simply cannot compete with bloggers and tweeters in terms of speed. Trained journalists on both sides of the Atlantic face anxious times as the new sources of news have exploited a lack of regulation, accountability and business model to create the impression of exciting and unfettered new distribution.

Truth, independence and accountability, are lofty ideals enshrined in Kovach and Rosenstiel's *The Elements of Journalism* (2007). The notion of independence is a contentious issue in international journalism as most bloggers and Internet amateurs profess independence from media owners and conglomerates, societal norms, commercial pressures, shareholders and government as the virtue behind their raison d'être. Few British journalists would argue they have true or genuine independence.

Newsrooms in the UK are run on the basis of top-down discipline, where the demands, desires and needs of owners, editors and shareholders come first. Most British journalists operate within these constraints. Even the BBC, which enshrines independence in its charter, is not independent. It is a state broadcaster dependent on a direct tax levied in the form of a compulsory licence fee, the acquiescence of the British public and the approval of the government of the day. As Murdock and Golding point out, journalistic outputs are determined by 'general economic dynamics of media production and the determinations they exert' (1974: 206). Commercial, socioeconomic structures, normative behaviours and market restrictions mean that journalists in the UK are fettered by a range of constraints which remove them from the claim of independence.

This independence is manifest in the work of WikiLeaks who are able to follow the principle of publish and be damned. However, the consequence of control for international journalism is that much of what is reported is bound by the economic dynamics described by Murdock and Golding. In the course of discursive practises the large news agencies such as the AP and Reuters do seek independence from those they cover, be it politicians or business interests, as a fundamental principle of the way the agencies work within western liberal democracies, according to Boyd-Barrett (1998).

That leaves accountability as an area where UK and US journalism can find common ground. Chalaby (1996) points to cultural, political, economic, linguistic and international factors which favoured the emergence of journalism in the UK and the US. It is the cultural, political and economic factors and the role of journalism in the public sphere of both countries that are most similar. In both countries journalists are accountable to myriad audiences, including consumers, owners, advertisers and the body politic. Citizen journalists may claim absence of control and accountability a virtue which can lead to the publication of pieces of journalism that are bold and unfettered by the commercial or political imperative. However, the lack of accountability also has the potential to lead to irresponsible, mendacious or malicious publication. In this respect, online journalism is yet to be truly tested in the courts on either side of the Atlantic. According to Kovach and Rosenstiel (2007), in the US traditional journalism should be accountable first and foremost to the reader. In practice most UK journalists see themselves as accountable to the editor or owner.

Newsworthiness – common ground?

News and information between the UK and US flows freely because of common ideas of what is newsworthy. The practice of the framing of news and news values in terms of proximity and prominence comes from assumed shared cultural, social and political values. British journalists and consumers tend to be more aware of American politics and politicians than say Belgium or Norway because of the US's cultural and linguistic proximity which define news values.

When assessing US newsworthiness, Shoemaker and Cohen found in a survey of journalists, PR practitioners and audiences that the stories considered to be the most important were the 'most deviant – statistically, normatively or in terms of their potential social change impact' (2006: 329). By deviance the authors meant anything unusual, odd or novel (2006: 49). Respondents cited the assassinations of John F. Kennedy (1963), Robert Kennedy and Martin Luther King (both 1968) as most important stories. They also mentioned the Moon landings of 1969, the death of Princess Diana in 1997 and the attacks on the USA on 11 September 2001. The stories combine elements of deviance and social significance. They share high degrees of political, economic, cultural and public significance, according to Shoemaker and Cohen. Their study included more than 2,400 news stories in 60 news media across ten countries, but did not include the UK. However, these key events all had prominence in the UK. The US and UK news media do not seem to have homogenous views on who or what is prominent, but do have common ideas of significance – what and who is significant based on common cultural, economic and political values. They also share common ideas of what is deviant or unusual, odd or novel. In terms of prominence, the election of Barack Obama in 2008 was a major story in the UK while the 2010 political crisis in Belgium where Prime Minister Yves Leterme tendered his resignation to the King hardly registered in British newspapers by comparison. The withdrawal of British troops from Iraq in 2009 became a story of deviance in the US. Britain had been the major ally in the war in Iraq and the decision was criticised in the US media and framed as a timid or cowardly act on the part of the UK.

Conclusion

From a shared understanding of significance and culture to economic and political interdependency, this article demonstrates that journalists and audiences on both sides of the Atlantic have at least some common or shared values of what is deviant and what is significant. There is no exact match for importance and some stories simply do not travel, but when some stories combine prominence and deviance, for example Donald Trump's golf course in Scotland or the release of the Lockerbie bomber in 2009, there are common threads that journalists and consumers understand innately.

The proliferation of banal journalism has lessened the impact of stories on the audience because the nuanced meaning is diluted or lost. International journalists now need an additional set of norms and values that will enable their work to stand out from the chatter of the Internet. Professional international journalists need to demonstrate legitimacy, meaning and veracity to give impact to their work, all while working at breakneck speed.

When engaging with the audience journalists need to show that the stories they write and produce are legitimate and a genuine pursuit of valid stories. Legitimacy comes from veracity in as much as it is original work based on news values and conventions of journalistic practise and factual reporting. By giving the work meaning, as in interpreting and contextualising events for an international audience, journalists can demonstrate the value of the work over straightforward headline facts. In terms of meaning making, the value in the work is giving the audience an understanding of what the story means to the country they are reporting from and the implications of the story to the home audience. This is the international journalist's 'line of sight', understanding the audience and translating meaning across countries divided by a common language or common beliefs.

Bibliography

Billig, M. (1995) *Banal Nationalism*. London: Sage.

Boyd-Barrett, O. (1980) *The International News Agencies*. London: Sage.

——(1998) *The Globalization of News*. London: Sage.

Chalaby, J. (1996) 'Journalism as an Anglo-American Invention', *European Journal of Communication*, September 1996, vol. 11 no. 3: 303–26.

Golding, P. and Elliot, P. (1979) *Making the News*. New York: Longman.

Kovach, B. and Rosenstiel, T. (2007) *The Elements of Journalism: What Newspeople Should Know and the Public Should Expect*. New York: Three Rivers Press.

Lewin, K. (1951) *Field Theory in Social Science: Selected Papers*. D. Cartwright (ed.) New York: Harper and Row.

McLuhan, M. (1964) *Understanding Media: The Extensions of Man*. New York: McGraw Hill.

Metykova, M. (2009) In Preston, P. *Making the News: Journalism and News Cultures in Europe*. Oxford: Routledge.

Murdock, G. and Golding, P. (1974) 'For a Political Economy of Mass Communications', in R. Miliband and J. Saville (eds), *The Socialist Register* 1973 (pp. 205–34). London: Merlin Press.

Rogers, E.M. (1994) *A History of Communication Study. A Biological Approach*. New York: The Free Press.

Rosen, J. (2006) 'The People Formerly Known as the Audience', Press Think, 27 June 2006. Accessed 10 October 2009 http://journalism.nyu.edu/pubzone/weblogs/pressthink/.

Shoemaker, P. and Cohen, A. (2006) *News Around the World: Content, Practitioners and the Public*. Oxford: Routledge.

Singer, J.B. (2008) in M. Löffelholz and D. Weaver (eds). *Global Journalism Research: Theories, Methods, Findings, Future*. London: Blackwell.

6 Environmental journalism

Sarah Lonsdale

Background and overview

When, as a young reporter working on the *Observer* newspaper I was sent to cover the 1991 Green Party Conference, my news editor growled after me as I was leaving: 'Count the beards. Count the sandals. And if David Icke shows up, go to town.' My news editor was referring to the former Green Party spokesman who famously claimed on television to be the son of God, and for a while would only wear turquoise. My instructions are an illustration of how much environment journalism has changed in 20 years. In 1991 even a 'serious' newspaper like the *Observer* was more interested in making fun of the 'Greens' than in addressing the issues the conference was raising. Back in 1991, carbon dioxide emissions, habitat destruction and air pollution were all on the Green Party's conference agenda. Beards were not.

The year after my 'beards and sandals count' – I gave up at 83 and David Icke did not show up – 10,000 members of the press and media attended the 1992 Rio de Janeiro 'Earth Summit'.[1] Environment journalism had arrived. From being a relatively minority interest for news organisations, dealing in 'spuds, bugs and floods', it is now a prominent specialist 'beast', covers a huge range of subject areas from economics to ecology, and is one of the most fiercely fought-over policy areas among business, pressure groups and politicians. Environment news now requires the journalist to have a working knowledge of high finance (carbon trading), the construction industry (low carbon homes), biotechnology (Genetically Modified crops), biodiversity, geography, global politics (fishing quotas and emissions reduction), meteorology (how many parts per million of CO_2 in the atmosphere is safe), anthropology (grass roots protests), hydrology (how a flood plain functions) and a working knowledge of physics (how a solar panel converts sunlight into electricity). 'There is no specialist political, business or feature writer who does not now regularly report on the environment ... we are all environment journalists now' (John Vidal, environment editor of the *Guardian*).[2] While there are several helpful publications examining the area of environment, communications and the media, there is little relevant in them for the journalist, starting out on his or her career as an environment specialist.[3]

Geoffrey Lean is Britain's longest-serving environment correspondent, having first been given that title while on the *Yorkshire Post* in 1969. Since then he has worked on the *Observer, Independent on Sunday* and *Daily Telegraph*.

The environment has raced faster and higher up the news agenda than any other specialism. Back in the early 1970s the issues were very different: ozone depletion, river pollution and whaling were all important. My 'big break' on the *Yorkshire Post* which led to my editor appointing me environment correspondent was about the amount of pollution factories were allowing to flow into the river system. These issues are no less important today, although ozone depletion is seen to have been 'dealt with' but they have been eclipsed, of course, by climate change.

(Geoffrey Lean, interviewed September 2010)

In the early days of environment journalism, it was an 'adversarial' specialism with campaign groups fighting to protect defenceless animals and plants portrayed as pitting their David-like wit against the Goliaths of big business and government. Anderson (in her 1997 book *Media, Culture and the Environment*, p. 127) describes how some groups such as Greenpeace were quick to pick up on the journalist's need for this kind of 'morality tale'. Unlike defence, where journalists always needed to work closely with the Ministry of Defence, or, in the days of the Labour correspondent journalists were famously close to the Unions, the environment has never really had its own dedicated government department, until the creation of the Department for Energy and Climate Change (DECC) in 2008. The other major government department dealing with environmental issues, the Department for the Environment, Food and Rural Affairs (DEFRA), caters for the needs of agriculture which very often comes into direct conflict with the needs of the environment. As a result, says Lean, 'Environment journalists have never been in the pockets of a ministry or industry. At one stage I counted up no fewer than fourteen Government ministries I was having dealings with.' But even the creation of DECC does not cover all the areas of the environment correspondent's remit. Stories about planning and 'nimbys' – 'Not in my backyard-ers' – are addressed to the Department of Communities and Local Government; stories on habitat, GM crops, flooding and wildlife are addressed to the Department for Environment, Food and Rural Affairs; stories on carbon trading are addressed to the Department of Business, Innovation and Skills and the Treasury.

One danger of this detachment from power is that the environment journalist may become easy prey to some of the dozens of environmental charities, NGOs or activist groups trying to spin a particular line, about the dangers of genetically modified food or the dangers of toxins in plastics for example. Some well-established organisations, for example Greenpeace and Friends of the Earth, have highly sophisticated media strategies which provide under-pressure reporters with facts and statistics, case studies, ready-made video footage and seemingly watertight evidence for their 'line'.[4] Another pressure is from industry press officers selling a 'greenwash' story – trying to promote their company as selling 'eco' products, or conducting business in a green way. BP for example campaigned very successfully with its 'Beyond Petroleum' slogan and became the preferred source of energy company funds for environmental groups, yet revelations in the aftermath of the Deepwater Horizon disaster show evidence of a dubious safety record for the company.[5] The way not to be duped by either side is to maintain high standards of journalistic fairness – and make sure your knowledge of scientific issues is strong.

Renowned nature writer Richard Mabey, author of several books on the environment, says in his view, the biggest pitfall for environment journalists is a lack of knowledge about how the environment works.[6] The vast majority of newspaper journalists are humanities graduates and the poor quality of science coverage in mainstream media is a constant source of complaint from the scientific community.[7] This complaint is not new – a wide-ranging report on the British Press published in 1938 complained.

> On parliament, law, sports, entertainments and other well organised news subjects the public are fairly fully and accurately informed about events and trends, but the same can hardly be said, for example of scientific, technical and industrial news.[8]

A good environment journalist needs to be an expert in the social and political sphere, but also needs to know how the environment works – how ecosystems function, what happens when there is a build-up of microscopic chemicals from plastic in plankton. 'It's a huge challenge – like studying for two PhDs,' says Richard Mabey. The way journalists can avoid misinterpreting data and thus looking ridiculous is, says Mabey (a Politics, Philosophy and Economics graduate), to

> swot up on the subject. Just read, read, read so you have enough knowledge at least to have an inkling when someone is trying to spin you a line, and also how various parts of Government policy impact upon and relate to issues like species conservation.

The bottom line is that as long as you apply the rules of good journalism – making sure all your facts tally, and come from a reputable source, that you have given all sides a fair hearing, you have taken accurate notes during interviews and you haven't been unnecessarily sensationalist – then you should get away with very few howlers.

Why is this important? Apart from your own personal credibility as a journalist, it is of course important that as a specialist – or as any kind of journalist – you get the facts right. Despite the current vogue for blaming the media for most of society's ills, studies reveal that serious newspapers and television channels still have a high believability factor with the reading and viewing public.[9] The quality of good environmental reporting is critical, particularly in view of the role the media can play in communicating the issues surrounding climate change, arguably the most important story of the twenty-first century. Media sources provide the public with the vast majority of their environmental information.[10] Other academics have concluded that because many environmental issues – and in particular climate change – are unobtrusive (i.e. most of us in the West have little or no first-hand experience of the effects of deforestation, for instance, or the disappearance of Arctic sea ice), the role of a credible media is even more important.[11] If the public is to be asked to insulate its homes, replace much-loved tungsten light bulbs with dim eco ones or reduce the amount of rubbish thrown into black bins each week as part of the government's pledge to reduce carbon dioxide emissions, then it needs to know why. Add to this the small yet nevertheless hard core of critics who remain ideologically opposed to any attempts by governments to reduce carbon emissions or mitigate the effects of climate change and who are ready to leap on any poorly sourced journalism on the issue, then the impetus to be as credible an expert as possible is huge. The increasing ideological war being waged over climate change, between the sceptics and the 'warmists' means the role of the responsible journalist has never been more important.

As any good journalist will tell you, regardless of subject matter, a successful piece of journalism must contain within it the fundamental elements of a story. Although environment journalists have that other big crowd pleaser – the cuddly animal – in his or her repertoire, stories about people have always been and will continue to be the most fascinating for the reader or viewer.

> It is hard, particularly when issues are far away or fairly abstract, for the environment writer to make the subject directly appealing to an audience. My advice to any environment journalist whether just starting out or well-established is to read or re-read Rachel Carson's *Silent Spring*.[12] It is the most exemplary mixture of powerful investigative journalism, deep green philosophy and a powerful appeal to readers, asking them to think about what life would be like if we never heard birdsong again.
>
> (Richard Mabey, September 2010)

Coverage of environmental issues

Environment subjects get good coverage in the mainstream media, relative to public concern. An Ipsos MORI poll of 990 British adults conducted on 4 June 2010, for example, reveals only five per cent of people place the environment top of their list of concerns. This compares to 65 per cent citing the economy, 29 per cent citing immigration, 26 per cent citing crime or law and order, and 21 per cent citing unemployment.[13]

However, an analysis of three national newspapers of varying political shades during the same week shows a wide range of environment stories and a depth of coverage that would seem to be out of proportion with the public interest as observed in the Ipsos MORI Poll.[14] This was the week immediately following the manhunt in Cumbria when a man killed 12 people, so a lot of attention was devoted to that tragic episode. It was also during the Deepwater Horizon Gulf oil spill crisis.

If we sort these findings into broad categories, the frequency distribution is this (Where the subject of the story is unclear I have put my explanation in parentheses.):

- pollution (including the Gulf oil spill and environmental pollution): 22 stories
- biodiversity (including bee stories and overfishing): 14 stories
- carbon emissions/climate change: 12 stories
- litter/recycling/local issues: 6 stories
- farming (including GM crops): 5 stories
- natural disasters: 4 stories
- population: 1 story.

The apparently surprising result that the *Daily Telegraph* carries more environmental stories than the *Guardian,* traditionally associated with more support, particularly for the climate change agenda, can be explained in that the *Telegraph* carries more farming, litter and bio-diversity stories, which are of traditional interest to its readers. In addition, several of the *Telegraph*'s 'climate change' stories are in fact from a sceptical angle, reflecting that newspaper's stance on climate change.

Although this is by no means a scientific survey – and bearing in mind pollution is probably over-represented because of the Gulf oil spill crisis during that week – these stories show the sheer range of subjects now considered 'environmental' from new ways of burning fossil fuels, and solar-powered festivals signalling the importance of stories about climate change, through the more 'traditional' type of environment stories such as the red squirrel, bee and elm stories. There is also a strong interest, particularly in the *Daily Telegraph* on waste disposal stories, as policy makers wrestle with ways of getting people to throw less rubbish away into landfill bins. GM crops are also a major concern. If we compare these articles and issues to concerns facing British journalists 15 years ago, a marked shift is detectable. Between 1991 and 1995, MORI (as it was then called) conducted regular surveys among environmental journalists on what they considered to be major issues to be tackled over the following years. The survey conducted in 1995 reveals that the two major concerns in 1995 were air pollution and transport-associated pollution.[15] Carbon dioxide emissions were third with 54 per cent of

Table 6.1 Environmental stories across three national newspapers

Newspaper	Pollution	Bio-diversity	CO2 emissions/ climate change	Litter	Farming	Natural disaster	Population	Total for each paper
Daily Mirror	5	2	1	1	0	2	0	11
Guardian	15	4	2	2	1	1	0	25
Daily Telegraph	2	8	9	3	4	1	1	28
Total for each category	**22**	**14**	**12**	**6**	**5**	**4**	**1**	**64**

respondents mentioning the subject spontaneously as an area of growing concern. Biodiversity, and more specifically species extinctions, now considered by many environment experts as almost on a par with climate change as posing a threat to the planet was cited by only 25 per cent of respondents as an area of concern.

In the twenty-first century, public concern about the environment peaked in late 2006 when the EC proposed cuts in carbon emissions of 20 per cent by 2020. Prior to 2006, the highest peak of concern was in autumn 2000, which was the wettest since records began and brought widespread flooding. Indeed a further poll tracking concern with a number of issues over a 13-year period reveals that relative to other major issues, particularly the economy and immigration, concern about the environment in 2010 was at its lowest ebb. In May 2000, the environment was top of the list of people's concerns and in late 2006 more people worried about the environment than unemployment or the economy.[16]

> The environment is not top of mind for the public when asked what they think the key issues of the day, however despite this there is a reasonable amount of coverage in the media. In the UK there is a certain amount of scepticism towards climate change, yet newspapers cover the issue quite thoroughly, albeit often focusing on where there is dissent. One area where the public is more engaged is in local environment stories such as litter, parks, open spaces and protecting greenbelt.
>
> (Edward Langley, head of environment research at Ipsos MORI)[17]

The budding environment journalist, then, will be guaranteed a big post bag if he or she concentrates on these issues.

Sources

Sources are the lifeblood of good reporting. Because the environment covers such a wide range of subject areas you could be talking to an ecosystems scientist one day and an elderly lady who has had an energy-efficient boiler fitted the next. Local activist groups are a good source of stories about the environment: from volunteers clearing out a rubbish-strewn river to parents anxious about clusters of illnesses in children near where crops are being sprayed. However, you will need to work hard to find reliable activists who trust journalists and remember that they have their particular line to spin.

> The environment can be a very emotive issue and you have to be terribly careful not to align yourself with one side or another. It's tempting to take the stance of being on the side of the activists/small guys who pit themselves against Government/big business but you have to be aware that every side has its own agenda to push. I've had on the one hand 'environment' groups like the RSPB and Friends of the Earth complaining that I have not been fair and I've had on the other hand the Atomic Energy Authority and the Ministry of Agriculture complaining, so I think I've probably got it about right.
>
> (Geoffrey Lean, September 2010)

Below then, with the above caveat in mind, is a list of reliable first sources of environment stories and web addresses. It is by no means an exhaustive list but may be a useful first port of call.

Government departments:

Department of Energy and Climate Change: www.decc.gov.uk
Department of Environment, Food and Rural Affairs: www.defra.gov.uk
Department for Business, Innovation and Skills: www.bis.gov.uk

Nature/wildlife conservation:

English Nature: www.naturalengland.org.uk
World Wildlife Fund: www.wwf.org.uk
RSPB: www.rspb.org.uk

Carbon emissions reduction:

Association for the Conservation of Energy: www.ukace.org
Friends of the Earth: www.foe.co.uk
Greenpeace: www.greenpeace.org.uk

Research:

Oxford Environmental Change Institute: www.eci.ox.ac.uk
Building Research Establishment: www.bre.co.uk
Centre for Sustainable Energy: www.cse.org.uk
Centre for Alternative Technology: www.cat.org.uk

Make the most of your own university or institution

At my own university, for example, academics are engaged in widely disparate forms of research but which are, nevertheless, environment focused. Our anthropologists have produced a paper on biodiversity in the Seychelles and another on environmental protest in the era of climate change, our business department are investigating dive tourism in Malaysia and our psychologists are researching the idea of public inaction in the face of mounting evidence of climate change. All these issues could form the basis of environment journalism and it would benefit journalism students enormously if they reach out and make links with other departments at their institution.

Global perspectives

Environmental issues for journalists are, more so than other areas of specialism that remain tied to domestic policy, becoming increasingly globalised. Air pollution, ozone depletion, over-fishing, carbon emissions, deforestation, species extinction:

all these issues transcend national borders. It is an irony in these days of awareness of carbon emissions from air travel that in order to cover all issues and international conventions, the thorough environment correspondent must travel thousands of miles a year. Although there is no established grouping or association of environment correspondents in the UK, there are two international organisations and both accept membership from British journalists. One is the American-based Society of Environmental Journalists (SEJ), founded in 1990. The Society has around 1,500 members. As well as providing a forum for journalists with a common agenda, the organisation publishes a bi-weekly 'tip sheet' which can help with generating ideas for stories. In polls of SEJ members, respondents say that the amount of space and time news organisations are willing to give environment stories is on the rise, but job security is also a major issue.[18] Beth Parke, chief executive of SEJ, says that with the trend for news organisations to reduce permanent staff and the concomitant rise of the freelancer one of the key issues for environmental journalists is the balancing act between journalism and activism.

> Journalists tend to become environment specialists because they have a keen interest in, and often a passion for, environmental issues. With the subject also becoming something of an ideological battleground it's vital that journalists stick to robust, accurate, reality-based reporting.
>
> (Beth Parke, interview with author September 2010)

The Mumbai-based International Federation of Environmental Journalists is mainly made up of journalists working in India and southern Asia although has members from across the globe. In southern Asia, journalism and activism are very closely linked and sometimes the two are interchangeable. President of the Federation Darryl D'Monte says one of the reasons why environmental journalism is so strong in this region is the quantity of man-made disasters, from Bhopal in 1984 onwards and now pressing issues such as the degradation of Himalayan river systems and the depletion of tropical hardwood forests. He also argues that the role of journalists in this region is vital because activist groups lack the resources of those in the West.

> ... avenues open in the West, like access to courts, not to mention direct protest, are often closed. This gives the media a heightened – one might even go so far as to say exaggerated – role in intervening in environmental controversies. Indeed, there is always the danger of the documenter mistaking himself – and being mistaken in the public eye – for the environmentalist.[19]

Case study: Charles Clover, *The End of the Line*[20]

Charles Clover is a columnist on *The Sunday Times*. Previously he had been the Environment Editor of the *Daily Telegraph* since 1987. He won the British Environment and Media's National Journalist of the Year award in 1989, 1994 and 1996. Previously, he was an editor at *The Spectator* and a features writer for the *Daily Telegraph*. He is a frequent contributor to BBC TV, Sky and BBC Radio news, as well as *Newsnight* on BBC2.

Story type: Over-fishing, fish stock depletion, biodiversity.

Medium: Originally a series of newspaper articles; then a book, *The End of the Line: how over-fishing is changing the world and what we eat* (Ebury Press, 2005) and finally as a film (2009).

Big break: I was covering the North Sea Conference in 1990 for my then newspaper, the *Daily Telegraph* and watched a Dutch presentation about the impact an industrial beam trawler had on the North Sea ecosystem. Its effect on the sea bed was like a tractor ploughing a field five times a year. This type of destructive large scale fishing means that for every 1lb of marketable sole, 16lb of marine organisms are destroyed. For me it was a Damascene moment and I began following fish stories with a more critical eye.

Top tips: Basic journalistic intuition based on personal interest and immersing yourself in a specialism so you can follow your hunches like a detective. I was able to link reports of vast sand eel catches in Denmark to the decline of bird populations and the Atlantic salmon off the Scottish coast.

Most helpful contacts: The RSPB, which tipped me off that the Danes were catching so many sand eels (a stock that is now collapsed) that they were burning their oil in power stations, something we would now regard as an obscenity; independent ecosystems biologists too.

Most unhelpful contacts: Government fishery scientists. They think it is their job to make industrial fishing possible and are pathologically secretive.

Outcome: The book *The End of the Line* has won a number of awards including the Derek Cooper Award for Campaigning or Investigative Food Journalism (2005) and the film, which has been an international success won the One World Media Environment Award (2010).

Parting shots: Specialist correspondents are tremendous assets to media organisations, particularly newspapers. They investigate enormously complicated subjects and come up with scoops time and again if allowed to get on with their jobs. The press and media must continue to invest in its specialists or it is effectively printing edited press releases.

Notes

1 www.un.org/geninfo/bp/enviro.html (accessed September 2010).
2 The *Guardian*, Media Section, 7 December 2009, p. 3.
3 Alison Anderson's book *Media, Culture and the Environment* (Routledge, 1997) provides a particularly thorough background on the complex links between media organisations, politics and campaign groups in an age of mass communications.
4 See for example Alison Anderson's analysis of Greenpeace's involvement in the disposal of the Shell Oil rig *Brent Spar*, in 1995, in her book *Media, Culture and the Environment*, pp. 111–14.

5 The Deepwater Horizon oil rig exploded in the Gulf of Mexico on 11 April 2010, killing eleven oil workers and causing what has been described as the worst oil spill in American history.
6 Richard Mabey, author of, among other publications, *Food for Free* (1972) and *Flora Britannica* (1996); interview with Richard Mabey September 2010.
7 See for example Dr Ben Goldacre's campaign on his website www.badscience.net.
8 Political and Economic Planning (PEP) *Report on the British Press*, 1938, p. 174.
9 Robinson, Michael J. and Kohut, Andrew, 'Believability and the Press', *Public Opinion Quarterly* 52 (Summer 1988) 174–89.
10 Atwater, A., Salwen, M. and Anderson, R., 'Media Agenda-setting with Environmental Issues', *Journalism Quarterly* 62 (summer 1995): 393–97.
11 E.g.: Liebler, C. M. and Bendix, J. 'Old Growth Forests and the Framing of an Environmental Controversy', *Journalism and Mass Communication Quarterly*, Vol 73, No 1 (Spring 1996) pp. 53–65.
12 Penguin Modern Classics new edition, 2000.
13 Ipsos MORI British Attitudes to the Environment, Climate Change and Future Energy Choices, June 2010.
14 *Daily Mirror, Guardian* and *Daily Telegraph* 4–10 June 2010. *Daily Mirror:* entire paper scanned. *Daily Telegraph* and *Guardian*: searched using 'Nexis' with search terms 'environment', 'pollution', 'climate', 'habitat' and 'species'.
15 Worcester, Robert, 'Cutting through the Greenery', article in *British Journalism Review*, Vol. 7 No. 3 1996.
16 Ipsos MORI poll May 1997 – May 2010 based on 1,000 British adults aged 18 plus each month.
17 Interview September 2010.
18 For recent polls conducted among SEJ members: www.tvweek.com/news/2009/10/newspros_sej_poll_job_resource.php.
19 D'Monte, Darryl, 'The Greening of India's Scribes', in Nalini Rajan (ed.) *Practising Journalism: Values, Constraints, Implications*, Sage: India, 2005.
20 Interviewed September 2010.

7 Automotive journalism

Andrew Noakes

The luckiest man alive today, according to motoring journalist Jeremy Clarkson, is motoring journalist Jeremy Clarkson. Armed with, he says, nothing more than 'half a qualification in journalism and the engineering ability of a sparrow' (Clarkson, 2005) he has risen from the obscurity of a local newspaper, the *Rochdale Advertiser*, to unrivalled prominence as an automotive critic. Luck may have played its part, but nobody should underestimate the talent and sheer hard work that made the most of the good fortune. Now, as mainstay of the BBC's *Top Gear* motoring TV show and its monthly magazine spin-off, and contributor of opinionated, anarchic columns to *The Sunday Times* and the *Sun*, Clarkson has become without doubt the best-known motoring journalist – in the world.

Clarkson's screen presence, comic delivery and (underrated) writing ability might make him a one-off, but his route into motoring journalism follows a well-beaten path. Many established motoring writers started their careers as trainee reporters on local newspapers, learning their trade reporting on the whole gamut of topics tackled by the regional press. Basic journalism skills were learned on the job, often topped up with some formal training in shorthand and media law through the newspaper's trainee system. Eventually they took on the paper's 'motoring correspondent' role or moved on to a specialist motoring magazine to write car reviews and motor industry stories. Alongside these career journalists came refugees from automotive public relations, significant examples including the late LJK Setright, a renowned technical writer, and Clarkson's *Top Gear* colleague, Richard Hammond. Others developed expert subject knowledge in engineering, motorsport or consumer affairs through formal study, industry experience or a combination of the two and then used that expertise in specialist areas of automotive writing. These are specialists, the likes of *Car and Driver*'s engineer/racer Patrick Bedard, car designer Robert Cumberford, the late Jeff Daniels whose background was in engineering and racing drivers Mark Hales and Tiff Needell. Often these subject specialists had little or no formal training in the craft of journalism.

Today the training of journalists in the UK has largely moved from the training courses operated by newspaper groups to degree courses run by universities. Though degree courses in media and journalism have seen a rapid rise in popularity in recent years and Master's degrees in specialist areas of journalism have been on offer for some years, there was no direct academic route into motoring journalism until 2004 when Coventry University introduced a Master's degree in automotive journalism. Established at the urging of Steve Cropley, editor-in-chief of Haymarket's motoring titles, the Coventry MA already has alumni working across a range of automotive magazines and websites.

But academic study of journalism in any form has its critics, and automotive journalism is no different. One online comment on an automotive article (Noakes, 2008) in the *Guardian* noted that the author was an automotive journalism lecturer and suggested students of automotive journalism would learn nothing more useful than, 'The role of high waisted overtight jeans in the mulimedia [sic] age'. Years before, a car magazine for hands-on classic car owners received a note from a reader suggesting that it should employ 'fewer journalists and more mechanics'. Both comments implied that automotive journalism required no particular skills or abilities, which is both an inaccurate view and a worrying one in an age when the value of any professional writing is being continually threatened.

Essentials for success in automotive journalism

Car enthusiasts looking for a way to turn their passion into a career are often attracted to automotive journalism. That can only be good, for them and for the profession: interested, excited people work harder and better for themselves, their employers and their customers. Journalists with a passion for their subject are likely to be better informed and more effective in their research and analysis, which can only be good for the reader. But endless enthusiasm for all things automotive is not enough. One of the keys to success in automotive journalism is understanding that you need to be as interested and excited and passionate about the 'journalism' part as you are about the 'automotive' part. The Guild of Motoring Writers offers advice for would-be motoring journalists on its website which cautions that,

> the ability to drive a car at its very limits, cornering at opposite-lock just like Tiff Needell does on the TV is NOT the number one requirement. Knowing the subject inside out, being able to list every MG paint code and the European car of the year for the last four decades might be useful, but again is by no means essential. The one skill you must possess is the ability to write.
>
> (Guild of Motoring Writers, nd)

Like any professional writer, an automotive journalist should be interested in the craft of writing and should read widely – not just within the automotive journalism field but also the best factual writing on business, culture, politics, the environment, even sport. The content might be interesting, or useful, but the reason for reading widely is not to absorb knowledge of the world but to examine the techniques the writers have used – to grab the reader from the very start of the article, to maintain their interest as the story develops and to ensure they read to the very end. The ability to catch and keep the reader's interest is important in any form of journalism, but particularly so in automotive journalism where the competition between writers and between publications is so great. That interest in the business of journalism should also extend beyond the process of getting the story and writing the words to the craft of making magazines, or websites, or video – and to embracing as many new content-production skills as possible.

That's not to say that an interest in and knowledge of cars is not useful. A familiarity with the history and development of the car can help to put new developments into context. Too few motoring journalists have a real appreciation of how the motor industry works, which can occasionally lead them to make inappropriate criticisms of the industry, or impractical suggestions for improvements to its products. Understanding how cars work can make it easier for the journalist to grasp the significance of new technology as it comes along – and over the next few years this will be more important than ever, as major changes in the way vehicles are owned, fuelled and driven are on the horizon.

New car road testing: launches and press loans

After the high-profile motoring TV shows like *Top Gear* – which the BBC exports to more than 100 countries, and which has been described as the world's most illegally downloaded programme – the most visible motoring journalists are those writing for the consumer motoring magazines. In the UK weeklies like *Autocar* and *Auto Express*, and monthlies like *Top Gear*, *What Car?*, *Evo* and *CAR* deliver a constant stream of news from and about new cars and the industry that makes them.

Magazines reporting on the motor industry are very nearly as old as the industry itself. Ancestors of the car can be traced back to the sixteenth century, but the motor car as we know it today took shape in the 1880s and the first magazines – *The Autocar* in the UK and *The Horseless Age* in the USA – were launched in November 1895 (Flink, 1990: 29). That there were just six cars on British roads did not deter *The Autocar*'s publisher William Isaac Iliffe and editor Henry Sturmey – not least because Sturmey had a variety of interests within the motor industry and was keen to promote the new-fangled horseless carriage. Sturmey was a member of the board of the English Daimler company while still editing *The Autocar*, becoming the company's chairman in 1897. It appears that his rather-too-close links to the industry eventually led to his departure from the magazine in 1901 (Taylor, 1995). Fundamental ethical issues have been a part of automotive journalism ever since.

According to Flink, the 'press launch' was invented in 1897 by Colonel Albert A. Pope of the Pope Manufacturing Co, who had diversified from bicycles into electric cars. Pope 'invited reporters to a private showing of his first electric cars, allowed them to operate the vehicles, and supplied pictures for publication'. The idea soon spread, until it was common for car makers to transport reporters from afar 'to be entertained and given a preview of new models in the hope that "free" publicity would follow' (Flink, 1990: 30). Little has changed since, except that manufacturers now foot the bill to bring journalists even greater distances and lavish on them even greater hospitality, leading to charges of bias against the reviews that result.

Car manufacturer press officers will, privately, tell stories of journalists who have insisted on upgraded plane seats or hotel rooms for launch events, or decided to attend an event only after confirming that the manufacturer would be presenting each journo with a suitably lavish gift. Such unprofessional conduct – which is not exclusive to automotive journalism – clearly conflicts with a journalist's responsibilities, which should be to the truth and to their audience. Good journalists work for the reader, not for themselves or even for their title's proprietor (Cropley, 2010). And readers can tell the difference: hacks who are more interested in the merits of their hotel room than the vehicle they have been invited to experience, who are in the automotive journalism business only for the perks, will find dwindling audiences for their lazy, uninformed reporting – and a long line of more committed and more capable journalists waiting to take their place in one of the most competitive areas of journalism.

Launch events usually include briefings on the new model from designers, engineers and executives from the car maker, plus an opportunity for the journalists to drive the car. They must drive hard enough to learn about the dynamic performance of the car, yet must also stay within the law and remember that the vehicle and quite probably the roads are unfamiliar – sometimes a difficult balancing act. The press office team prepares a test route in advance and provides a road book with directions and maps. Often two journalists share a car, one driving and one navigating, and they swap over half way so both get the chance to drive. If a publication sends a journalist and a photographer, they will share a car and stop along the route for photography. These days a journalist might also be expected to produce a short video review to be posted online.

Major press launches for new car models are often conducted in warm climates, not just to put journalists in a good mood but also for practical reasons. Changeable weather could play havoc with the launch schedule, which is inevitably tightly packed due to the number of journalists likely to be attending (which could be several hundred for a pan-European event) and a limit on the press office's car fleet, manpower and budget. Dependable sunshine makes life easier for photographers, a lack of rain keeps the cars cleaner and minimises the potential for accidents. But motoring journalists are finding it more and more difficult to justify trips to press launches which take them away from their desks for two or three consecutive days, thanks to ever greater productivity demands from their publishers. On top of that, the new car market has fragmented in recent years, with many more different models on sale – so the number of launches has increased. As a result, there has been a trend in recent years towards shorter, more flexible and more local driving events which can be completed within a day. But even so a reporter single-handedly attempting to cover every launch could be expected to attend as many as five or six events a month, at least some of which could involve international travel. In addition they might also need to be present at some of the major motor shows (Geneva, Paris and Frankfurt in Europe; Detroit, Chicago, New York and Los Angeles in North America; plus Tokyo and, increasingly, Beijing and Shanghai) or whichever of the 80 or so national and international motor shows is closest to their home territory. Some will also attend specialist trade shows like SEMA in Las Vegas and Autosport International in Birmingham. Events like the Pebble Beach Concours and Goodwood Festival of Speed are also now used for new product announcements by manufacturers, making them essential newsgathering opportunities for some journalists. With such a packed travel schedule, an automotive writer could find it difficult to spend much time driving cars on his home patch – which is more important than it may at first appear. Road conditions vary, and a car which impressed on the smooth tarmac of Germany or in the balmy climate of the south of France might show up unexpected shortcomings on a typically potholed British B-road in the grim grey drizzle of winter.

When journalists or motoring publications do conduct more extensive car tests they generally rely on car manufacturer press offices to supply cars. Each press office runs a fleet of press demonstrator vehicles which are loaned to journalists, often for a week at a time, at an average cost to the manufacturer of around £700–£1,000 per loan (Brownlee, 2010). The most exclusive, and expensive, makes like Ferrari have only a handful of cars available to journalists in each sales region, while mass-market makes will have dozens of vehicles covering all the main choices of model and specification. Usually the cars are delivered and collected, fully insured, arrive topped up with fuel and, of course, are impeccably presented. In the past there have sometimes been suspicions that some press cars were rather too well prepared – that is they were somewhat better in their fit and finish, or even in their performance, than the machines rolling off the production line. Few manufacturers would be likely to attempt anything of that sort today, as the backlash from dissatisfied customers would undo any good PR achieved by the favourable road test comments. In fact, practicality dictates that most press demonstrators are brand new cars and sometimes they come to journalists with only a few hundred miles under their wheels – too little to fully run-in the engine, gearbox and other components, which might mean their performance and economy are marginally less than a normal customer could expect.

Most journalists conduct their tests exclusively on the road, quoting the manufacturer's figures for performance and economy rather than carrying out their own tests. Only a very few publications have the resources to conduct properly scientific performance tests, which *Motor* magazine claimed to have pioneered in 1925 (Pearce, 1985). *Autocar*, which absorbed *Motor* in 1988, takes its road test cars to the Motor Industry Research Association (MIRA) Proving Ground near Nuneaton in Warwickshire or the Millbrook Proving Ground in Bedfordshire to be 'figured' – put through a well-established series of tests to establish their performance. Both venues have absolutely level one-mile straights ideal for acceleration tests, and banked tracks for high-speed testing. The equipment used to measure speed and distance for these tests has evolved enormously over the years: in the past a cumbersome and expensive 'fifth wheel' measuring device had to be strapped onto the car, but modern GPS systems now provide all the required data at a fraction of the cost. Maximum speed, acceleration in each gear and acceleration through the gears from a standing start are all measured. The latter requires the most skill from the driver (in a manual gearbox car, at least) and will be repeated several times until the driver is satisfied that the car has reached its potential. The standing start tests can be tough on the car and are generally carried out last so that if something breaks – broken driveshafts and fried clutches have been known – the rest of the data is already recorded and the story can still be completed by the deadline.

Motoring journalists who write regular road test articles and columns for print or online publication have to keep up to date with new models as they come along, and will usually have a continuous stream of press loan vehicles throughout the year. Add cars they drive during launches and other events and they could easily drive more than 100 different cars in a year. Road testers on specialist car magazines would often drive a different car every day.

Sub-specialisms: other areas where automotive journalists operate

New car testing might be the most obvious branch of automotive journalism and it is certainly one of the most attractive for those seeking to enter the profession, but it is only one of many sub-specialisms. Even magazines concentrating on new car news and reviews will include a variety of other strands of journalism.

Genuine investigative reporting, for instance, is alive and well in the industry pages of the specialist car magazines, which largely bypass the car makers' press offices and get their information from sources close to the engineers, financiers, product-planners and decision makers at the business end of the motor industry. For these stories a journalists needs plenty of well-placed contacts, good judgement and perseverance.

There is also a healthy strand of consumer journalism within many specialist car magazines, offering advice on buying, selling and using cars but also campaigning for motorists' and car buyers' rights. In Europe, for instance, car magazine groups were carrying out their own independent crash tests years before the independent EuroNCAP test programme made car manufacturers take safety more seriously. It was a Swedish journalist, Robert Collin, who uncovered the unstable handling of the Mercedes-Benz A-class in the now-infamous 'elk test' in 1997 (Puchan, 2001). Nearly four decades earlier, the technical editors of the rival weeklies *Autocar* and *Motor* joined forces just once, to present their damning judgement on the handling of the new Morris Marina to the management of British Leyland – prompting the company to make hurried revisions before the car was released for sale (Daniels, 1995).

Beyond the all-make new-car magazines there are titles which are more tightly focused on specialist areas, such as motorsport, modified cars, classic cars, 4x4s and off-roaders, diesel cars, and even kit cars, along with dozens of publications dedicated to single makes or models. Generally these titles have smaller circulations, lower ad revenues and smaller budgets than the generalist new car titles, and standards of journalism vary widely. They can, however, be rewarding to work for and great places for new journalists to learn, because they have smaller editorial teams and even junior writers will often be involved in major decisions like cover design, commissioning and flatplanning. Car testing for these titles often requires a different approach because cars will generally come from individual owners rather than manufacturers' press offices. While a car maker would happily submit its product for even the most extreme testing, the owner of a cherished classic or painstakingly customised car would expect a less aggressive approach – yet the reporter must still find out enough about the car during his test drive for him to write about it.

Business-to-business titles covering the motor industry or vehicle fleet management also often have small editorial budgets and small editorial teams. Writers from automotive B2B titles have gone on to write and edit prestigious consumer magazines like *CAR*, proving that these non-newstrade titles can be a good starting point for new entrants to automotive journalism.

Networks: associations for automotive journalists

Seven motoring journalists met at the Press Club in London on 9 October 1944 to discuss the formation of the Motoring Correspondents' Circle, which became the Guild of Motoring Writers two years later. The Guild is the largest motoring writers' group in the UK and now has more than 400 members who 'strive constantly by whatever means … to raise the standard of motoring journalism' (Guild of Motoring Writers, 2010). Other UK-based groups include the Motoring Journalists Division of the Chartered Institute of Journalists, and nine independent regional motoring writers' groups. Operating under an umbrella body, the Association of Motoring Writers Groups, the regional groups support the work of motoring journalists around the country.

Motoring writers' organisations have also been set up in other countries, notably Italy, South Africa and New Zealand, while the USA boasts two major associations – the Motor Press Guild on the west coast and the International Motor Press Association in the east – and several other groups covering geographical areas or subject specialisms.

All of these organisations vet prospective members to ensure only bona fide members of the media are admitted, giving the car makers' PRs an easy way to weed out the fly-by-nights interested in nothing more than the freebies that might be on offer. All have rules by which member journalists must operate and some, like the Automotive Journalists Association of Canada, have a formal code of ethics. The groups provide opportunities for members to meet each other and key motor industry professionals, and provide support in times of crisis. The larger groups often organise their own track test days, which give members the chance to drive newly announced cars under controlled conditions. The Guild of

Motoring Writers' test days ran until 1979, when the organisation was taken over by the Society of Motor Manufacturers and Traders. In the US, the two main motoring journalists' organisations both operate track days.

Many of the groups offer annual awards to promote high standards of journalism and to encourage new writers into the motoring field. The highest-profile prize for young writers is the Sir William Lyons Award, presented annually by the Guild of Motoring Writers and sponsored by the Jaguar car company (which Lyons founded). It is open to anyone under the age of 23 and many former winners have gone on to successful careers in automotive journalism. The Guild's comprehensive range of annual prizes also includes awards for technical, consumer, regional and environmental reporting within the automotive sphere. The two major US associations have their own annual awards recognising excellence in automotive journalism.

The motoring journalists' associations do a useful job in identifying working motoring journalists and supporting them in their work, roles which are likely to become more and more important as the publishing industry goes through technology-led change.

The future for automotive journalism

Automotive journalists face more changes over the next few years than any other branch of the profession. The practice of journalism is changing and developing, while at the same time the motor industry is facing radical changes to its products and manufacturing processes.

Like all journalists, those in the automotive field are watching a gradual decline in print publishing, particularly in newspapers, and the migration of content to online outlets – together with new content platforms such as Twitter. Some will leave automotive journalism because they will be unable or unwilling to embrace new types of content and new methods of working. The rest will have to be ready to give the reader the kind of content they want.

In addition the automotive journalist has to face an uncertain future for the motor industry, as it deals with the rising cost of oil and the increasing concern over the environmental impact of the motor car. Designing alternatives to conventional cars is easier than getting the customer to understand them, and accept them not as simply a direct replacement for their existing car but a new and better form of personal transport. Automotive journalists will play a crucial role in explaining these new technologies, guiding readers through a host of new and difficult choices, and assessing the merits and demerits of new cars and new technologies as they appear.

There has never been a more challenging time for automotive journalism, nor a more important time for automotive journalists to be working to the highest possible standards. To survive this turbulent era automotive journalists will need to learn new skills and understand new automotive technologies – and they might just need a little bit of luck.

Case study: Steve Cropley, editor-in-chief of Haymarket motoring publications

Steve Cropley fell in love with cars, and car magazines, at an early age. Twice a week, a train would roll into the mining town of Broken Hill in New South Wales where he lived as a boy, carrying thousands of gallons of drinking water.

> I used to sit in school and I'd hear the train, and I'd know it took approximately two and a quarter hours for the newspapers that were also delivered on the water train to get to the town's newsagent. I would start looking at my watch.

Cropley told an audience of journalism students at Coventry University (Cropley, 2008), 'I knew what time to bunk off school to pick up the motoring magazines.' His earliest contact with the media came when he supplied lists of share prices to 'the local rag', the *Barrier Daily Truth*, then he studied engineering for a year before joining *The Advertiser* in Adelaide as a trainee journalist. After four years he moved to a specialist car title, *Wheels Magazine*, in Sydney, where he worked for five years before moving to the UK – because 'it was obvious that all the good things that happen in the motor industry happen on this side of the world'.

Cropley worked for the iconoclastic *CAR* magazine from 1978, taking over as editor in 1981 (from another Australian, Mel Nichols) and guiding the magazine through an era where its popularity and authority climbed steadily. He left in 1988 and founded a new magazine, *Buying Cars*, which was sold to Haymarket in 1991. Since then he has been editor-in-chief of Haymarket's motoring titles, his main outlet the flagship *Autocar*, for which he writes news, features and a weekly column. Cropley is also keen to find and nurture talented young motoring journalists, offering work experience placements to dozens of young writers every year. He was instrumental in setting up the Automotive Journalism MA course at Coventry University in 2004 and remains a visiting professor there.

Despite his many years at the top of his profession, he maintains that he is 'merely a reporter', using his privileged access to new cars and the people who design and make them to ask the questions the reader wants answered. It is an approach which has won him many friends in the motor industry, in automotive publishing and amongst the readers of his magazines. In recent years he has picked up both the Guild of Motoring Writers' Pemberton Trophy for contribution to motoring and the Headlineauto Journalist of the Year award – both voted for by fellow journalists.

Cropley offers two golden rules for budding writers. First, always remember you work for the reader. 'You do not work for the proprietor, you certainly don't work for the advertising department, you don't even work for the editor.' Second, make sure you retain your reader's attention to the last line of your copy. That, he says, is fundamental: 'If you don't do that you have failed.'

References

Brownlee, S. (2010) *Press cars* [interview by A. Noakes] by Twitter, 2010.

Clarkson, J. (2005) 'The luckiest man alive?' *Top Gear* [online] available from www.topgear.com/content/features/stories/2005/03/stories/01/1.html [23 October 2010].

Cropley, S. (2008) *Coventry Conversations* [lecture] available from http://coventryuniversity.podbean.com/mf/web/r4af2e/stevecropley161008.mp3 [30 October 2010].

——(2010) *Coventry Conversations* [lecture] available from http://coventryuniversity.podbean.com/mf/web/b8aic9/stevecropley290910.mp3 [24 October 2010].

Daniels, J. (1995) *Morris Marina* [interview by A. Noakes] St Tropez, 1995.

Flink, J. J. (1990) *The Automobile Age* (Cambridge, MA: MIT Press).

Guild of Motoring Writers (nd) 'Becoming a Motoring Journalist' [online] available from www.gomw.co.uk/information/show/pagename/journalism [31 October 2010].

Guild of Motoring Writers (2010) *Who's Who in the Motor Industry* (Bournemouth: Guild of Motoring Writers).

Noakes, A. (2008) 'So a Model T was Greener than a Modern Car? No Way!' *Guardian* [online] 17 October available from www.guardian.co.uk/commentisfree/2008/oct/17/automotive-carbonemissions [23 October 2010].

Pearce, L. (1985) 'Road Tests Explained', *Motor Road Test Annual 1985*, 2–5.

Puchan, H. (2001) 'The Mercedes A-class Crisis', *Corporate Communications: An International Journal* 6 (1), 42–46.

Taylor, S. (1995) 'The Story of Autocar', *Autocar* 1 November, 6–9.

8 Fashion journalism

Julie Bradford

There has been a huge growth in fashion coverage. Once the preserve of the women's pages and high-end glossies, it is now picked over and analysed in newspapers, supplements, weeklies, websites and the thousands of fashion blogs that have sprung up since 2005. Fashion brands and retailers are getting in on the act, publishing their own magazines with circulations to rival the most established titles.

Consumers are joining in, too. They can watch a live-streamed catwalk show and post their comments online, engage with brands on forums, Twitter and Facebook, upload pictures of their day's outfit on photo-sharing websites and show off their latest shopping haul on YouTube.

No wonder Jess Cartner-Morley, fashion editor of the *Guardian*, says there is no better time to be in fashion journalism. 'Fashion coverage has absolutely exploded,' she says (Cartner-Morley, 2011). 'Fashion has become part of the national conversation, much more so than even a decade ago when I started.'

For her, the unprecedented interest in fashion is a result of social and cultural changes. 'Woman have an increasing voice in public life. It's also part of the blurring between the public and domestic sphere. We want to know what people in public life are wearing, and why. And people understand it more.'

Media developments have undoubtedly helped promote fashion coverage – increased pagination, improved colour printing for newspapers and the move online. Fashion is also a big draw for advertising for beauty and clothing, which guarantees it pre-booked slots in print and prominence online. And fashion will always have an appeal for news editors who want to inject glamour and colour into their pages.

The appeal to the audience can be relied on, too. Previously considered an elite world, fashion has become much more accessible and consumers feel they have more of a stake in it. Dirk Standen, editor-in-chief of the website Style.com, said:

> One of the things that Style.com has done over the years ... is open up what was a closed system to a lot of people; to millions of readers. There is a huge fascination out there and amongst the public for what goes on inside fashion.
> (Amed, 2011)

The harnessing of celebrity to fashion, with designers vying to dress music and film stars for awards ceremonies and get them in the front row at their catwalk shows, has its detractors but has undoubtedly helped turn designers into household names.

The fashion industry has played its part. Consolidation by the three big luxury companies, LVMH Moet Hennessy-Louis Vuitton, Pinault-Printemps-Redoute and Richemont, who together control more than 500 of the best-known luxury goods labels, and the emergence of vast new markets in China, India, Russia and Brazil, fuelled the epic careers of the late Alexander McQueen and John Galliano which swept fashion onto the front pages. At the other end of the market, collaborations between High Street stores and designers – Giles Deacon for New Look; Christopher Kane for Topshop; Karl Lagerfeld, Stella McCartney and Versace for H&M – brought fashion's elite to within reach of most shoppers. It's a serious business, too. British fashion contributes nearly £21 billion directly to the UK economy each year, making it similar in size to the telecommunications or real estate sectors (British Fashion Council, 2010).

'Fashion has everything for a journalist – money, industry, beauty, history, drama, intrigue, big characters,' says Jess Cartner-Morley of the *Guardian* (Cartner-Morley, 2011). 'I feel incredibly privileged to do what I do.'

Ask her what the downsides of the job are, though, and she replies, 'having to explain this to people'. Her words point to a striking disconnect in fashion journalism. Despite its importance to the media, and despite the fact that it is one of the most sought-after jobs for female journalism graduates (Hanna and Sanders, 2007), it is accorded a uniquely low status in UK journalism both academically and anecdotally. How it is represented in studies, books and films and why that might be will be explored later in this chapter.

Where fashion journalists work – the market

Print magazines

Fashion is inextricably linked with women's magazines and has been from their very start in the eighteenth century. Fashion plates, engraved with the latest styles from Paris, could be reproduced in periodicals like the *Lady's Magazine* or *Entertaining Companion for the Fair Sex*, launched in the UK in 1771. New leisure time, mass literacy, railways and improvements to colour publishing led to a surge of new titles in the late nineteenth century, including *Harper's Bazaar* and *Vogue*. Launched in New York in 1892, *Vogue* was initially a social gazette, but it was turned by its new owner Condé Nast from 1909 into one of the first specialist magazines targeted at a wealthy niche audience in order to deliver high-end advertising. By shunning a mainstream audience, *Vogue*'s circulation in 1910 was only 30,000 but it had 44 per cent more advertising pages – at the highest prices – than any of its competitors (Oliva and Angeletti, 2006).

Today, *Vogue* and other high-end fashion glossies pursue much the same strategy. Though their circulations appear small (in the first half of 2011, British *Vogue* sold around 210,000 copies a month, *Harper's Bazaar* just under 120,000 and *Tatler* 88,000, according to the Audit Bureau of Circulations (Press Gazette, 2011), the spending power of their readers and the luxury advertising this attracts gives them profitability and credibility. Quite what a priority this is for them is brought home when one reads their media kits or packs – the information they compile about their readers to attract advertisers. '*Tatler* delivers … a glamorous environment, a rich audience, an acquisitive attitude' (Tatler media pack, 2010). Even the more mainstream glossies secure around 60 per cent of their revenue from advertising (McKay, 2006), and it is this reliance that has led to accusations that their editorial is compromised, as will be discussed later.

The British Fashion Council estimates that fashion magazines employ 3,101 people and contribute £205 million to the UK economy each year (BFC, 2010). They can be roughly divided into three types: the biannuals, monthlies and weeklies. The biannuals include the likes of *Love Magazine*, *AnOther Magazine*, *Fantastic Man* and *The Gentlewoman*, and tend to feature high production values, luxury brands and lavish photoshoots with top models and photographers, together with wider arts and culture coverage.

The weeklies were once associated with traditional older women's magazines and downmarket titles, but the past decade has seen a wave of fashion-and-celebrity titles for younger women, including the 2005 launch of *Grazia*, billed as the UK's first glossy weekly. Not only are they popular with supermarkets because of their quick turnover, they have also become renowned as big sellers of product; when *Grazia* wrote about the Houlihan trouser range by American firm J Brand, Selfridges sold out its entire stock the following week (Grazia Daily, 2010). Whereas monthlies produce their issues three months ahead of publication, weeklies turn around their content in days. Paula Reed, then *Grazia*'s style director, said:

> The freedom we have – to see somebody on the streets, to spot something in a newspaper or to pick up on gossip in the office, and get it into the magazine – feels incredible, and that's what readers are responding to.
>
> (Cordero, 2011)

The monthlies, squeezed in the middle, have suffered. *Marie Claire*'s circulation fell 21 per cent and *Company*'s dropped 36 per cent between 2008 and 2011 (Press Gazette, 2011). They have responded by extending their brands – into biannual runway editions, offshoots like *Company High-Street Edit* and *Cosmopolitan*'s free *Cosmo on Campus* magazine, websites, apps and events. This has inevitably led to more pressure for journalists. One glossy editor said that six years ago she had twice the staff, twice the budget and one magazine to produce, whereas now they have to stretch their resources to produce two magazines, the website, apps and events.

Another factor to throw into the mix is the growth of customer magazines, online (see below) and in print. Following in the footsteps of supermarket magazines like Tesco and Asda, fashion brand magazines contain editorial showing how to get the latest looks using the label's range. Available to pick up in stores or sent out directly to customers, some have achieved huge circulations – *John Lewis Edition* was second only to *Glamour* in the women's lifestyle sector in the first half of 2011, distributing 474,579 copies. Third was *Asos* magazine, with 452,000 copies circulated

(Press Gazette, 2011). The appeal for the consumer is that they are getting a free magazine with well-funded content – paid for by marketing budgets, rather than shrinking ad revenue, and sometimes featuring top photographers and writers. The appeal for companies is that the magazines 'give depth to a brand in an environment they can control' (Association of Publishing Agencies, 2010).

A different type of magazine is the trade journal *Drapers*, considered vital reading for anyone in the fashion industry as well as an excellent training ground for fashion journalists.

Newspapers

Fashion coverage in newspapers was largely a post-war development, but even then it was largely limited to a weekly slot in the qualities (McRobbie, 1998). It was generally in the form of a fashion editor's report on couture shows, trends and on what to wear for various social occasions (Polan, 2006). From the 1980s, however, fashion reporting grew more prominent along with other forms of lifestyle journalism as newspapers sought female readers and introduced colour printing. Fashion stories began to appear on news pages, stylists were hired to produce shoots for feature pages and colour supplements became a natural home for extended coverage. The likes of *Sunday Times Style* and the *Mail on Sunday*'s *You* magazine have strong followings, and the *News of the World*'s *Fabulous* supplement was the only section to survive the newspaper's closure in 2011 when it moved to sister publication the *Sun*.

Newspaper fashion writers – and they are mainly writers, rather than stylists – see their role a little differently to magazines. Cartner-Morley describes it as 'relating fashion to the reader … everyone communicates through fashion, but it's not verbalised. I have to find a way of putting that into words' (Cartner-Morley, 2011). She also says she has a different relationship to the fashion industry than magazine journalists: 'We can be independent because we are not supported by their advertising. I can go to a show and write a review saying it's rubbish – a magazine can't do that.'

Websites

Fashion was slow to make the jump to online, but by the late noughties the benefits were clear. Not only is it an ideal subject for the media-rich formats of the web, with videos and photo galleries, fashion has been revolutionised by the fact that news can be updated instantly or events live-streamed. Online advertising has also been encouraged by the fact that consumers spent £4.27 billion on fashion online in 2010, a rise of 152 per cent over five years (Mintel, 2011), and developments in e-commerce – where audiences can click on a product to shop it directly – allows publishers to monetise their editorial content.

The growth of editorial online has worked two ways. Established brands in print have developed their websites to make the most of the visual and financial benefits. The *Daily Telegraph*'s fashion website, relaunched in 2010 with directly shopable content, is the work of 30 editors and is the most popular part of its online offering with advertisers (Kansara, 2010). Fashion magazines also have associated websites, which allow them to publish up-to-date news between their monthly or weekly issues, though they were comparatively slow to make the most of digital channels – US *Vogue*'s site was basic until a big relaunch in 2010.

Then there are the big stand-alones like Style.com, launched by Condé Nast in 2001 and once dubbed the online home of *Vogue*. Now it has its own huge audience base – 4.6 million unique visitors during New York's A/W shows in 2011 (Moses, 2011) – and was so confident it was planning to launch a print magazine and a designer e-commerce section the same year. 'I don't think media brands can afford to be tied to one medium anymore ... You want your content to be available in as many places as possible,' editor-in-chief Standen said (Amed, 2011).

As print publications sought to bring shopping into their sites, in the other direction retailers were becoming their own publishers, putting together shopable digital magazines. Former *Tatler* editor Natalie Massenet led the way with luxury online retailer Net-a-Porter, launched in 2000. It now has three million monthly visitors, a digital magazine and iPad app, and a menswear site, Mr Porter. *Asos* launched a digitial version of its customer magazine in 2008, and My-Wardrobe.com and Harrods followed suit in 2011. Shopping centres around the country have their own blogs and online magazines made up largely of fashion and beauty editorial.

The good news for journalists is that they, rather than traditional copywriters, are being employed on this new breed of magazine. This includes high-profile appointments – Mr Porter, for instance, is headed by former *Wallpaper* and *Esquire* editor Jeremy Langmead. 'Journalists have a different skill set. They know how to engage the readers, and engage communities of readers,' says Julia Hutchison, chief operating officer of the Association of Publishing Agencies, the trade body for consumer publishers (Green, 2011).

As a result, retailers' magazines retain credibility in the world of fashion journalism. 'They are the competition for us, no doubt,' Cartner-Morley believes (Cartner-Morley, 2001). 'A lot of the more interesting ideas are coming from them. They are attracting people that have taken the leap ahead into the digital future more quickly than those on print publications.'

Commentators also warn against squeamishness over the merger of commerce and editorial content. Vikram Alexei Kansara, managing director of Business of Fashion, wrote: 'In the real lives of fashion consumers, magazines and shopping are already integrated. People have used magazines as inspirational product guides since their very inception,' (Kansara, 2010).

Blogs

Fashion blogs began to take off after 2005. Written either by anonymous 'insiders' (fashion editors like Sasha Wilkins of Liberty London Girl) or outsiders (Style Rookie's 11-year-old Tavi Gevinson of Chicago or Bryanboy, Bryan Grey Yambao from the Philippines), they were viewed with derision and then suspicion by a fashion industry long used to controlling access to and coverage of its people and products. UK designer Christopher Kane spoke for many when he complained, 'People can say what they want about anyone on a blog without consequences and that's quite scary' (Milligan, 2009).

However, as some blogs amassed large followings, fashion houses and brands began to see the potential of getting them on board – both to influence coverage and to tap into their new young, global audiences. The tipping point was the D&G Spring/Summer 2010 catwalk show, when Garance Dore, Scott Schuman of The Sartorialist, and Bryanboy were invited onto the front row. Now bloggers are regular features at the shows and street style blog photographs are a staple of fashion week coverage for most newspapers, magazines and websites. The industry is working with bloggers in all sorts of ways – to shoot ad campaigns and to front fashion brands, to name but two – and they have generally been accepted as a new wave of fashion influencers.

Meanwhile, traditional media outlets have hired bloggers to write and shoot for them and have gamely started their own blogs, with varying success; *The New York Times* commented, 'reading them, you often sense a generational disconnect, something like the queasy feeling of getting a "friend" request from your mother on Facebook' (Wilson, 2009).

As a result, the arguments about whether bloggers will replace traditional fashion journalists have generally died down. The consensus appears to be that bloggers have the advantage of speed, accessibility and a degree of authenticity – despite the growth of corporate 'seeding' – but do not have the training, resources or time to produce the interviews and fashion stories that magazines and newspapers excel at.

Microblogging and social networks

Social media have emerged as a critical influence in fashion, and by 2011 many brands and publishers were experimenting with ways to harness them. Fashion journalists were already a big presence on Twitter and microblogging site Tumblr. Founded in 2007, two years later Tumblr became the first social network to appoint a full-time fashion director when it found that almost one in five of its 1,000 most popular blogs were fashion related.

Next on the horizon are social curation sites, where users share content and product selections, either from all over the internet (sites like Pinterest and Svpply) or from a range of fashion partners (Lyst – tagline, 'Lyst is your own fashion magazine. Be your own editor'). On Polyvore.com, 1.4 million users create digital mood boards using clothes from runway shows and retailers and share them online; from this, the company compiles a daily top 20 list called 'Zeitgeist' of top brands, trends and celebrities. The *Daily Telegraph* planned to add social curation to its fashion website, with readers recommending products alongside the newspaper's experts. Going further, Lookk.com, launched in 2011, invites users to vote for their favourite pieces by new designers that will then go into production and be sold on the site. 'It's where design, buying, editorial and retail all meet. The consumer wants to take an active part in the process now,' says Laura Naylor, editor-in-chief (Naylor, 2011).

The potential implications for fashion brands and fashion media were brought home by a report by Italian luxury foundation Altagamma in 2011, which said that one in two customers turned to Facebook or Twitter for advice before buying luxury goods. 'Blogs and social media are setting trends more than fashion critics, especially in emerging markets like China,' the report said (Ciancio, 2011).

How to get into fashion journalism

Compared to other areas of journalism, there are no set routes into fashion journalism – no specific qualifications or apprenticeships. Moreover, it is marked by high labour mobility and a strong freelance culture (McRobbie, 1998). Because fashion is a fairly self-contained community, fashion journalists are more likely than others to move between media, PR and fashion houses or brands (Tungate, 2008).

It is important first to note the difference between stylists and writers. Most fashion editors, directors or assistants on a magazine are primarily stylists, though they do write captions and accompanying copy when required. Stylists tend to have fashion or other arts-based degrees, though there are foundation degrees specifically for styling at places like the London College of Fashion. The profession was relatively obscure until fashion editors began to be credited on magazine pages in the 1980s, thanks to the new wave of style magazines like *The Face* and *i-D*, and the influence of Anna Wintour at British *Vogue* (Soames, 2009). Big names include Grace Coddington at US *Vogue*, ex-French *Vogue* editor Carine Roitfeld and *Love Magazine* editor Katie Grand.

Fashion writers are generally separate. On magazines, they will appear on the masthead as fashion features or fashion news editors, writers or assistants. On newspapers, most of the fashion desk will be writers, with perhaps one stylist on staff or freelance stylists brought in for shoots. However, this division might change with the influence of bloggers, who often do both writing and styling.

Ten or 20 years ago, fashion journalists generally did not have a specialist qualification. Cartner-Morley, for example, had a history degree and joined the *Guardian* as a researcher before moving to the fashion desk. However, she has seen that change. 'None of my peers had specialised training, but the younger ones coming through tend to have either a journalism or a fashion qualification' (Cartner-Morley, 2011). Some have both – *Look* magazine's fashion news editor Lucy Wood did a fashion journalism course at the London College of Fashion. Other fashion journalism undergraduate degrees are on offer elsewhere at the University of Sunderland, the University for the Creative Arts in Surrey and Southampton Solent University. The balance between fashion and journalism varies between institutions: at the time of writing, the course at the University of Sunderland is the only one to lead to journalism industry qualifications.

While fashion knowledge is required – not least as a sign of interest and engagement – for fashion writing, journalistic qualities are considered at least as important. 'To be a decent fashion journalist you need the same qualities that are needed to be a regular journalist – an eye for a story, an ability to write, a sense of fairness,' says Charlie Porter, former deputy fashion editor on the *Guardian* and editor of *Fantastic Man* magazine (Press Gazette, 2003). *Company* editor Victoria White put her number one requirement as 'being a good writer (let's not forget this is what it's ALL about)' (webchat, 2010). A good 'eye' and the ability to think visually are also key.

The most common path into fashion journalism is through an internship. That is how would-be writers and stylists learn how to do the job, make contacts and get themselves known. Hannah Almassi, fashion reporter for *Grazia* (see case study), set up a year's worth of internships as soon as she graduated and from that was hired as assistant to *Grazia*'s fashion news editor. Lucy Wood, *Look*'s fashion news editor, worked as an assistant at *Grazia* during the final year of her degree – something she says was tough but necessary. 'My advice is to start as quickly as possible because it's inevitable that you'll have to work for free at first' (Roy, 2009).

But the internship route and its importance in the industry are contentious. The Institute of Public Policy Research warned in 2010 that failing to pay interns for work beyond the normal length of a placement was illegal, and editors have complained that the guidelines are unclear. Moreover, requiring young people to work for free to prove themselves favours those who have London-based family to live with and who can fund themselves, with harmful consequences for diversity. London College of Fashion graduate Liz Lamb, whose family is from Darlington, worked for three years for practically nothing before giving up and returning to the north-east. Liz says, 'A lot of people on my course were from London and were living with parents, but I just couldn't sustain it. You also get a lot of society girls and it doesn't matter if they don't get paid that much' (Lamb, 2011). Liz took a vocational journalism course to get into the industry a different way, and is now a senior features and fashion and beauty writer for *NCJ Media*.

Many internships involve working in a magazine's fashion cupboard, logging, looking after and returning clothes and accessories called in for shoots. But *Company*'s Victoria White has urged students to look beyond the glossies, either for internships or first jobs. Her first job was *Inside Soap* magazine, while she points out that the editors of *Red* and *Grazia* started out on *Chat*, and the *Glamour* editor on *TV Hits* magazine. She argues that weeklies, customer and business-to-business magazines often have bigger staff and offer better training than the more glamorous glossies (webchat, 2010). Other useful variations on internships, especially outside London, are going to newspapers, teaming up with local photographers and building up a portfolio, and helping out at fashion shows (Lamb, 2011).

Many editors also advise would-be fashion journalists to maintain a blog, because it shows commitment, improves writing skills, gets them known and helps to create and hone a 'voice' and a point of view. 'I would question any aspiring journalist who doesn't have a blog these days,' says White (webchat, 2010).

What fashion journalists do

This will vary enormously depending on the journalist's publication and role, but these are some of the most common routines and practices.

Runway shows

The biggest dates in the fashion calendar are the twice-yearly ready-to-wear fashion weeks in New York, London, Milan and Paris, as well as the haute couture shows in Paris. They involve thousands of journalists, stylists, PRs, buyers and photographers from around the world and cost hundreds of thousands of pounds to stage. Most of a designer's clothes are sold at pre-collection gatherings in showrooms, months beforehand (Tungate, 2008), so the catwalk shows are more of a publicity than a trade event. And in these days of internet video, photo galleries and live-streaming, not to mention shrinking budgets and environmental concerns, why does anybody still bother attending the shows?

The simple answer is that they are a great story for journalists. They provide the hook for months' worth of trend reports, there are celebrities on the front row to write about, there are theatrical stunts and outlandish clothes, designers to interview, and models, other fashion editors and bloggers to photograph and analyse. A more complex answer, posited by academic studies, is that the shows are 'cultural' events through which 'particular groups of fashion elites reproduce themselves' (Kawamura, 2004: 62). There is certainly something of that in the way journalists talk about the shows. 'It's where you get to see everybody, what the fashion crowd are wearing, it's a really important way of keeping the industry together,' says Hannah Almassi, *Grazia*'s fashion reporter (Almassi, 2010).

A reporter will take down notes and sketches during the show and can snap outfits on his or her phone. Instead of slavishly noting down every detail – there tends to be 40–50 pieces in a show – they will look for a couple of themes, illustrated by references to a handful of particular outfits. They will also look at the basic silhouette of the clothes, the cut, fabric, colour and texture. They look at how the clothes are styled and the models' hair and make-up. They also take in the production of the show – the catwalk, the models, the music, lighting, special effects – as well as the general atmosphere and details of who is there. On top of that, they must note where the designer's influences are coming from; from their own impressions, from visiting the designer in his or her studio ahead of the show, from press releases and from interviewing the designer backstage afterwards.

It is a lot to take in during a 15-minute show, but help is at hand from the designers' show notes and from PRs present at the shows. The journalist might get backstage afterwards to talk to the designer and others involved in the show, and can also make an appointment to see the collection in a showroom. They will also have carried out research beforehand on the designer's situation, signature styles, history and previous shows – all useful context for a report.

For newspapers and websites, a catwalk report has to be written and sent within hours, so clarity of thought, a strong angle and sharp writing is key. For magazines, the timing is more complex, bearing in mind that the autumn/winter collections are shown in February/March, and the spring/summer collections in September/October. A weekly might report quickly on the shows, but will have to wait six months before writing up the seasonal trends or featuring the pieces in fashion shoots. A monthly magazine won't be able to include the shows in its pages for three months, because of its lead-time, but will be looking at which pieces to call in for shoots within a month or so.

Trend reports

A staple of fashion writing is the trend report, which can range from a lengthy analysis complete with social, economic and cultural context to a quick couple of paragraphs surrounded by pictures of product, depending on the publication. The angle might be a particular fabric (lace, say, or leather), a colour or a pattern (polka dots, neon), some aspect of cut, shape or silhouette (ruffles, skinny jeans, bodycon), parts of the body (emphasis on the waist, or shoulders), a past era (Edwardian, 1990s) or a particular aesthetic (grunge, military, androgynous).

Trend forecasting is a huge industry, and a publication might have a subscription to a company like WGSN which uses style scouts around the world, consumer research, reports from trade and catwalk shows, retail trends, textile development, cultural indicators and colour forecasting to predict trends 18 months to two years ahead.

But because the art of fashion journalism is relating fashion to people's every-day lives, writers will generally look closer to home. Runway shows are an obvious starting point, but Cartner-Morley says, 'It has to have got beyond the catwalks for us for it to be a trend. We look at films, too, television shows, exhibitions, generally what's in the air' (Cartner-Morley, 2011).

Hannah Almassi at *Grazia* is constantly striving to spot trends just ahead of the curve. As she is young (in her mid-20s), she keeps tabs on what her friends are interested in and looks closely at what she spots on people in London. She checks blogs every day, scours Australian and American magazines for new looks or brands, goes through the trade press and keeps an eye on what style leaders like certain celebrities or models are wearing. Once she has identified a trend, she needs to validate it with a runway or celebrity picture. 'You need something to hold the page rather than just products,' she says. 'You need to explain where it's come from, who did it on the catwalk, who's been wearing it, why it works now, how you keep it looking right, where are the best items to get the look.' She finds the products by going through lookbooks and websites, and contacting the PRs of likely brands and retailers.

For other magazines, celebrities' red carpet and off-duty looks might be the main source of trend reports. Lucy Wood of *Look* says one of the first things she does every morning is 'go through all the new paparazzi pictures that have come in overnight and spot emerging trends' (Finnan, 2010).

Press days, where journalists are invited by High Street stores to view a new season's collection, can also be a useful reference point for trends. Cartner-Morley says that even if she cannot get to others, she will try to make the Marks & Spencer press day as it is an important barometer of the High Street.

Street style

The increased focus on celebrity pushed street style features out of magazines, but by the late noughties they were making a comeback thanks to the success of photo-bloggers like Tommy Ton, Streetpeeper, The Sartorialist's Scott Schuman and Facehunter. Schuman sees them as a valuable genre of fashion journalism: 'Previously fashion was so alien and so hierarchical. Bloggers show the average person that they too can be part of it' (Copping, 2009).

Magazines have found that street style photos are one of the main drivers of traffic to their websites, and in 2010 were working on ways to allow users to upload their own pictures. When *Grazia* saw how popular street style was becoming, it revamped its Style Hunter page and tasked reporter Hannah Almassi with finding the 'right' four women each week. She tries to avoid the street style photographers – not always easy – but says that because of the magazine's appeal 'we do pick some people that others wouldn't notice. We're not just going for the cool kids down at Spitalfields, we might get a 40-year-old woman down Bond Street who looks fantastic' (Almassi, 2010).

Almassi agrees that street style is a valuable way of making fashion more accessible to readers, and less didactic.

> Sometimes when you look at models or advertising, you don't think you could look like that. Whereas when you look at a real girl, you realize you may already have the clothes and you can. And it shows girls wearing trends in lots of different ways – it's not about making everyone into a fashion machine.
>
> (2010)

Fashion spreads

Fashion photoshoots, spreads or stories are a sign of prestige in a fashion publication. While the glossies may have several stories, shot in interesting or far-flung locations with top models and big-name photographers, more general women's magazines, weeklies and newspapers may be restricted to fewer stories, more studio shoots, or even just pages of unstyled product pictures.

The job of the fashion editor or director is to come up with a theme or 'story' for a shoot. This can be as simple as a particular trend, type of garment or season, or as complex as a reference to film, literature or world events (*Vogue Italia* caused controversy with a 'Water & Oil' shoot in August 2010 inspired by the BP oil spill in the Gulf, featuring oil-coated models draped on rocks). Fashion storytelling can spark the readers' imagination, and weave a whole story, mood or magic around the clothes featured, but it has become common to bemoan its decline in magazines now. A contributing editor to *Vogue Italia*, Debra Scherer, wrote: 'The truth is, for the most part, we now take pictures of clothing in order to optimize merchandising' (Scherer, 2011).

The fashion desk will put together a mood board for the shoot, and the clothes will be booked and called in from fashion houses and brands. How easy it is to secure the pieces depends on how prestigious a publication is. Models, photographers, make-up artists, hair stylists, location and perhaps set designers, are arranged for the day(s) in question, with the shoot presided over by either the fashion editor or freelance stylist. Editorial shoots are paid far less than advertising campaigns, but bring with them credibility and the chance for work to be seen. On local publications, models, hair stylists and make-up artists might do the job for free as long as they are credited in the captions.

Other events and sources of ideas

Other events that fashion journalists attend include meetings with PRs, often organised around breakfasts, lunches or dinners, as well as trade shows, launches, parties and award ceremonies. They might have regular features like how-to-wear articles, opinion or advice columns, product pages, product reviews and news round-ups, as well as who-wore-what-best or hits-and-misses, especially during awards seasons. Other common features are interviews and profiles with designers or celebrities, often organised by their PRs, especially when they have something to promote. Another staple of newspaper coverage is the analysis of what a public figure or someone in the news has chosen to wear at an important time, and what they might be trying to convey. Colourful first-person pieces – like Polly Vernon's efforts to get snapped by street style bloggers, in *Grazia* (March 2011) – and other one-off features, perhaps investigatory in nature, are rarer in fashion journalism but are welcomed by magazines looking for fresh ideas, and are a good way in for would-be freelancers.

To come up with a constant stream of ideas, fashion journalists keep up to date not only with fashion news and trends, but what is going on in the arts, entertainment, business and political news too. Almassi of *Grazia* says: 'On a Sunday I read as many newspapers and blogs as I can, pulling out tears of things that are interesting, not just fashion' (Almassi, 2010). The best advice she was ever given was to 'do things you wouldn't normally do and meet people you wouldn't normally meet, because ideas are everywhere and you learn from other people'.

Bouncing ideas off colleagues is also very important, perhaps especially in fashion where consensus has to be reached on aesthetic judgments and links have to be made to perceive a trend. 'My main source is my desk – we'll rabbit on about what we have seen and heard, and that's how we pick up on things, batting ideas about, establishing connections,' says Cartner-Morley (2011).

Ideas are then pitched at conferences with editors and a stories list will be drawn up for journalists to work on. Those journalists working across media platforms must also decide how best to tell the story. It might still be words, but it could equally be a photo slideshow with captions or audio, or an interactive graphic, or a video. Even those only working in print must focus on sourcing visuals as well as words – stories will be ditched if they cannot be represented by, say, a catwalk or celebrity picture.

Issues in fashion journalism

One of the most vexed issues is magazines' relationship to their advertisers and how far it affects editorial. Anecdotally, tales abound of fashion houses threatening to pull advertising because they haven't had enough mentions in the editorial, or have had criticism; of clothes switched at the last moment before a fashion shoot to include something from an advertiser; of magazines doling out perfume credits to keep advertisers happy; of glossies only using advertisers' clothes on the cover. In his book on branding, Tungate writes: 'The vast percentage of fashion journalism is at best effervescent, at worst fawning. Could it possibly be because magazines need to keep their advertisers sweet?' (2008: 130). And in a study of newspaper specialists, Tunstall (1971) found that fashion journalists were ranked lowest in respect by other specialisms because of their advertising function.

In their defence, fashion journalists argue that the advertiser-editorial relationship is a little more balanced than is sometimes made out, not least because magazines have to retain some credibility to be worth advertising in. French *Vogue* ex-editor Carine Roitfeld said she tried to promote young designers on the up, and added: 'Even the biggest advertisers accept that their clothes and advertisements look better in a dynamic environment. It can be best described as a sort of mutual understanding' (Tungate, 2008: 132). British *Vogue* editor Alexandra Shulman takes a pragmatic approach. 'Although there is this feeling sometimes that creatively it's not pure, well – magazines are a business, you're not sitting there writing poetry' (Barber, 2008). As discussed earlier, journalists on newspapers and websites feel they are not constrained by advertisers in the same way.

A related complaint is that fashion journalism is too close to PRs, who are accused of spoon-feeding stories and doling out freebies to ensure positive coverage. There are an estimated 200 PR companies with fashion clients in London alone, and many are in daily contact with journalists. Critics say the personal relationships forged make it difficult for journalists to write negative things, on top of PRs' control of access to collections, designers and events like runway shows. Political journalist Andrew Marr wrote in his press history *My Trade*: 'Fashion journalists work so closely with the PRs of the big houses that they are constantly in danger of becoming virtually their employees' (2004: 109). Again, though, journalists argue that their dealings with PRs are more subtle than critics will allow. Cartner-Morley says: 'Some are too close, as in all fields are journalism. PR contacts are essential – they are invaluable colleagues. If you let yourself get turned into a mouthpiece for them, that's sheer laziness' (Cartner-Morley, 2011). Almassi of *Grazia* says her stories are sometimes too specific and too forward-thinking to be fed to her by PRs – rather it's her chasing them up when she is trying to source products.

The main thrust of all these complaints – about advertiser influence, PRs and freebies – is that they lead to uncritical and frivolous coverage. In a book about British fashion, cultural studies writer Angela McRobbie said fashion writers were scared to step out of line, ignored social and political issues, confined themselves to information or praise, and didn't adhere to journalistic notions of impartiality. 'The fashion media thus secures the marginalized trivial image of fashion as though it cannot be bothered to take itself seriously or to consider its own conditions of existence' (1998: 174), she concluded, adding that it kept fashion journalism in a 'ghetto of femininity'.

But fashion journalists often argue their job is dismissed as trivial precisely BECAUSE it is largely staffed by women. Writing about the portrayal of fashion journalists as shallow and appearance-obsessed in the 2006 film *The Devil Wears Prada*, Hadley Freeman of the *Guardian* complained:

> This is what movies about the fashion industry always do: they make fun of or punish – or both – women devoted to a job they enjoy ... There is the added crime that they work in an industry run, very successfully, by other women.
>
> (2006)

Fashion journalists can be slightly baffled by the accusations of relentless positivity, too, perhaps because of how they see their role. Fashion is based on desire, not need, so it does not require the kind of rigorous consumer reviews other products are subject to. In addition, because they are writing largely about trends, they are necessarily pointing readers to what is desirable. Almassi says of *Grazia*:

> If there's a collection that's not so good, you almost edit it out as it's not relevant for people to know. Why not show them something that's really good instead? And if you're constantly going on about 'this is out, this is uncool', that comes across as horrible and puts pressure on people.
>
> (Almassi, 2010)

Cartner-Morley believes that fashion coverage suffers when journalists write for the people they're featuring, instead of writing for the reader (2011).

Looking ahead to the future, of concern to many in fashion journalism is how print publications will survive. In 2011 they had been hit by an advertising downturn, both because of recession and a move to online, and they have to compete against free and faster editorial on the web. Social media are vying for the attention of readers, and some question the viability of the role of the fashion editor when consumers are seeking styling inspiration, recommendations and validation from their peers online. But fashion journalists are on the whole confident that magazines have enough brand credibility to survive, whatever the format. They cannot imagine the fashion landscape without the beautifully put-together photoshoots and cultural commentary of the high-end glossies. And even in the online world, they argue, an expert eye is required. 'You can't just go online and search black trousers. You need someone to edit, someone to say "Zara are doing fantastic black trousers in the style of such-and-such a designer". So fashion writers and editors will always be needed,' says Cartner-Morley.

Case study: Hannah Almassi, fashion reporter for *Grazia*

Hannah Almassi was studying for a degree in fashion design at Nottingham Trent University when she realised she was more interested in how her clothes would be reported in a magazine than actually making them. 'I based my final show around it. I'm still really interested in the design process, and it does help me now because when you see something beautiful and exquisite you can fully appreciate just how long it's taken to get to that stage.'

Hannah organised a year's worth of work placements at magazines for when she graduated, but struck gold with the very first one.

> I went to *Grazia* literally the week after I finished uni – I was very determined. It was supposed to be a month, and I was working in the fashion cupboard, helping call things in for the shopping pages and fashion shoots. I loved it there, and on the last day got pulled aside and asked if I wanted to be (fashion news editor) Melanie Rickey's assistant for six months.

Assisting Rickey meant doing background research for news and features, finding catwalk pictures, sourcing the right products for a page, helping with styling and attending interviews with her. Hannah began to write pieces and contribute ideas herself, and the six months turned into 18 months. She ended up being promoted to junior fashion news editor, and now fashion reporter.

> When you turn up at *Grazia* you are non-stop from the minute you walk in, because it's a weekly and there's so much content to turn round in just five days. Most people have monthly deadlines – we have daily deadlines, hourly deadlines.

Hannah is responsible for the Style Hunter pages, and goes out with a photographer each week to spot and interview around ten suitable street style subjects. She also writes for the magazine's 10 Hot Stories at the front of the book, and contributes to the shopping pages at the back if required. She comes up with story ideas at the weekend, shares them with the fashion team on Monday, then helps pitch fashion's ideas at the main conference with all the editors the same day. They're whittled down to a final list, and her stories have to be researched, written and shot by Wednesday morning to go to the sub-editors and art team. The magazine is printed on Thursday evening.

Her long-term ambition is to be some kind of fashion commentator, predicting trends and consulting for designers or brands on where their businesses should be heading. In her spare time she does test shoots to keep her hand in with styling and writes a blog.

> I'm fortunate to be in a position where I do see a lot – meet great people, see collections, go to fashion shows, meet PRs, and that does seem to interest a lot of people. So it does seem silly not to share that. It's good practice, too   I'm still learning to write. I'll always be learning to write, forever and ever.

References

Almassi, H. (2010) *Interview with the author*, 18 December.

Amed, I. (2011) 'Style.com to Launch Magazine and "Dip Toes" in E-Commerce', *Business of Fashion*, 22 August. Available: www.businessoffashion.com/2011/08/bof-exclusive-style-com-to-launch-magazine-and-dip-toes-in-e-commerce.html.

Association of Publishing Agencies (2010) 'The Boom in Branded Magazines', 11 January. Available: www.apa.co.uk/news/the-boom-in-branded-magazines.

Barber, L. (2008) 'The World According to Garb', *Observer*, 2 February. Available: www. guardian.co.uk/lifeandstyle/2008/feb/10/fashion.features1.

British Fashion Council (2010) 'Value of the British Fashion Industry', *British Fashion Council*. Available: www.britishfashioncouncil.com/content.aspx?CategoryID=1745.

Cartner-Morley, J. (2011) *Interview with the author*, 14 September.

Ciancio, A. (2011) 'Fashion Bloggers to Spur Online Luxury Sales – report', *Reuters*, 15 September. Available: http://uk.reuters.com/article/2011/09/15/uk-italy-luxury-idUK TRE78E4LA20110915.

Copping, N. (2009) 'Style Bloggers Take Centre Stage', *Financial Times*, 13 November. Available: www.ft.com/cms/s/2/89f8c07c-cfe0–11de-a36d-00144feabdc0.html#axzz1 YQMXDg2r.

Cordero, R. (2011) 'Musing on the Pace of Fashion', *Business of Fashion*, 18 May. Available: www.businessoffashion.com/2011/05/musing-on-the-pace-of-fashion.html.

Finnan, S. (2010) *How to Prepare for a Career in Fashion*. London: Adelita.

Freeman, H. (2006) 'Prada and Prejudice', *Guardian*, 6 September. Available: www.guardian. co.uk/commentisfree/2006/sep/06/film.comment.

Grazia Daily (2010) 'Grazia Ignites Houlihan Fever!' *Grazia Daily*, 10 June. Available: www.graziadaily.co.uk/fashion/archive/2010/06/10/grazia-ignites-houlihan-fever.htm.

Green, L. (2011) 'Online Retailers Discover the Joy of Journalism', *FT.com*, 4 February. Available: www.ft.com/cms/s/2/4dc5e92c-2fe3–11e0-a7c6–00144feabdc0.html#axzz1YV docvRP.

Hanna, M. and Sanders, K. (2007) 'Journalism Education in Britain: Who Are the Students and What Do They Want?' *Journalism Practice* 1(3), 404–20.

Kansara, V. (2010) 'Fashion 2.0: Magazines Capitalise on Shopable Content', *Business of Fashion*, 26 March. Available: http://businessoffashion.com/2010/03/fashion-2-0-magazines-capitalise-on-shopable-content.html.

Kawamura, Y. (2004) *Fashion-ology: An Introduction to Fashion Studies*. London: Berg.

Lamb, L. (2011) *Interview with the author*, 18 April.

McKay, J. (2006) *The Magazines Handbook*. 2nd edn. London: Routledge.

McRobbie, A. (1998) *British Fashion Design: Rag Trade or Image Industry?* London: Routledge.

Marr, A. (2004) *My Trade: A Short History of British Journalism*. London: Macmillan.

Milligan, L. (2009) 'Kane and Able', *Vogue.com*, 1 December. Available: www.vogue.co.uk/news/2009/12/01/christopher-kane-interview.

Mintel (2011) 'Online Fashion Clicks with Brits as Market Increases 152% Over Past Five Years', Mintel Press Release. Available: www.mintel.com/press-centre/press-releases/695/online-fashion-clicks-with-brits-as-market-increases-152-over-past-five-years.

Moses, L. (2011) 'At Fairchild, Consumer Is the New Black', *Adweek*, 31 March. Available: www.adweek.com/news/television/fairchild-consumer-new-black-126130.

Naylor, L. (2011) *Interview with the author*, September 7.

Oliva, A. and Angeletti, N. (2006) *In Vogue: The Illustrated History of the World's Most Famous Fashion Magazine*. New York: Rizzoli.

Polan, B. (2006) 'Fashion Journalism', in Jackson, T. and Shaw, D. (2006) *The Fashion Handbook (Media Practice)*. London: Routledge.

Press Gazette (2003) 'Fashion Journalism: Tips of the Trade', 27 June. Available: www.pressgazette.co.uk/story.asp?storyCode=28220&sectioncode=1.

——(2011) 'Mag ABCs, Women's Monthlies: *Glamour* stays top', 18 August. Available: www.pressgazette.co.uk/story/asp?sectioncode=18storycode=47722&c=1.

Roy, R. (2009) 'Working at *Look* Magazine – An Interview with Lucy Wood', *Stylist Stuff*, 12 January. Available: www.fashion-stylist.net/blog/2009/01/12/working-at-look-magazine-an-interview-with-lucy-wood.

Scherer, D. (2011) 'Op-Ed: Why Do We Take Pictures of Clothes?' *Business of Fashion*, 7 September. Available: www.businessoffashion.com/2011/09/op-ed-why-do-we-take-pictures-of-clothes.html.

Soames, G. (2009) 'Why Every Girl Wants to be a Fashion Stylist', *Sunday Times*, 20 December. Available: www.thesundaytimes.co.uk/sto/style/fashion/art192.

Tungate, M. (2008) *Fashion Brands: Branding Style from Armani to Zara*. London: Kogan Page.

Tunstall, J. (1971) *Journalists at Work: Specialist Correspondents*. London: Constable.

White, V. (2010) 'Webchat', *Company.co.uk*, 17 September. Available: www.company.co.uk/community/forums/thread/990916.

Wilson, E. (2009) 'Bloggers Crash Fashion's Front Row', *New York Times*, 24 December. Available: www.nytimes.com/2009/12/27/fashion/27BLOGGERS.html.

9 Food journalism

Steve Jones and Ben Taylor

Introduction

On 13 November 2010, the *Guardian* newspaper carried an article – 'A tale of two herds' – about 'plans for an enormous super dairy, home to 8,000 cows' (Lewis and Vidal, 2010). The article explored concerns about 'intensive farming which has almost totally separated food and nature', and contrasted the scale of the proposed farm with a herd of 44 cows tended by a Hare Krishna community on a farm in Hertfordshire. Producing much lower yields than the super dairy, the Hare Krishna milk, 'at £3 a litre […] will be the most expensive cows' milk in Britain'. The article then carried out a taste test, inviting a panel to compare the Hare Krishna milk with regular milk. The panel consisted of the *Guardian*'s environment editor, John Vidal; Sam Clark, the proprietor-chef of London restaurant Moro; and Rosie Sykes, a chef, food writer and contributor to the *Guardian*'s *Weekend* supplement. All the panellists agreed that the Hare Krishna milk was superior, with Clark explaining how it could be used to make excellent cheese and yoghurt, and Sykes commenting that a 'white sauce or a custard' made with it 'would be incredible'.

The article neatly broaches a number of the issues we wish to explore in this chapter. First, insofar as the article is written by two of the newspaper's environment editors, Vidal and Juliette Lewis, it demonstrates that journalistic interest in food isn't restricted to recipe columns and restaurant reviews. Indeed, the article's discussion of animal welfare issues, and of apprehensions about the relationship between food and nature, gestures towards broader anxieties about the food we eat. Increasingly intensive forms of food production have generated a growing sensitivity towards food as an object of individual and social risk, and food journalism is often to be found addressing these apparent risks. Second, in spite of this, the taste test allows the issue of intensive farming to be brought back into the kitchen. Clark and Sykes, the panel's food experts, treated the Hare Krishna milk as though it were a new and exotic ingredient. Sykes, for example, claimed that she had 'never drunk milk like that before. It even moved in a different way', while Clark noted that 'there's not just a marginal difference' between it and normal milk: '[I]t tastes like you're on a farm […] There's no comparison.' While contemporary food production and consumption carries risk, then, it also brings with it the excitement of novelty. The speeding-up and stretching-out represented by global food sourcing has generated new forms of diversity in contemporary food journalism, as writers attempt to explain new or rediscovered foodstuffs and food practices to consumers. This is often presented as a pleasurable search for new eating and drinking experiences, and the pursuit of cooking and dining as expressive lifestyle practices is regularly valorised.

In this chapter we look at the various forms taken by food journalism, an increasingly 'crowded field' (Hughes, 2010: 2) and one whose subject matter has become widely reported and discussed within print, television and online media. Far from being the marginalised '"women's page" stuff' (Brown, 2004) of the past, coverage of food has begun to merge with other news issues such as health, business and celebrity, such that it now 'occupies an unrivalled centrality in all our lives' (Bell and Valentine, 1997: 3). Despite this 'mainstreaming', however, food journalism has received little academic scrutiny in comparison to other forms of leisure and lifestyle journalism. We aim to correct this here by outlining the origins of food journalism, the size and composition of the specialism in the UK, and by analysing the textual strategies deployed within it. We will argue that food journalism is frequently bound up with developing middle-class tastes, and their separation from 'popular' tastes, while also being strongly marked by gender differences.

Although these divisions continue to be an important way of conceptualising food journalism, the field has been subject to processes of development and change. In the later part of the chapter we therefore show how major shifts in the classed and gendered dimensions of cuisine have provoked a response within food journalism as the field has sought to shape tastes and behaviour in new ways. Moreover, as well as being conscious of the changing attitudes of its readership, food journalism has had to respond to shifts in the organisation of the industry it reports on, and whose advertising revenue it seeks. Furthermore, food journalists are not the only intermediaries within this enlarged field. Not only are challenges coming to traditional journalism from the blogosphere, but also from the restaurant industry itself. As high-profile chefs seek to diversify their brands, they pursue media careers on television and in print, sometimes appropriating the role of investigative food journalists for themselves.

To understand how the specialism operates in the present, we need to have some understanding of how it came into existence in the first place, and how these origins continue to exert influence in the present (Benson and Neveu, 2005: 13). It is to this that we now turn.

The making of the food journalism field

While in formal, newspaper, terms, we could place food journalism as a regular feature item, contrasting 'in tone and length to the news coverage at the front of the newspaper' (Niblock, 2008: 48), this description tells us little about the content of the genre, the changes it has undergone over time, or about its relationship with adjacent cultural forms. We find it useful, therefore, to follow the sociologist Pierre Bourdieu in describing food journalism as a 'field'. For Bourdieu, a field is a relatively durable and consistent set of cultural practices governed by its own internal laws, a 'particular social universe endowed with particular institutions and obeying specific laws' (Bourdieu, 1993, 162–63). Fields possess their own autonomous codes of conduct and modes of behaviour and their own forms of reward (not just monetary reward, but also symbolic recognition in the form of awards and, crucially, the acknowledgement of one's peers) so that they become 'self-regulating, self-validating and self-perpetuating' (Ferguson, 2001: 5). At the same time as drawing our attention to the internal dispositions of a cultural activity, the notion of 'field' also points to its external relations with related cultural fields. In the case of food journalism, for example, it explores how this activity is bound up with the larger journalistic field, with other forms of food media and with the food industry.

Although there are scattered instances of food writing throughout recorded history, a persuasive case can be made that, the organised translation of culinary production into journalism occurred in the social flux that followed the French Revolution, as new classes, tastes and intermediaries emerged. '[T]aken as the systematic, socially valorised pursuit of culinary creativity', argues Priscilla Parkhurst Ferguson, 'gastronomy began in the nineteenth century, and it began in France' (Ferguson, 2001: 10).

The most comprehensive discussion of this moment has been provided by Stephen Mennell (1996). Mennell argues that it was the appearance of a food writer, the gastronome, which was the decisive contribution to eating as a social activity (1996: 266–90). Only by translating the experience of eating publicly into news did tastes become first national and then international. The gastronome, he argues, is someone who cultivates both his own refined tastes and, through writing, the tastes of others of his class. He 'is more than a gourmet – he is also a theorist and propagandist about culinary taste' (1996: 267).

Two authors, Alexandre Grimod de la Reynière (1758–1838) and Jean Anthelme Brillat-Savarin (1755–1826), were the effective founders of this genre of writing since 'virtually everything of the sort written since quotes or harks back to these authors' (ibid.). As 'men of letters', both authors belonged to a pre-existing and much broader literary field. Gastronomic journalism was therefore, in the first instance, a primarily aesthetic or philosophical field, rather than one closely linked to professional cookery or domestic practice. Mennell argues that, rather than simply offering a set of instructions to the reader, Grimod's *Almanach des Gourmands* (1803–12) and Brillat-Savarin's *Physiologie du Goût* (1826) blend these instrumental requirements with discursive reflections on etiquette and nutritional health, meanwhile providing 'a brew of history, myth, and history serving as myth' (ibid.); and nostalgically evoking 'memorable meals' (271). By writing in this way, argues Ferguson, these authors provided 'culinary texts of indirection', which served to redefine the prosaic activity of dining out as a phenomenon of a higher moral and intellectual order (Ferguson, 2001: 13).

By articulating the superiority of a form of culinary taste, these 'disinterested' works of journalism worked to reinforce the class and sex advantages of their social group. The culinary landscape evoked by the *Almanach* was a public one of shops, restaurants and cafes and this was a sphere open primarily to middle-class men. It was, moreover, a metropolitan one, with each edition including as its centrepiece a 'gourmand's itinerary' around Paris, evidence of the growing consolidation of the city's position as the nation's culinary and cultural centre. For Grimod, 'superior culinary achievement begins in Paris, then spreads to the provinces, and eventually to the rest of the world' (Garval, 2001: 63)

Some decades after the appearance of gastronomic journalism, a parallel development, taking place primarily in England, sought to inculcate new culinary dispositions in a predominantly female readership. Negotiating both the increasing home-centredness of 'respectable' women's lives (Mennell, 1996: 234) and a 'tendency in industrial societies to rely […] on formal instruction' (Mennell, 230), a 'women's press' emerged, focusing on the cultivation of middle-class women's domestic skills. The cookery column, dispensing advice on matters of both the kitchen and the table became a small but indispensable element of these magazines' content. Although emerging around 1850, this style of publication gathered momentum in the late nineteenth and twentieth centuries with the publication of weekly and monthly titles such as *Woman's Life* (started 1895), *Good Housekeeping* (1922) and *Woman's Own* (1932). While these publications, with their depiction of home catering as dull routine and moral obligation seem to stand outside the aestheticised food journalistic field we have described, Mennell's analysis describes counter-tendencies in which the pleasures of new forms of food, culinary creativity and entertaining could be addressed. Certainly by the late twentieth century, he argues, there were a great many ways in which magazines demonstrated how 'cooking and eating [could] be de-routinised for enhanced enjoyment' (Mennell, 265). Moreover, it was this form of food journalism which generated one of the more significant shifts in the field as the dependence of magazines, and increasingly weekly newspapers, on advertising revenues opened up new forms of food representation as written copy was increasingly accompanied by food imagery created by the publication's own stylists or by advertisers.

The preceding historical analysis has demonstrated how the nascent field of food journalism achieved coherence through its education of a growing middle class in matters of culinary taste. Yet it was marked from its outset by key divisions between the public and private spheres, and correspondingly between masculinity and femininity. It has been further shaped by its relationship with the food industry on which it comments. Clearly, the great expansion of food journalism over time has brought new issues into focus, and complicated these structuring divisions of the field. It is to this contemporary landscape that we now turn.

Forms of food journalism

The market for food journalism in the UK is varied and expanding, and can be divided into three categories. First there are trade publications aimed at the food retail and hospitality industries. Some of these are long established: *The Grocer* magazine, for example, began in 1862, and, with a weekly circulation of around 30,000 in 2010, is the market leader in the sector. Others represent a response to more recent developments within the food industry: *Speciality Food Magazine*, for example, was launched in 2002, and focuses on developments within delicatessens, farm shops and supermarkets stocking 'fine foods'.

The second category is magazines aimed at food consumers, many of which are branded. Most of the large supermarket chains, for example, publish their own monthly magazines which feature recipes and food products, but operate as marketing vehicles for each supermarket brand. The largest circulation within this market segment is the free-to-customers *Tesco Magazine*. With just over two million readers a month it is the publication with the fourth highest circulation of all magazines in the UK. In a similar fashion, articles in the *BBC Good Food* magazine revolve noticeably around chefs, series and recipes appearing in the BBC's own food-related broadcasting. The launch of *Jamie Magazine* in 2008 saw a magazine tied to the brand of the celebrity chef Jamie Oliver and, as we shall see, this link between food journalism and celebrity is growing. Elsewhere, there are a number of more specialist titles, such as *Taste Italia* and *Great British Food*, which focus on particular traditions and cuisines.

The final category is newspaper-based food journalism. Most newspapers publish features devoted to food, including regular recipe columns and restaurant reviews. Increasingly, this material finds its place in supplements or sections devoted to issues such as homes, gardens and fashion. Some newspapers – the *Observer*, *The Times* and the *Telegraph* – have their own specialist food supplements, and it has been argued that these publications are used to 'build circulation' more generally for each newspaper (Parker, 2006). Given the increasing interest in food, and the 'explosion of lifestyle media' (Bell and Hollows, 2006: 1), William Sitwell, the editor of *Waitrose Food Illustrated*, has predicted that the number of newspapers with 'spin-off [food] magazines' such as these is likely to grow (Parker, 2006). The appearance of online versions of newspapers and food magazines has allowed such publications to address their readership in new ways.

Having described the market for food journalism, we will now identify the different forms such journalism takes. An initial distinction worth making is between food journalism published in trade magazines and that published in consumer-oriented titles, whether magazines or newspapers. Undertaking a comparative analysis of an example of each category, – the trade magazine *Caterer & Hotelkeeper* and the food magazines *Taste* and the BBC's *Gourmet Good Food* – Joseph Fattorini (1994) has argued that there is significant distance between the manner in which food, and the industries which produce it, are represented. In particular, he notes how food magazines frequently deploy a 'lack of realism' brought about 'by inaccurate representations of the world of professional catering in the media' (Fattorini, 1994: 28). While trade publications represent food as 'just one part of the job', for the consumer-oriented publications food is related to 'pleasure, enjoyment of the end product, [and] cooking as a leisure activity' (Fattorini, 1994: 27). In the rest of this section, we want to focus on consumer-oriented food journalism, and to identify some of the different ways in which food is constructed as a site of pleasure. In doing so, we assume that there are three principal manifestations that these forms of journalism might take: first, the cookery column; second, the restaurant review; and third, the feature article about food. We will deal with each of these three categories in turn.

As we have shown, the cookery column emerged in women's magazines and in newspaper sections targeted at women, and endorsed the idea that domestic cooks are female (and, implicitly, that professional chefs are male). From Elizabeth David, to Jane Grigson, to Amanda Grant, the cookery column was a place where female writers could share their culinary wisdom with female readers. However, a number of developments have begun to reconfigure this arrangement. First, the cookery column is increasingly breaking free from its traditional location in the women's section. As Robert Hanke notes, by the 1980s the cookery column had migrated to the lifestyle sections of newspapers, and much greater emphasis was now placed on the enjoyment of food (Hanke, 1989: 223). As David Bell and Joanne Hollows (2005) observe, 'contemporary consumer culture encourages us to play with lifestyle' (Bell and Hollows, 2005: 5), and the cookery column increasingly invites readers to think about cooking not as a household chore, but as an activity which belongs to a broader array of lifestyle choices spanning interior decorating, gardening and fashion. In the course of this trajectory, the gendered nature of the cookery column has been eroded. Today, the columnist is just as likely to be a man as a woman, and is often likely to have worked as a chef (such as Hugh Fearnley-Whittingstall in the *Guardian* and Heston Blumenthal in *The Times*). Finally, there is now an increasingly strong relationship between cookery columnists and other media outlets. Fearnley-Whittingstall and Blumenthal have both had success with a number of cookery books and television series, as have writers such as Nigella Lawson (who was a restaurant critic for *The Spectator* and a food columnist for *Vogue* before moving into cookery books and television) and Delia Smith (whose early television career went hand in hand with a cookery column in the *Evening Standard*). In this way, the cookery column has increasingly become a site where the identities of celebrity cooks are established and sustained.

As with the cookery column, there is an important gendered dimension to the restaurant review which, notwithstanding the handful of female reviewers (such as Fay Maschler, who writes for the London *Evening Standard*), has tended to provide a vehicle for male commentators – most prominently A.A. Gill and Michael Winner, both of *The Sunday Times* – to enter the world of the restaurant and to proclaim publicly and authoritatively on matters of taste. As our discussion above of the prehistory of food journalism suggests, the contemporary restaurant reviewer, like the gastronome, is invited to cultivate his readers' culinary taste. Hanke argues that restaurant reviews thus perform an important intermediary function, educating 'a body of informed eaters' who are trained to handle developments in the restaurant industry (Hanke, 1989: 229). For David Williamson *et al.*, restaurant reviews 'demonstrate an extreme level of exclusion' in undertaking this task, and tend to be concerned with questions about the quality of the food and drink and the ambience of a particular restaurant, rather than the more prosaic matters of service and cost (Williamson *et al.*, 2009: 55). Drawing on Bourdieu, Roy Wood concurs, arguing that a discourse of snobbery extends from the restaurant review to other forms of food commentary (Wood, 1996: 10). Just as the gastronome maintained a sense of metropolitan authority, contemporary UK restaurant reviews are largely London-centric, for all that they occasionally venture into the

provinces. Reflecting on a disappointing meal in a Nottingham restaurant, for example, the *Observer*'s restaurant critic, Jay Rayner, 'defended the occasional London
bias of [his …] column by arguing that, outside the capital, standards are patchy'
(Rayner, 2005). The restaurant review can therefore be seen as a space within which
the boundaries of metropolitan good taste are policed and conveyed to others.

The feature article about food has, according to Hanke, grown in popularity
since the 1970s, and now appears regularly in the lifestyle section, or weekend
magazine supplement, of national newspapers. According to Wood, food-related
feature articles range from 'articles on aspects of food supply (ingredients, usually
fairly exotic …); [to] features about cooks (usually male chefs operating in the
higher reaches of the market)' (Wood, 1996: 7). What Wood suggests, then, is that
feature articles contribute to the lifestyling of food, and look to pass on emergent
forms of taste, and knowledge about food, to the aspiring reader. The manner in
which they do this, however, is often rather complex. As we have seen, the risks surrounding contemporary food production and consumption are often the focus of
food feature-writing. But we have also seen that food is widely represented as a
source of pleasure. As a result, a tension between risk and pleasure often operates
across feature articles about food. In the *Observer*'s monthly food supplement
(*OFM*), for example, a regular feature sees the nutritionist Dr John Briffa scruti-
nising the contents of a celebrity's shopping basket. Thus, in May 2009, the actor
John Hurt's love of blackberries and green tea were praised by Briffa, but his
penchant for chocolate cake and vanilla ice-cream were questioned. 'The sugar
and refined flour in [the] cake will disrupt John's blood sugar and insulin levels,
which in turn can lead to weight gain, heart disease and diabetes' (Briffa, 2009).
Nevertheless, *OFM* is also regularly to be found extolling the pleasures of indul-
gent food. In the same edition, for example, there were articles on fried breakfasts,
celebration cakes and a cocktail bar. If consumer culture invites us to make lifestyle choices about the sort of foods we might want to prepare and eat, then food
journalism often addresses the risks and pleasures we need to negotiate along the way.

We have thus identified the contours of the current market for food journalism,
and outlined the principal forms which that journalism takes. In the next section,
we consider the impact of online formats on food journalism.

Challenges and changes

As we have established, food journalism emerged historically in the figure of the
gastronome. Its subsequent developments, through newspapers and magazines,
have deployed the same sense of authority which the gastronome possessed, to
convey the appropriate boundaries of culinary taste. However, this position of
authority is arguably threatened by the emergence of online forms of 'participatory
journalism' (Paulussen and Ugille, 2008), where ordinary readers are able to
submit their own recipes and restaurant reviews to websites. A website such as
TripAdvisor.co.uk, for example, markets itself as 'The world's largest travel
review site', and by late 2010 was claiming to carry '2 million ratings on more
than 670,000 restaurants in over 35,000 cities' across the world, all submitted by

regular restaurant-goers. The site trades on its wide coverage and on the honesty of its correspondents, who often eschew the sense of metropolitan confidence found in newspapers' restaurant reviews. Thus a visitor to a Russian restaurant in Bradford notes in their review that they 'were quite nervous and had no idea what to expect'. In addition to restaurant review websites, there are online recipe-sharing networks, such as MyDish, where users can upload their own recipes. Elsewhere, bloggers such as greedygourmet and gastrochick, comment on restaurants, recipes and other culinary matters. As Dan Gillmor suggests, the emergence of these forms of 'citizen journalism' threatens the power of 'Big Media' because 'technology has given us a communications toolkit that allows anyone to become a journalist at little cost and, in theory, with global reach' (Gillmor, 2004: xii). If the recipe columns and restaurants reviews of the past provided a vehicle for authorising certain forms of taste, then citizen journalism would seem to challenge that authority.

Doubtless, these participatory forms of food journalism will reconfigure the field in some ways. Nevertheless, there are a number of reasons why any changes will be slow. The first of these is that newspapers and food magazines increasingly incorporate these practices within their own publications. For example, the BBC's *Good Food* magazine has a food blog covering 'foodie news, gastronomic gossip and culinary titbits', while the *Guardian*'s Word of Mouth blog performs a similar function. As Neil Thurman notes, a number of online news organisations now allow users to submit reviews themselves. For example, ThisisLondon.co.uk, the London *Evening Standard*'s website, carries a number of 'reader reviews' which are 'spread across' topics such as 'books, computer games and restaurants' (Thurman, 2008: 141). Second, as online newspapers and magazines develop in this manner, and as blogs and food-oriented social networks increasingly acquire commercial support through advertising, so there is less distance between them. The images of different categories of food on the home page of mydish.co.uk, for example, share the same production values and a similar aesthetic to the images found in the majority of food magazines. Finally, we have shown that, food journalism today is inextricably linked both to broader forms of lifestyle journalism and to celebrity, and these are features which citizen journalism cannot replicate on its own. Food is envisaged as a pleasurable part of a range of lifestyle choices, and celebrity chefs extend their brands as a means to endorsing certain ways of cooking, just as newspapers and magazines trade on the cachet of having celebrity chefs as their columnists. In this context, the internal structure of food journalism appears to rest precisely upon a sense of authority; upon the ability of journalists or celebrity cooks to operate as cultural intermediaries, instructing their readers in novel ingredients, or rediscovering old ones; recommending new restaurants, or calling into question the reputation of long-running establishments. As Tania Lewis argues, these intermediaries acquire the status of popular experts, constructing 'food as a site of pleasure and "productive play"' (Lewis, 2008: 56) and distancing it from any idea of domestic drudgery. In short, she suggests, such 'expert advice also potentially offers "reassurance in a world of culinary confusion"' (Lewis, 2008: 64). While citizen journalism potentially turns everyone into a cookery columnist or a restaurant reviewer, the important relationship between food, celebrity and lifestyle media ensures that the forms of expertise upon which the authority of food journalism depends look set to endure. Despite the field of food journalism having undergone a number of reorientations, then, its central coordinates, as outlined here, and the position of the gastronome, will doubtless remain intact.

Case study: Nigel Slater

Nigel Slater (1958–) is a British newspaper and magazine journalist. His career touches on several themes raised in the chapter.

He trained at catering college, equipping him with 'an unsurpassable knowledge of French classical cookery [but no understanding] of how to roast a chicken … or make a decent green salad' (Slater, 2003: 222) and worked at various restaurants. These experiences pre-date the widespread practice of chefs rebranding themselves through the media: instead, his route into journalism came via work as a magazine recipe tester.

Slater was appointed *Marie Claire*'s food writer in 1988. By then, such publications were balancing traditional, domestic representations of femininity with new priorities: the need to have fun and the assumption that working women's lives were subject to time constraints. In this context, he presented himself as a domestic cook who was able to combine the care associated with the preparation of a meal from scratch with the convenience associated with busy lifestyles. An early newspaper column recounts that he had grown tired of prepared food: 'it takes a good half-hour to reheat a cook-chill dish of sole Veronique, and yet only six minutes to pan-fry a fillet of sole and a further two to pour a little wine and cream into its pan-juices' (Slater, 1992: 18).

Despite this commitment to 'real fast food', Slater's writing style invokes gastronomy's sensuous and scholarly disposition towards food. His columns conform rather to what Mennell calls the 'ill-defined margin' (Mennell, 1996: 271) where (masculine) gastronomy and (feminine) recipe writing meet, or what Slater himself describes as a format of 'yum yum yum and three recipes' (Adams, 2003: 18). This was confirmed when, in 1993, he took over from Jane Grigson as the *Observer*'s chief food writer.

Whereas the traditional gourmet drew authority from his familiarity with classical standards of good taste, Slater adopts a more 'omnivorous' style of cultural authority which freely mixes legitimate forms of cookery with more popular cuisine. Thus, a column on the pasty acknowledges both tradition and novelty while licensing experimentation: 'If your pasty has the word "Cornish" in front of it, then it comes with rules [otherwise] … the world is your oyster … cod and parsley sauce; mixed wild mushrooms; even blackberries and apples' (Slater, 2009).

Slater is a prominent advocate of seasonality, and this relates to the centrality of a discourse of risk to food writing. His local, seasonal food sourcing and use of produce from his own garden generate reassurance and pleasure. His work on *The Garden* magazine demonstrates the cultural intermediary's ability to write across different lifestyle fields.

Despite the challenge for online journalism, the field continues to cohere around the authority offered by the food journalist, and Nigel Slater is no exception. An archive of his *Observer* columns since 1999 is accessible via www.nigelslater.com.

Although he has worked as a TV chef, at least as important to his celebrity has been his ability to cross over from the culinary to the literary field. His bestselling childhood memoir *Toast* (2003) was adapted for film in 2010.

Bibliography

Adams, T. (2003) 'Nigel Slater: The Interview', *Observer*, 14 September, 18.

Bell, D. and Hollows, J. (eds) (2005) *Ordinary Lifestyles*, Aldershot: Ashgate.

——(2006) *Historicizing Lifestyles*, Aldershot: Ashgate.

Bell, D. and Valentine, G. (1997) *Consuming Geographies*, London: Routledge.

Benson, R. and Neveu, E. (eds) (2005) *Bourdieu and the Journalistic Field*, Cambridge: Polity.

Bourdieu, P. (1993) *The Field of Cultural Production*, Cambridge: Polity.

Briffa, J. (2009) 'What's in Your Basket?' *Observer Food Monthly*, 24 May, 30–31.

Brown, D. (2004) 'Haute Cuisine', *American Journalism Review*, 26, February/March, www.ajr.org/article_printable.asp?id=3545 (accessed 16 November 2010).

Fattorini, J. (1994) 'Food Journalism: A Medium for Conflict', *British Food Journal*, 96 (10), 24–28.

Ferguson, P. (2001) 'A Cultural Field in the Making', in L. Schehr and A. Weiss (eds) *French Food on the Table, on the Page and in French Culture*, London: Routledge.

Garval, M. (2001) 'Grimod de la Reynière's *Almanach des Gourmands*', in L. Schehr and A. Weiss (eds) *French Food on the Table, on the Page and in French Culture*, London: Routledge.

Gillmor, D. (2004) *We the Media: Grassroots Journalism, By the People for the People*, Sebastopol: O'Reilly Media.

Hanke, R. (1989) 'Mass Media and Lifestyle Differentiation', *Journal of Communication* 11, 221–38.

Hughes, K. (2010) 'Food Writing Moves from Kitchen to Bookshelf', *Guardian Review*, 19 June, 2–4.

Lewis, J. and Vidal, J. (2010) 'A Tale of Two Herds', *Guardian*, 13 November, 12–13.

Lewis, T. (2008) *Smart Living*, New York: Peter Lang.

Mennell, S. (1996) *All Manners of Food: Eating and Taste in England and France from the Middle Ages to the Present* (2nd edn), Chicago: University of Illinois Press.

Niblock, S. (2008) 'Features', in B. Franklin (ed.) *Pulling Newspapers Apart*, London: Routledge.

Parker, R. (2006) 'Newspaper Supplements', *Media Week*, 25 July, www.mediaweek.co.uk/news/571459/Newspaper-Supplements-Papers-mags-ad-share/ (accessed 16 November 2010).

Paulussen, S. and Ugille, P. (2008) 'User Generated Content in the Newsroom', Westminster papers in Communication and Culture, 5 (2), 24–31.

Rayner, J. (2005) 'Raw Deal', *Observer Magazine*, 28 August, 52.

Schehr, L. and Weiss, A. (eds) (2001) *French Food on the Table, on the Page and in French Culture*, London: Routledge.

Slater, N. (1992) 'Recipes for Instant Success', *Times*, 19 September.

——(2003) *Toast*, London: Fourth Estate.

——(2009) 'Nigel Slater's Modern Day Cornish Pasties', *Observer Magazine*, 27 September, 50.

Thurman, N. (2008) 'Forums for Citizen Journalists?', *New Media and Society*, 10 (1), 139–57.

Williamson, D., Tregidga, H., Harris, C. and Keen, C. (2009) 'The Working Engines of Distinction', *Journal of Hospitality and Tourism Management*, 16 (1), 55–61.

Wood, R. (1996) 'Talking to Themselves', *British Food Journal*, 98 (10), 3–10.

10 Music journalism

Paula Hearsum

Introduction

In July 2009, DrownedInSound.com, the online music magazine, posed the question, 'is music journalism dead?' (Adams, 2009). The article opened a discussion week on the topic, which raged around the impact of online music journalism, the closures of print magazines and depressed state of the industry as a whole. Echoing other concerns at the 'demise' of the profession, the debate pivots on a belief there has been a golden age of music journalism, which no longer exists.

That era in the UK was almost 40 years ago, when, at its peak in 1973, the iconic music weekly, *NME*, was selling 300,000 copies. The year 1973 represents a point in time when most currently employed music journalists, of which only a handful have had that as a full-time title of permanent employment, were either too young to read or not even born and online journalism was a mere twinkle in computer programmers' eyes. As DiS wrote the equivalent of an obituary for the profession, those very same rose-coloured spectacles were also being worn by popular music academics who were concomitantly answering a call for papers from *Popular Music and Society* to examine the shifting sands of the profession. Inglis (2010a) suggests the overwhelming response he received as journal editor, was both broad and engaging. It is a testament to continual interest in the combination of the subject with the professional form, and represents a particularly pertinent moment to pause for reflection:

> … as new forms of journalism emerge, as new musical genres combine and re-combine, as audiences become more skilful, as other sources of information become commonplace, and as access to music itself is transformed, the nature of the relationship between popular music and journalism stands at a critical point.
>
> (Inglis, 2010a: 241)

However, despite facing similar current economic pressures the two professions appear historically to have had a long tradition of either holding each other in contempt, or at least regarding one another with suspicion. Yet they have much to offer us in understanding as they both verbalise the same subject matter, popular music, albeit with different sensibilities.

By looking at the relationship between experience, engagement and meaning this work forms part of a body of thought that began life as a paper delivered at IASPM (Cardiff, September 2010). This chapter considers the critical reflections of those on seemingly opposing sides. It does so from within an understanding of the body of work that has been undertaken in the field and hopes to explicate some fruitful contributions to both professions. It utilises both journalistic and academic voices of those involved in the professions, including personal interviews and discussion that took place over the course of this research. It will examine both disconnects and connectivities in order to suggest that putting down the boxing gloves might offer more than continuing with the fight.

With 320,000 unique monthly visitors, the US-based (and globally produced) Drownedinsound.com seemed well-placed to discuss dwindling sales of other print competitors. In the UK, nme.com now drives forward the NME brand (Wiseman, 2009) with 5,342,246 unique users (June 2010) at a time when its print circulation took a 17 per cent tumble to 33,875 copies a week. This new generation of online music journalists suggest their inspiration came from their print predecessors rather than any formal music education:

> For me, reading about music was not just what ignited my passion for music but what doused it in kerosene. It wasn't just reading what these fit-to-burst enthusiasts had to say about releases which informed both my knowledge and taste but it was their ability to articulate it. For a few hours each week I was captivated by their combination of words which would never be found in any of the books on the school reading list.
>
> (Adams, 2009)

A far cry from what must be the two most keenly quoted (mis)understandings of music journalism:

> Rock journalism is people who can't write interviewing people who can't talk for people who can't read.
>
> (Zappa, 1980: 74)

> Writing about music is like dancing about architecture.
>
> (attributed to multiple authors)

Educational bodies have grappled inconsistently with the inclusion of popular music within the UK school curriculum. At its best it has been marginalised institutionally through governing structures of the education system. The future of music within formal education is under review by the Henley committee and music educators fear severe cuts to the current £82.5 million Music Standards Grant (Richardson, 2010). In higher education the state of affairs for popular music study appears stronger. Its once conspicuous absence is now addressed. Take a look through undergraduate options through UCAS, type in 'popular music' and 149 courses pop up, for Journalism 668 and 15 degrees on 'music journalism' itself, and this doesn't include the myriad opportunities to study the areas in, say, Media Studies, Communication or Cultural Studies degrees where popular music forms elective options within a wider degree (UCAS, 2010). While academic journal publishers (including those who publish journalism and popular music journals) have comfortably accepted that the vast majority of their readership will be online, some publishers of music magazines have been reluctant to seek new distribution methods. So it does appears to be apposite to explore the balance and tensions between music journalism experience and theory. The crisis facing the journalistic profession has been acutely felt in specialist arts areas and music journalism is no exception. Like their academic counterparts, on a basic level, both offer a way to understand the meaning(s) music can create using words as their currency. They are both relatively small professions, which organise individually (freelancer/visiting lecturer), locally (music staff writer/popular music academic within a department) and globally (IASPM – 700 members, formed 1981 and the International Federation of Music Journalists with 2800 members in 85 countries).

Having spent ten years as a music journalist practitioner and 20 as a music and journalist academic, I continue to enjoy this balancing act. Daily work in the lecture room involves the continual engagement of my popular music and journalism students. Facilitating their meaningful exploration of the two areas. As a writer *and* reader I am intrigued to understand how my journalistic craft can continue to have relevancy and support its future existence in a format which both respects the musician, author and reader in terms of meaning making and quality. While personal experience sees no disconnect between writing about popular music and teaching about it, one individual chequered CV is not sufficient for analysis alone, and supplementary support and critical ears were drawn upon from others who have been on both sides of what I suggest is an artificial divide.

This chapter suggests that reading about music will increasingly rely on an understanding of and within, what Anderson (1991) called an 'imagined community' for its continued existence. The imperative is for us to collaborate and understand how this musical reading community has shifted so we can be in a better place to secure its future. For music journalism to continue to be meaningful the requirement to be fulfilled is to create a shared musical discourse with a purpose. In order to re-evaluate the original principles of music journalism we need to understand the three aspects of its communicative functions listed below.

1 How we *experience* music journalism through its various platforms and discourses.
2 How we *engage* with the content through the connection between the words and the music itself, both individually and collectively.
3 And finally how together this creates particular *meaning(s)*.

Let us accept that there is a current erosion of the cultural gatekeeping role of a music journalist. The next step is to elucidate the profession's key drivers and its reception to better offer a way of extracting what is critical about the functionality of that role, what useful purpose it serves and what level of quality (in writing and content itself) we desire to be retained. Undertaking the re-evaluation and celebration of those three purposes is one contributory step towards music journalism's survival.

Experience, engagement and meaning – all three words are significant motivators and have an elemental personal resonance both in my previous incarnation as a music journalist as well as in my current role as an academic. The practitioner/theorist divide is one I find artificial. Having enjoyed, and survived, a decade as a full-time music journalist in the 1990s at *Vox* (a now defunct monthly music and film magazine, and sister title to *NME*) I recollect it as a great time to be in that part of the industry because the *experience* itself was utterly immersive and fulfilling.

It never was, and probably never will be, a financially lucrative profession. At a recent reunion it was horrifying to note that despite pressure from the NUJ, music writing word rates have barely changed in 20 years. Something the *Guardian*, which hosted a forum on music journalism, concurred with:

> In my view, the days of making a living from pure music journalism are behind us all.
>
> (Britten, 2010)

Let's face it, this is a pretty wonderful way to make a living. How extraordinary to be paid to listen to, discuss and write about music. During my interview for *Vox*, a row erupted with the managing editor, Alan Lewis, about the value of studying popular music academically. 'You don't want to be reading all that stuff by that Simon Frith' was one comment thrown my way. At the time of my undergraduate study in the late 1980s, the newly emerging field of popular music theory, headed by the likes of Simon Frith and Dave Laing, were every bit as inspiring as the weekly musings to be found in *Sounds*, *NME* and *Melody Maker*. However, the 'academic critic' was a teasing point throughout my stint in the music press but to Lewis's credit he always gave me the space to nurture this 'dark side'; this other way of enjoying music … and I spent the decade also lecturing on the subject around various higher education establishments around the country.

On reflection, music journalism aimed at the student market (i.e. the *NME*, *Kerrang!* bracket as opposed to *Q* and *Mojo*) is a job for a particular period in a lifetime. Nearing my 30s I experienced disengagement from the surrounding lifestyle rather than from the subject itself. I listen to, and read about, music as much now as I did then, but I don't particularly want to see bands every night. Quite frankly the shift from two key festivals a year to tenting it every weekend during the summer, was a wet soggy sleeping bag and exposure to trench foot step too far. A space, which I felt I once inhabited as a native, now became an external viewing position; I was on the outside looking in. If music journalism was seen by some as a place for 'failed musicians' (or 'failed groupies' – True, 2008: 37) then music academia was the ghetto of 'failed music journalists'. Obviously, not my view.

Chewing the academic cud is a strangely familiar terrain. It continues to concern engaging an audience in a meaningful exploration of popular music and words. Not such an imaginative leap of faith from one profession to another and enjoyably it regularly leads to questioning the currency of the use of words to make sense of music. Each cohort offers a sharp reminder to seek its relevance to new generations. Probing this from both sides forces us to see what the two professions offer.

So this chapter comes to you with a purpose. To make journalistic *experience* a *meaningful* and useful present-day academic tool for the analysis and understanding of popular music. The student body come to study popular music already armed. They bring their own set of musical knowledges and experiences. Not just as absorbers and listeners (as perhaps those who study film are also cinema goers, but many as 'makers' of music, festival attendees and creators of Spotify playlists; the new personalised DJs). To echo Raymond Williams (1921–1988, a well-known figure within cultural studies), musical culture might well be ordinary but its beauty lies in its EXTRA-ordinary nature, which gives conceptualisations around it an extraordinary 'structure of feeling'. As the next generation move us forward, we need to learn from, and connect with, the ways in which they consume their musical knowledge. Musical experiences we can share across generations and professions as we peer into each other's musical spaces. Last semester, a student rushed up to me before a session to say she'd been listening to an online personalised radio station. She'd been recommended a Joni Mitchell track because she liked Regina Spektor. This generation who listen to music musically multitask. They can listen, read archived interviews and purchase albums like *Blue* simultaneously. She had been blown away. Older and younger generations, sharing that experience of listening to *Blue* for the first time. A communal musical moment across time and space. Amazing: eyes, ears and brain now have the musical world and its archive at its fingertips.

Reading music and reading about music now rely on this 'imagined community'. The possibilities of mining such information occur in an a-synchronous universe. Using archived journalism for older releases alongside more current non-peer reviewed online opinions; complexly interwoven. Which brings up two, familiar questions. First, do the 'Google generation' have hierarchy of believability and trust in the music journalism they consume and, second, are those mechanisms imbued within the production of those words? It is that process which needs unpacking, requiring a critical analysis beyond the scope of this chapter; but the first question returns us to the role of a music journalist as a trusted cultural guide or gatekeeper who plays a part in the way we attain musical knowledge or cultural capital. What has shifted is that it is not just about 'the kids', this same world is inhabited by professional journalists *and* older listeners who share and co-create.

The place for strong writing has not gone but must now fight for its future among the hubbub and information overload. Writing about popular music and teaching about it *both* require an understanding of the contextual landscape. Marc Brennan, whose PhD and consequent book (2008) compared UK and Australian popular music writing, suggests the warmth of music journalism is something academics could learn from:

> It seems that a lot of academic writing tries to evacuate emotion especially … for me it is usually an emotive tie that gets me wanting to write about something anyway. Contextualisation to me is the most important aspect of both. It

helps address the 'so what' factor both in reading academic work and music journalism. ... And (this might be offensive, sorry) but a lot of academic writing about music leaves me feeling cold inside. It often has this 'outside observer' feeling ... But really – isn't the purpose about leisure and pleasure? Give me a beer and the latest copy of *Q* over Foucault any day.

(Brennan, 2010)

Barney Hoskyns wrote in *NME* in 1984, and you'll get the dated reference in a moment, that music journalism has a very particular role:

I think we are simply in the business of discussing what we take to be a sub-culture, constructed partly by – and partly for – young people of different sexes, classes, races ... Nothing in this life is any more 'important' than Paul Young, for the 'Philosophical Investigations' do not change the basic facts of life any more than 'No Parlez' does.

Hoskyns goes on to say that what is important about our culture is not the music in itself but how we use it to relate to others, how we communicate through it or interpret it. He beautifully described music journalism as a METAMUSIC; a music about music. A point similarly made by music critic, Everett True, who suggested that at its best, it is 'an art to rank alongside the medium it evaluates ... to enhance the experience of listening to music in every respect' (True, 2008: 38). Hoskyns produced a structure for such 'metamusic', which should cover these four things, which works well for review writing in particular:

- distinguish musical form
- give explanation of production style
- explore emotion
- contextualise.

Lucy O'Brien, who has written across many music titles and also now lectures in the area, agreed that it was a 'very useful formula'. In considering what she draws on from her professional practice into her teaching she noted the power of contextualisation in generating meaning for her students:

Journalism has given me a strong, working knowledge of bands and artists across a range of genres, plus 'insider' knowledge about the ... industry. I understand implicitly how music is mediated and marketed ... not just so I can give students entertaining anecdotes, but also ... ground their work with a practical approach.

(O'Brien, 2010)

Laing (2010), while noting its prescriptively, suggests that academic analysis puts more emphasis on contextualisation:

... to analyse the aesthetic, social and cultural forces that have produced the music under discussion.

(Laing, 2010)

However, what Hoskyns does do in line with academic research is:

> ... stand outside the process of journalism and theorise his practice, which is the kind of activity that academic work is supposed to include. In sociological terms his research methodology is 'participant observation'.
>
> (Laing, 2010)

Seeing journalism as a metamusic, where the combination of words, create an artistic form in their own right, was an analogy much echoed by those interviewed. Simon Reynolds, himself much taken by Hoskyns's piece, was equally influenced by the ideas of Simon Frith and Dick Hebdige as by American music writers (Lester Bangs and Griel Marcus). In describing rock criticism's 'performative aspect' embedded in the work rather than within the person he suggested another dimension to be added into the formula:

> The writer, who most likely in person is not terribly impressive or commanding a figure, manages to create a kind of charismatic effect through language and through the creation of a persona, a sort of super-self [like] fronting a rock band, or ... being a rapper. There's a whole range of personae – fabulously hip and in the know and 'down with the scene', or an authority in terms of knowledge, or a prophet with a messianic line of patter, or the gonzo persona who's a little out of control and brutally honest (Lester Bangs to Everett True), or wry, ironic ...
>
> It's about rhetoric and the art of 'suasion. There's skill and tricks but there is also, as with a rapper, just confidence, the arrogance to make a categorical statement about an artist or genre's worth. To be a judge. The first person I got this buzz off was Julie Burchill in NME, the absolute certainty with which she decreed things, and the vehemence and viciousness, and also the way you were hypnotized by the cadence of the prose into believing she was right, at least for the duration of reading the piece. Years and years later, when I started to think critically about music journalism itself, I realized that a lot of this 'truth' effect was achieved simply through her use of alliteration and other word tricks. It was the music of her writing as much as its meaning.
>
> (Reynolds, 2010)

The impact of personality journalism in this field was raised recently after the death of a fabulously talented and much missed colleague, Steven Wells (better known as Swells), in 2009. Swells belonged to another 'golden era' of music criticism in the UK of the 80s and 90s. His acerbic commentary built on the 70s and early 80s 'serious' music journalism legacy. Both Brennan (2008) and Forde (2001) discuss the particular shift away from personality journalism with the charisma Reynolds noted, to a more brand focused singular voice, which occurred in the 00s. Swells' death opened a wave media commentary lamenting the demise of the profession. One written by former rival *Melody Maker* writer, Everett True, suggested the focus should be to: 'Engage, argue, inform, irritate ... but above all entertain' and not to be 'impartial' or 'objective' but to be a 'tastemaker' after all. He suggested:

> Believe in us, and we have the power to change worlds. Stop believing in us and we cease to exist. Do the public really require – or even want – a faceless 'meta' critic, the lowest common denominator of countless opinions, where all opinion is reduced to a mean average mark? Isn't that taking all the fun away?
>
> (True, 2009)

The article formed part of the DrownedInSound.com discussion. Articles anchored around one particularly heated debate inspired by a talk by freelance music journalist, Christopher R. Weingarten, at the '140 Characters conference'. Weingarten discussed Twitter culture's impact on music journalism suggesting we were currently in the third phase of 'music journalism 2.0'. The first had been in 1999 with online DIY culture (such as *Pitchfork*), which opened up the listening mindsets of consumers. By 2004 blog culture emerged and encouraged magazines to merely report on trends in blogs. Finally, phase three, he suggests, is where music promos turn up online without the 'gatekeeper' or what Weingarten calls a 'filter' which has stratified listening habits where the new 'link economy' has closed us down when we should open our ears because it celebrates musical commonality not difference. Taking up the challenge he posits current music twitterings can be 'poetic and informative' but only if we go beyond the 'who' of the music questions and into the 'because' and 'why'. Coming full circle to Hoskyns' last two points.

The purpose of music journalism has also had a long history connected to what appear on the surface to be the antithesis of one another; consumerism and alternativism, but actually have an interesting symbiosis. Atton (2009) suggested that rock journalism offered an alternative to conventional discourses and using Bourdieu's work on cultural producers and their activities, he critically compared reviews between fanzines and 'ideological' magazines. Within the small field of academic writing in this arena, there are many references to the trust held in terms of an authenticity being an imperative to the success of a music writing – we need to believe in the writer to follow their thoughts, a point that academia, with its peer-reviewed, cited, referenced and 'stamp of authority' also uses to give worth to writing.

> The purpose of music journalism is to let you know what music is out there and what is good/worth getting excited about. It's also a valuable alternative culture. Right from the '60s with its roots in the counterculture press, music journalism has long been the 'rebel' in the journalistic world, offering an alternative viewpoint on mainstream consumerism. Good music writing is about seeing beyond record company hype.
>
> (O'Brien, 2010)

Reynolds ponders a disappearance of this value:

> I think this is where music criticism comes closest to matching the music itself. I read pieces growing up that would actually make me tremble with excitement. Or cheer at the end. Things that I read over and over again, cut out and kept, and know by heart ... Very much in the way that people in the 18th or 19th Century could recite long stretches of poetry. The greatest of these pieces have had an effect very nearly as powerful as listening to the music they're about. I don't come across music writing like that much anymore, that has that effect on me – and this may partly be a result of not being as impressionable as I was as a teenager and a student ... But mainly I think it's because people aren't writing this kind of stuff anymore ... Perhaps music culture simply can't sustain that particular kind or degree of seriousness, the sense that music is central in the culture and that it has this transformative or catalyzing power.
>
> (Reynolds, 2010)

So the question is to ascertain whether the qualities of writing about music (academically and culturally) have overlaps. Inglis (2010b) suggests academic writing has 'originality, insight, knowledge, research' and journalism's unique quality is to be 'concise and give an understanding ... provide information ... add enjoyment'.

Frith (2010) feels they have similarities and strong writing of both fields is that in which he 'learns something or which makes me think' and he reopens a common terrain of definition variance:

> ... there was always a distinction between music (rock) critics and music journalists, one group's critically reviewing records/gigs, the other reporting music news (or recycling press releases) and even now in broadsheets tends to be a distinction between the critics' page and the puff page ... just as one can in film coverage in which the same distinctions apply. I would guess the situation now is that most people read the music critics in whatever newspapers/ magazines they read ... a smaller number read critics in specialist music mags (whether *NME*, *Kerrang!*, *Gramophone*, *Roots* or one of the jazz mags), and a larger number use the web rather loosely to check out reviews of a record or act by Googling and trawling a variety of possible sites (including Amazon). So there are more critics out there than ever but not many with much power to influence a significant audience.
>
> (Frith, 2010)

Instead of moaning that music journalism as a profession will hit a financial end – a new generation writing/blogging for nothing ... like Weingarten (2009) has done with his 140 character Twitter reviews – we could rise up to see it as a rich opportunity to meet those challenges. Music journalism has needed a reality check for some time. The stiff competition is not for column inches and by-lines but for commodities based on time, in terms of attention, as well as money. The key demographic has little of either. Most of our students hold down more or less full-time jobs to keep their degree afloat. Cash and time poor – the ethics of buying either music or words about it, have altered. However, they do desire a broader exposure too as they are less concerned with trends. Unlike Weingarten though, I suggest they happily absorb knowledge, their cultural capital, via any source. What was a monogamous bond, the mediation of music through the traditional inkies has become an open relationship, and writers and their publishers have either had to willingly embrace this polygamy or fold.

> I'm not sure the music press (or at least the weekly music press of previous decades) will survive. Glossy/nostalgia-laden publications like *Mojo* and *Q* will continue to appeal to an older audience. And specialist publications like *Kerrang!* will continue to secure a loyal audience. But for young audiences, I'm not sure the concept of a regular music press is something they're familiar with.
>
> (Inglis, 2010b)

NME's once magazine-closeable ABC figures continues to exist because it is now a brand first and a music paper second and forms part of a portfolio (online, radio, TV and marketed events). It's also much more comforting to announce you 'reach 1 million music fans every week' than refer to the 20 per cent printed circulation drop. Music journalism 2.0 changed the rules for its creators. Just as Web 2.0 changed the way we locate and absorb music itself and how we *experience* it.

The discourse that holds the discussion of that experience has more possibilities. We are currently in a world which allows us to read anything from a one-word response to a piece of music from an unknown posting on YouTube to a feature piece in a printed form written by a 'professional'. We can have all options simultaneously. But is there something fundamentally unique about the skill requirements of a music journalist? Inglis suggests not:

> … being a music journalist is not fundamentally different from any other branch of journalism.
>
> (Inglis, 2010b)

The process by which those words (music press or blogs) are put together is worth deconstructing. Just because one goes through a commissioning and editing process through a series of, for want of a better phrase, peer-review suggestions, and another goes out individually at the push of a button; what makes one command more attention than another? What purposes do they respectively serve? What reach and potential do they have? Arguably they all fuel consumption of 'extra musical information' and enhance the listening experience, and that purpose is always driven by the same things: it heightens our *engagement* with the *experience* of music itself. It helps us make *meaning* out of it. It was the reason I went into music journalism in the first place. It's something that is at the heart of both my research and my teaching. If we don't connect music with the three words of this chapter: *engagement*, *experience* and *meaning* … then what's the point?

However, (inverted) snobbery can be at play from the two corners of the ring Frith suggests:

> Being an academic still gets knee jerk negativity from practicing music journalists.
>
> (Frith, 2010)

Perhaps an echo to previous discussions on his two careers:

> I may have spent the last twenty years writing pop and rock criticism, judging records for a living, but I have tended to keep such arguments, (plunging assertively into fan talk at the bar and in the record store) out of my academic work. I am well aware ... why value questions are difficult to raise in the cultural studies classroom, journal and textbook.
>
> (Frith, 1996: 8)

Martin James, a seasoned music journalist who moved across from music performer to music journalist and then into academia, also noted the variance in the two fields during writing his current research which is aimed at two diverse audiences as theoretically diverse as music academics and yet accessible; where terminologies are translated but yet still be accepted in the academy. Now as the course leader for BA in Popular Music Journalism at Southampton Solent University, he draws on journalism for:

> ... context. The dense theory brings to live and useful for social aspects and to evidence inconsistencies and myths, historiographics and show e.g for Punk the press (*Sounds*, *Melody Maker* and *NME*) had different takes but now there are singular voices and yet it is many voices that make musical history.
>
> (James, 2010)

A view shared by Hoskyns, whose immense popular music journalism archive project, Rocksbackpages (RBP) encapsulates the polysemic voices. RBP describes itself as the 'ultimate archive of music journalism' with over 13,000 articles (RBP, 2010). In order to differentiate itself from what Hoskyns called the 'Wiki-sised' history of music journalism, the archive offers a 'more rounded and multi-dimensional' array of writing so future generations of music journalism readers can delve deeper and that multiple-voices and views are read in parallel. For him, the two professions are 'closer than they once were' (Hoskyns, 2010) and RBP has bought the academic arena into a commercial sensibility:

> Academics have come out of their ivory towers and an increasing number of students are studying culture. The time (Frith's) *Sociology of Rock* was a pinnacle moment was a moment where an intelligent discussion of popular culture was allowed.
>
> (Hoskyns, 2010)

During Hoskyns' *NME* time (early 1980s) he saw a marked opening of possibilities to write in a 'psuedo-intellectual' way but also that it could be a turn-off as much as a turn on. He stands by the point that music journalism should deepen an appreciation and experience of a song/music and it can be informed by the musicological. He wrote 'subbed culture' when *Smash Hits* was at its peak and everything had come full circle to pre-gonzo journalism. The most typical question asked of a band was 'what is your favourite colour':

> We were at a crossroads where pop music was becoming commodified to celebrate it in a non-commercial way. Let's accept that in the current *X-Factor* culture, teenagers just want to consume pretty faces and disposable grooves, why should educated farts make them stop and think. We are all trapped in this web of commodifcation and it's hard to get excited when all the festivals are beamed into your living room.
>
> (Hoskyns, 2010)

Hoskyns mused on a nostalgic return for his youth where finding new music required a graft by the listener. The new process of music retrieval/access, whereby a reader/listener can instantly find writing and music has typified the crisis in the industry as a whole. This 'graft', he suggests, offers a way of going against the grain of everyday cultural experience, and he asks of this new retrieval:

> What is the pay off, the cathartic experience when there is an instant download? Where is the sense of the forbidden? Pop stars were the pied pipers leading us from innocence to experience and the MP3 is a soulless bit of information like gum drops where all the flavour disappears.
>
> (Hoskyns, 2010)

Integrating theory and practice straddles the academic/practitioner divide. In practice-based lectures, we can focus work on readership and utilise research to better understand the reader. Perhaps what publishers can learn is the con-textualisation that ABC/ABCe/NRS figures lack. A critical analysis of language using a variety of discourse theory methodologies can bring statistics to life. James (2010) cites the utilisation of Talbot's 'synthetic sisterhood' (1995) to better understand the shifting dynamics of reader identity. An elusive concept to both online and offline producers who have the bare minimum of data with circulation figures and litmus test focus groups. Like Anderson's notion of the 'imagined community', what the academic profession can offer the practitioner world, Talbot suggests, is that a discourse is used to construct the readership. It is one in which the reader becomes actively involved. Holding tightly onto an imagined notion of control, however, is not the way forward. James suggests that the space held by Reynolds, who wrote utilising the likes of Baudrillard ('whilst everyone else was reading a copy of the Melody Maker and all trying to outsmart each other') has gone:

> There was a time when the challenge was for a journalist to see how many theoretical terms they could get through the subs … in the early 90s the key buzzword was 'jouissance' and the real trick was to use it in the correct way.
>
> (James, 2010)

When trying to unpack his own style, with eloquent self-reflection, Reynolds intimates that the relationship between academic understanding of music and writing about it within the guise of a music journalist, is more complex – that while Deleuze and Guattari can be much better understood through the music of Can or early 90s jungle:

> ... it's more like I'm selling the reader on theory and philosophy, than elevating and dignifying and legitimizing the music. If you apply Marxism to hip hop, it's not that hip hop suddenly seems more weighty and interesting, it's that Marxism seems to have more purchase on reality, because hip hop provides evidence to substantiate it. You can see the effects of money and reification and commodity fetishism on human relations. But all this is written large and clear in hip hop already, the Marxist gloss in a way is superfluous. So why bring it into play, then? The compulsion to connect theory and music just comes from indulging my own interests, amusing myself to an extent. But also I do it when I think it's 'true' – when a theoretical concept just seems to fit what's going on in the music or the subculture.
>
> (Reynolds, 2010)

O'Brien noted that while there was a particular shift in acceptability of that crossover in the weeklies during the 1990s it is the reach of the audience itself which shapes the content:

> In the 70s and 80s the weekly music press (particularly *NME* and *Melody Maker*) quite happily featured academic or intellectual writing – but by the early 90s there was a move to simplify the music press, bringing it in line with the rest of the consumer press. Since then writers have been encouraged to keep the theory to a minimum and 'just talk about music'. I write for *Mojo*, a music monthly that probably has a high number of graduates in its demographic ... and there is room for a few sophisticated ideas. However, it is still a consumer magazine, so we have to keep the tone 'accessible' and anecdotal.
>
> (O'Brien, 2010)

As suggested earlier, the most precious commodity of any author (whether that be a lecturer in a classroom talking about popular music or a music journalist writing about popular music) is their time; representing a commitment of a portion of the lifespan of reader or student. So the need for a 'trusted guide' in that relationship between wordsmith and music fan remains. The general consensus from the interviews compiled for this work agreed that music writing was becoming generalised at a point when time constraints and online reading requires brevity or sensationalism:

> Coming up with a contrived, inflammatory or polarizing angle, in order to increase your clicks through tweeter-isation.
>
> (Reynolds, 2010)

But is it what we want? Journalists and music academics alike all suggested that the traditional skills of prose, which offers agency, invokes passion and has clarity of musical explanation would continue to have value.

> What I find disconcerting is how many young writers are very reasonable and sane in their approach, and overly fair-minded. It's not what I want to read, at all. I'd much rather read a very fierce denunciation of something, even if it was attacking something musically dear to my heart.
>
> (Reynolds, 2010)

The way we can restore meaning to music is appreciating analysing music, in either profession potentially offers in terms of payoffs:

> Whilst there is no obligation to intellectualise, there is enormous reward in stopping to reflect on music's social function. That is its healing property and it makes it easier to bear the agony of existence ... The use value of both music journalism and academic analysis of popular music must go beyond the good/bad paradigm.
>
> (Hoskyns, 2010)

Reynolds goes further to consider that what the right application can extend is a 'buzz' for the mind, which gives an understanding of the meaning of music a clarity and the structures at play in socio-culture are made visible to which O'Brien advocates that:

> Generally, it's important to keep standards of rock writing high – and you can only do that with good, in-depth research and perceptive writing. Academia enhances those skills. I think there is a natural link between music journalism and academia – the both involve thinking and writing.
>
> (O'Brien, 2010)

Finally the analogy of the 'gatekeeper' that Frith (1978) first called music journalists; our 'ideological gatekeepers' or 'privileged type of fan' (Laing, 2010), has a comparative with music theorists – both are in the business of writing and retelling our musical history, shaping our past which has an impact on our present and future. Just as Forde (2003) mapped the impact of turbulent economics within the publishing industry on the sector itself, so the academic body, faced with repercussions of the Browne Review (2010), must readdress and support arts and humanities in general and popular music and journalism studies itself. Laing (2010) has observed the rise of popular music courses in contrast to the declining numbers for old style music courses – the latter of which now incorporate popular music as a lure for applicants.

Without investment in either the future looks uncertain. Atton (2010) proposes that we need to turn the model on its head to examine it again; where once those who 'write about music' were the 'tastemakers' who informed audiences, now it is the audience themselves who are informing the writers. Not so much *user-generated content* but *user-pitched content*. The bloggers and online contributions are taken more notice of than the streams of written mail sent physically to the music press. Atton suggests that actually the voice of the amateur, which to all intense and purpose, most music writers at least start off being, (traditional route into music writing from fanzine/student magazine into the more widely distributed press remains a strong path in) is no different but that process itself has intensified and is now 'hyperspecialization', where the amateur becomes the expert.

> Microgenres are only comprehensible to those in that culture. ... where in the 1980s *Melody Maker*, *NME* and *Sounds* was all there was. Now the field is becoming more specialised commercially and socially. Where the 1980s saw a bust of highly experimental writing with writers such as Ian Penman and Paul Morely drawing on post-structuralism currently most fans are engaging IN popular culture.
>
> (Atton, 2010)

It is also an era where the web creates the space for 'fans to speak out too' (Laing, 2010). Interviews for this research certainly demonstrated an internal hierarchy of use of academia in popular culture and Atton's point is echoed by Reynolds' suggestion that the two writers were the 'pale theory boys' (Reynolds, 2009). It has been intriguing to note the moves by some music journalists into the academic arena, with few going the other way. Forde (2010) is an example of the latter, and he reflects that music journalism is 'a young person's game' and that the churn is a positive one as the music generational baton is naturally handed on. As the printed format struggles to translate, the traditional 'inkie' demographic moves to find intelligent music journalism very much alive and kicking in the online world through the likes of The Quietus (http://thequietus.com/), Drownedinsound (http://drownedinsound.com/) and Pitchfork (http://pitchfork.com/). In addition to that layer, in watching the shift into digital formats with interest, Forde suggests that there is another way in which the traditional gatekeeper is being eroded and that is through 'crowd sourced' music writing such as the music blog aggregators The Hype Machine (http://hypem.com/) and Elbo.ws (http://elbo.ws/) which offer new ways of filtering of music discussion through popularity.

However, in his introduction to his edited collection, Frith (2007) compellingly reminds himself, and us, that our musical repository of exchange very much comes from a history of overlap between the professions:

> Rock was first theorised by practitioners rather than academics, by journalists, musicians and audiences, by record companies and their PR departments, by radio producers and deejays. The key to an understanding of popular music, I had come to realise, not high but low theory. The importance of such writers as Dave Laing and Charlie Gillett in Britain, Greil Marcus and Robert Christgau in the USA, lay less in their books (which are, in fact, of the highest academic standard) than in their weekly journalism, their everyday

engagement with music and musical institutions as critics and reporters. They were the models for my own attempt to combine the academic study of popular music with rock journalism.

(Frith, 2007: xi)

Music journalists and academics of popular music both take on the 'cultural intermediary' role to an extent – whether that be the music 'critic', the 'music journalist', the 'music writer' (Forde, 2010) and the more encompassing title of those who 'write about music' (Atton, 2010) it can operate as the space in which both corners of the boxing ring meet. It is also where they will thrive and flourish because the desire to continue to do something as wonderful as telling someone how music makes you feel sees no signs of diminishing.

References

Adams, S. 2009. 'Music journalism RIP: An introduction' on: Drownedinsound (http://drownedinsound.com/in_depth/4137359-music-journalism-r-i-p-an-introduction).

Anderson, B. 1991. *Imagined Communities: Reflections on the Origin and Spread of Nationalism.* London: Verso.

Atton, C. 2009. 'Writing about listening: Alternative discourses in rock journalism', in *Popular Music*, Vol. 28 No. 1, 53–67.

——2010 (*personal interview*).

Botts, L. 1983. *The Rolling Stone Interviews: Talking with the Legends of Rock & Roll 1967–1980.* London: Omnibus.

Brennan, M. 2008. *Writing to Reach You: An Exploration of Music Journalism in the UK and Australia.* VDM Verlag Dr. Muller Aktiengesellschaft & Co. KG.

——2010. (*personal interview*).

Britten, A. 2010. 'Breaking into music journalism' on: Guardian.co.uk forum: http://bit.ly/9C5vml (accessed 14 November 2010).

Browne, J. 2010. 'Securing a sustainable future for higher education: An independent review of higher education funding and student finance'. 12 October 2010. Available: http://webarchive.nationalarchives.gov.uk/+/hereview.independent.gov.uk/hereview//report/

Forde, E. 2001. 'From polyglottism to branding: On the decline of personality journalism in the British music press', in *Journalism: Theory, Practice, Criticism*, Vol. 2, 37–56.

——2003. 'Journalists with a difference: Producing music journalism', in Cottle, S. (ed.) 2003. *Media Organization and Production.* London: Sage.

——2010. (*personal interview*).

Frith, S. 1978. 'The music press', in *Sound Effects: Youth, Leisure and the Politics of Rock 'n' Roll.* London: Constable.

——1996. *Performing Rites: Evaluating Popular Music.* Oxford: Oxford University Press.

——2007. *Taking Popular Music Seriously: Selected Essays.* Simon Frith, University of Edinburgh, UK. Series: Ashgate Contemporary Thinkers on Critical Musicology Series.

——2010. (*personal interview*).

Hoskyns, B. 1984. 'Subbed culture', in *NME*. October.

——2010. (*personal interview*).

Inglis, I. 2010a. 'Introduction', in *Popular Music and Society* Vol. 33 No. 4, October 2010, 431.

——2010b. (*personal interview*).

James, M. 2010. (*personal interview*).

Laing, D. 2006. 'Anglo-American music journalism: Texts and contexts', in Bennett, A., Shank, B. and Toynbe, J. (eds) *The Popular Music Studies Reader*. London: Routledge, 333–39.

——n.d. (*personal interview*).

O'Brien, L. 2010. (*personal interview*).

Popular Music & Society. 2010. Vol. 22 No. 3, October 2010.

Reynolds, S. n.d. (*personal interview*).

——2009. 'Music and theory'. Available: www.frieze.com/comment/article/music_theory/ (accessed 15 November 2010).

Richardson, H. 2010. 'Fears for future of school music lessons', BBC Online 19 November. Available: www.bbc.co.uk/news/education-11796636 (accessed 22 November 2010).

Talbot, M. 1995. 'A synthetic sisterhood: False friends in a teenage magazine', in Hall, K. and Bucholtz, M. (eds) *Gender Articulated: Language and the Socially Constructed Self*. London: Routledge, 143–65.

Toynbee, J. 1993. 'Policing Bohemia, pinning up grunge: The music press and generic change in British pop and rock'. *Popular Music*, Vol. 12 No. 3.

True, E. 2008. 'Is there anything left to say about music?', in *Rolling Stone*, December 2008, 37–40.

——2009. 'You write to make an impact: a tribute to Steven Wells'. Available: drownedinsound.com 14 July 2009, http://drownedinsound.com/in_depth/4137352-you-write-to-make-an-impact-a-tribute-to-steven-wells (accessed 14 November 2010).

Weingarten, C. 2009 'Last rock critic standing'. Available: http://twitter.com/1000timesyes (accessed 19 November 2010).

Williams, Raymond. 1958. 'Moving from High Culture to Ordinary Culture', originally published in N. McKenzie (ed.), *Convictions*. London: MacGibbon and Kee.

Wiseman, E. 2009. 'Behind NME lines', in the *Guardian*, 9 November 2009. Available: www.guardian.co.uk/music/2008/nov/09/nme-wiseman-conor-mcnicholas-musical-express (accessed 19 November 2010).

Zappa, Frank. 1980. in Botts, L. (ed.) *Loose Talk: The Book of Quotes from the Pages of Rolling Stone Magazine*. New York: Quick Fox Press.

Websites

Rocksbackpages – www.rocksbackpages.com

UCAS – www.ucas.com (accessed 14 November 2010)

11 Media reporting

Paul Bradshaw

The media is one of the UK's most important industries. In 2008 the 'creative sector' (which also includes related fields such as fashion) employed almost two million people across over 150,000 companies. According to the Department of Culture, Media and Sport those companies contributed 5.6 per cent of the UK's Gross Value Added in 2008, and accounted for exports totalling over £17 billion. Despite the gloom that permeates parts of the industry, it is a fast-growing sector that is covered not just in the media press but in the financial press.

The media is big business – and media journalism is at its heart business-to-business journalism; the same as reporting on any other industry – with one key difference: you are part of the industry on which you are reporting.

This 'embedded' quality of media reporting is both a strength and a weakness: on the one hand, you will already be connected to a network of contacts and experts in your field; stories surround you. On the other, there is an obvious risk of self-censorship for fear of offending current or potential employers.

This is a fear that you should overcome: if you fail to report important stories through fear, you are not doing your job as a journalist. And if you cannot do that, no one will want to employ you anyway. Potential employers will be more offended by a cowardly journalist than one who has the courage to report an important story.

Another weakness of the media reporter is short-sightedness: it is easy to mistake the media industry for your part of it. The media is not 'national newspapers', or magazines; it is not limited to what happens in London, or even the UK. Nor is it merely the creative side of the business – because it is a business. And that business requires not just writers and producers and celebrities, but lawyers and regulators, marketing and PR, printing and distribution, manufacturing and research.

Part of your role is to connect those dots, to tell the story of how a regulator's decision might affect the day-to-day work of a producer or journalist; to spot manufacturing problems that are likely to cause problems for your readers – and provide others with a new opportunity. And of course you will chronicle the creative successes and failures and celebrity tiffs. In short, if it affects your audience or is merely something for them to talk about round the water cooler, it's news.

Setting the rhythm of the job: the diary

Like any industry, the media business has an annual rhythm made up of everything from the 'silly season' to the key conferences that litter the year. A first task, then, will be to create a calendar of events that make up that rhythm, and continue to add to that as you come across new examples. To begin with you will need to identify the following:

- **Results**: Audit Bureau of Circulation (ABC and ABCe) numbers, Rajar figures (radio) and other metrics of audiences and advertising success will be released at various times of the year, and you will be expected to spot the stories in the numbers. Likewise, you will need to monitor the filing of financial results of individual companies, and annual reports by Ofcom and other industry bodies.
- **Industry conferences and events** such as the Edinburgh and Cannes TV festivals, the Oxford Media Conference, and the Society of Editors.
- **Awards**: from the glamour of the Royal Television Society and BAFTAs to the likes of regional media awards and ad-hoc awards organised by online communities.
- **Parties**: such as the various office parties held by employers over Christmas.
- **Seasons**: such as the 'silly season' in late summer when newspapers compensate for a lack of hard news with odd stories, TV's autumn season when many of its most important shows are launched, or the Christmas season which is always a crucial time for the music, publishing and games industries.
- **Political events** with implications for the industry, such as the budget (which may include incentives such as tax breaks for particular parts of the media, such as the game or film industry) and consultations in the UK, EU and US on legislation such as libel law, privacy or Freedom of Information.

You will need to be one step ahead of these events, preparing material ahead of time and anticipating material that will be needed afterwards (such as follow-ups).

Planning for diary events

Different events will require different strategies, but planning will be key for all of them. In the case of releases of results such as ABCs and financial results, key personalities will be in demand from various outlets for an official response, so make sure to approach them before then to arrange an interview. In some cases you may need to interview them before all the information is available, and anticipate that information by asking how they might feel in various scenarios.

In the case of larger events and conferences you will be looking out for surprises and insights: who was the unexpected winner – or loser? Who provided the most insightful comment – or the one that set everybody's teeth on edge? Of course, reporters from other outlets will be looking for similar things, so make sure you arrange one-to-one interviews and chat with a wide range of people to get unique reactions and angles – and stories that may have nothing to do with the conference at all.

With many events you will be expected to report proceedings live online – whether that is via tweets on Twitter, a liveblog embedded on your employer's website, or audio clips and streaming video from your phone. Make sure you have spare batteries, 3G dongles (the conference Wi-Fi will struggle under the demand of all those smartphones), all the leads you need – and an eye for a plug socket. Arrive as early as possible to 'recce' the venue, check the signal strength on your phone, the power points, lighting, and where you will need to be to capture the best video, the best photos, and the clearest audio (these will all be different places).

When large reports are released you will need to digest them quickly and identify the most newsworthy or useful pieces of information buried within. For Patrick Smith (see case study later), for example, digesting reports was key in his time on paidContent:

> It was all about brevity. It may have been a 56-page report you've just read, but that's no reason you should bore the reader. I learned a lot of about keeping it short – the managing editor Ernie Sander was keen on telling reporters that two paragraphs is normally enough. If you write more than that, that's telling the readers that it's a really important story and deserving of their attention.

To focus your reading, first ask yourself what the key issues are facing the industry at the moment, and go straight to the sections dealing with that (the 'Find' function on PDFs and Word documents comes in very handy here).

If the report is stuffed with graphs and charts, they will contain valuable insights: what is top? What has risen the most, or fallen most dramatically? What is the biggest change? Make sure to read the text that explains the charts – there may be methodological issues or unusual factors that change your interpretation, or that you can highlight as your angle – and of course there may be quotes that explain it better than you could.

Monitoring the buzz: using alerts and feeds

If your diary establishes the annual rhythm of your reporting, the use of alerts and feeds sets the daily tone of your work.

In order to stay on top of developments in your field and spot the most newsworthy angle in a story or interview, you need to be aware of what is happening, and what people are talking about. In the pre-internet era this was based on pub chatter and that day's industry headlines – now there are a range of tools to also keep in touch in real-time – but both sorts of sources are important.

Email alerts are an obvious place to start. Most specialist media outlets offer these – but you can also subscribe to Google News Alerts to be informed whenever a particular person or company is mentioned in a news story on any news outlet. If you are planning to interview someone or write a feature on an organisation, for example, you should ensure that you are receiving alerts for any mention of them to make sure that you don't miss any possible issues you should be asking them about.

But email alerts involve a certain time lag, and Google News only covers a small part of the news being discussed online. In addition you should be using an RSS reader (such as Google Reader) to stay in touch with the latest news as it is published not just in specialist media but also on blogs and other platforms. Jemima Kiss, who reports on media and technology for the *Guardian*, says she looks to a range of industry blogs in her work, particular in the USA, for trends and direction that will later influence the wider media:

> *The Wall Street Journal* is consistently impressive, as is their startup-style digital wing AllThingsD. I really rate GigaOM for his calm insight and experience, TechCrunch for comprehensive coverage and a dozen or so other blogs and sites I check regularly. More than that though, I increasingly rely on the opinions and observations of like-minded contacts through Twitter so keep an eagle eye on links and discussions being shared.

This monitoring of real-time channels such as Twitter forms the final piece of online information. Desktop tools like Tweetdeck allow you to be constantly informed of any mentions of particular terms, and web-based services like Hoot-suite offer similar functionality. Patrick Smith says he particularly recommends Twitter as a reporting tool:

> I'm puzzled by people that don't get it. If contacts are the most important part of reporting, then what better way to find and connect with people? Many stories of mine have come from Twitter, though mostly through the private direct message facility. And many leads have been made that way. Facebook is just as important – if only magazine offices would stop banning it.

If you do not already use Google Reader to follow RSS feeds and Tweetdeck or another Twitter 'client' (software or website) to follow mentions of key people, companies or terms, there are lots of resources online – including videos – to help you do so. Search for 'Following searches on Twitter' and 'Using an RSS reader' to get you started.

Spotting news stories

The attention of the media industry changes depending on what affects it most at any particular time, and the power struggles of various actors within it. People in the advertising industry will be particularly interested in how their work is affected by waves of new laws and regulations, for example: music industry workers may be particularly interested in any news around commercial opportunities such as merchandise or licensing, or plans to tackle 'piracy' (a loaded term that you should be careful about using if more neutral terms are available). Newspaper employees may at one point be obsessed with paywalls, at another with user-generated content, and then with libel laws.

At a time when most parts of the industry are suffering commercially, anything to do with commercial success will be newsworthy. When an industry is booming, failure will make headlines.

Here are just a few suggestions of qualities to look out for as you look around you and talk to contacts about industry goings-on.

The 'new'

New launches, from magazines and games to companies and campaigns, are obvious places to look for news stories. *When* something becomes 'new' will vary between industries: as far as the industry is concerned a TV programme is 'new' when it is commissioned, for example, not broadcast – and an artist is new when they are signed, or generating competition for their signature, not when their first single is released.

New reports, new laws and regulations, new deals and contracts, new decisions and new appointments are all other examples of newsworthy events to look out for. Keep in contact with people at the Department for Culture, Media and Sport (DCMS), the Press Complaints Commission (PCC), Ofcom, and any other regulators, campaign and consumer groups, lawyers and civil servants whose work affects the parts of the media that you report on.

Scour the media job ads – the more senior the position, the more important (speak to your own advertising department, too, to get a head-start on possible stories). But less senior roles – particularly unusual ones, or unusual elements buried in an otherwise unremarkable job description – can also offer clues to organisations' plans. You should also remember that not all media jobs will be advertised in the media press: positions in marketing, accounts, law, production and research might all be advertised elsewhere.

When you talk to contacts in the industry, ask them about changes to people's roles, the formation of new internal teams, or executives who are 'busy' on other projects – any of these might be a useful lead.

Reaction

As soon as people absorb the newness of something, they will want to know how it has been received. If there is a lag between the two (as, for example, between a key TV series being commissioned and critical reception or audience figures upon broadcast) then this may merit a separate article – you may want to set a reminder in your diary to seek reaction out when that happens. Fan communities can be a good source here – and they can also be a good source of leads on problems in production, so don't just lurk in these communities: make contacts and build relationships so that they come to you first with the best stories.

More broadly, unexpected reactions can be particularly newsworthy: an outburst by a company CEO; uproar on Facebook about a casting decision; consumer anger about a new product. Watch for these, but make sure it's not a one-sided story – they can read that for themselves. Add context, analysis and counter-reaction.

Trends

Are there a number of companies launching similar products or initiatives – or making plans to? Are they recruiting in particular areas? Frantically training staff in new skills? Commissioning similar research? Examples might include record companies signing new talent from MySpace, or adding contract clauses covering merchandise; newspapers launching iPad apps or recruiting in mobile.

Trends are a great example of the value of simply talking to lots of people in your field and being in touch with what's going on. While they might not be able to talk to you on the record about what's happening (and therefore you will not spot this on social networks), you may still be able to report on the overall trend, or prepare material for when projects are announced.

Reporting trends will often require you to answer the 'Why?' question. Why this? And why now? You will often need industry leaders or academic experts to provide insight into those questions, but along the way you should be developing your own expertise to provide instant analysis when stories break.

Features

Trends can often be the basis of lengthier features – whether they explore the trend in more depth or explore a case study or interview which will have broad appeal within the industry. If increasing numbers of radio stations are going into partnership with local newspapers, for example, you might want to pitch the idea of a full-page interview with one of the project leads. Likewise, you may pitch a double-page spread intertwining several interviews with industry leaders, analysts and representatives of other factions, such as consumers, fans or employees. You might commission a 'How-to' piece on a particular skill – or an analysis piece from a respected expert. Which of all of these you decide to do will obviously depend on your audience and what else has been done by your publication and your rivals.

Conversely, *unique* experiments that buck the trend will justify deeper feature treatment too – as the industry looks for pioneers in new ways of doing things, especially if it is making – or saving – money. Here the focus will be on all that is innovative about the project, and the key questions that your readers will want answered include how they are doing it – and why? What exactly are they doing – and who with? Where are they doing it – and when?

Ongoing issues – especially worsening ones – that affect a part of the industry will always justify a feature. Is reality TV dead? How do you make money from content online? What's the next big thing in music? But beware: some of these questions can be overdone, so if it's been an issue for a while you will need a new treatment to breathe new life into it – a newsworthy angle, or an emerging personality, that makes it 'different this time'.

Patrick Smith says:

> It's important to get behind the spin and look at the trends. Is print really dying, or as a printed medium across all society is it pretty much stable? Is online really changing media habits or is TV by far the more important channel in terms of growth? It shouldn't be so much 'this is what happened last week' as 'this is what will happen next year'.

Finding sources

Media reporting, like most journalism, is a mix of reactive and proactive work: you have to be able to react to events and approaches, but also seek out leads and information. For Jemima Kiss leads come through a mix of sources: 'Interesting conversations, planned and otherwise, with people, tips through email and Twitter and the inevitable PR.' For Patrick Smith the best stories come from contacts:

> It's a boring and perhaps predictable answer, but the definition of a blockbuster story now is the same as it's always been: something big and important that isn't in the public domain. While company reports and analysts can shed light on subjects and help with analysis, they are available to everyone. Nothing beats the opinion or advice of someone in the middle of a story or business. Some of my biggest stories have simply come from asking people, sometimes company CEOs at the centre of a big story what's going on. I'm often surprised that no one has got there first.

Finding contacts in the media industry can appear easier than it actually is when you notice that media workers tend to be such prolific users of social media. Facebook allows you to find others who have worked for the same company as you, while LinkedIn's advanced search facility allows you to search by employer as well. MySpace is well known as a place to find bands and artists in the music industry – or aspiring to be – and Twitter is populated by both media personalities and the people behind them.

You should familiarise yourself with the etiquette of each of these platforms: for example, people do not tend to mind you following them on Twitter (unless their account is private), but a contact request on LinkedIn is generally only advised if you have already met them. Facebook falls somewhere in the middle, while a contact on MySpace may get buried in the spam that the site suffers from.

Don't underestimate the value of a simple mailing list – there may be one that allows members of a particular sector to talk about issues that affect them. And don't treat all these channels as places to find contacts only when you need them – you should treat them as places to slowly get to know your contacts, and to understand who knows who within the field. Then when you do meet them you will have common points of reference to talk about.

As professional communicators, many media workers also maintain blogs either about their work or their interests. Familiarise yourself with the leading voices in each field – and follow their RSS feeds. The BBC, for example, has an 'Editor's Blog' where senior staff talk about their work – but there are also personal blogs maintained by journalists and web developers within the organisation. Similar examples can be found in other sectors.

Take any opportunity you can to reach out to a new contact – whether that's answering a question on Twitter or posting a comment on their blog. Don't overdo it – a little goes a long way.

But your contacts book should not begin and end on social media. There will be key figures in your sector – indeed, whole parts of it – that do not have any regularly updated presence online. Senior figures will often want to avoid making it easy for people to contact them on Facebook, or may simply not see the point of 'wasting time' online. Similarly, the parts of the media whose work relies less on talking in public – law, accounts, production – may not have any interest in – or opportunity to – express themselves online. These are also often the best leads for the biggest stories: companies being bought and sold, titles being bought or shut down, staff being laid off or hired.

Have your own space

Needless to say that having your own blog (and accounts across various social networks) can be extremely useful in providing a space for potential sources to get to know you and contact you. Use it to write about the things that don't conveniently fit into your published or broadcast work – the stories behind the stories, or small observations, or links to interesting posts elsewhere (linking is a good way of reaching out to contacts too).

There's nothing wrong with including the odd personal piece too, as it allows others something to connect with you over – but obviously remain professional, and don't blog while drunk!

Jon Slattery, former editor of *Press Gazette*, sees 'a real passion for media and interest in the changes that are taking place' as a key asset for aspiring media reporters:

> When I interviewed staff for *Press Gazette* I looked for people that had experience and/or contacts in a media sector they wanted to write about (i.e. newspapers, magazines, broadcasting). Today it would be a good knowledge of social media, blogs, Twitter, etc.

The modern media reporter: multiplatform, engaged – and live!

It is a rare journalist these days who only writes or broadcasts. Whether you are working for a newspaper, magazine or broadcast institution, you will be expected to produce material for websites, mobile and social media platforms – and to be at least willing to produce simple video or audio footage, liveblogging, or managing user-generated content (UGC).

Jemima Kiss feels that an understanding of how these technologies can serve a story is essential:

> Curiosity, inventiveness and a desire to tell a strong story in the best possible way should drive all reporters to some extent – so if you're not interested, maybe you're in the wrong job. Thinking of it as technology is not the right approach – all of these are just tools for your work.

Recognising that every medium has its own qualities and language – and that people consume them in different ways – is important. Blogging is a very different art to writing an article or column, and Twitter is not just a channel to throw headlines on – it is a place to have conversations and ask questions, invite reaction and opinion, and share interesting links (not just those that you have written). Equally, online audio is not radio, and online video a very different creature to broadcast TV.

There are an increasing number of books that explain these differences – and dozens of blogs and online videos to tell you more. But the key thing is to start building your experience – and assets (a blog and a network of contacts) – now. Josh Halliday, who joined the *Guardian* as a media reporter in 2010, says he owes his job to the blogs he ran while studying a journalism degree.

His colleague Jemima Kiss agrees that having these assets and experience is important, but also adds that specialisation is important – whether in a particularly format or technology, or in a subject area.

> It will be much easier to establish a profile, make contacts and focus your work around a subject area you can get your teeth into, even if you build up knowledge and an attractive portfolio of work on your own blog to start with.

Looking forward, Kiss feels that there is still a lot of change to come, and aspiring journalists should continue to experiment.

> Many of the changes and innovations in our news reporting started with unnoticed and seemingly inconsequential fiddling – Twitter, for example. It slowly became more and more central to our coverage and how we promote our work, but that took time. Likewise the new innovations that will change our work probably seem quite modest now.
>
> I do think that this period is one of the hardest for journalists in that we still work under many of the conventions of a traditional newsroom but with a relentless development pace and barrage of unfiltered, highly demanding content that makes our jobs extremely pressurised. Within five years, I would hope, we will have evolved enough that technology will be far more intelligent, selective and targeted, even before we get to the stage of editing it ourselves. There will always be a role for the human reporter, editor and journalist but technology has a much smarter role to play to free us from the grunt work and allow us to do the important stuff.

Case study: Patrick Smith, reporter, Media Briefing, formerly at *Press Gazette* and paidContent

I started at *Press Gazette* in 2006: the magazine was weekly and like hundreds of other weekly trade mags across the country today, it's raison d'etre was to fill the front eight pages (particularly page one) with juicy news that no one else had. We focused on the comings and goings of Fleet Street, regulation and phone tapping, court cases and sackings, regional press collapses and the occasional campaign.

I moved to paidContent in 2008, where the emphasis was entirely on reporting online. There was and is no legacy print product to protect. A seven-year-old company – newly under the ownership of Guardian News & Media – paidContent was all about growth in new platforms: into web, mobile, research reports and real-life events. Reporters were expected to be across every development in media, with a strong, ceaseless focus on digital media. With no deadline to speak of, the deadline was always different versions of 'now'.

Aggregation has become increasingly important. *Press Gazette* has launched a blog and uses that to link to other sources and give a commentary on what else was being reported across the media world. But at paidContent linking and aggregating other sources became the core job. The company's founder Rafat Ali liked to call it 'intelligent aggregation': not just linking to another report, but adding some context, relevance, links to past paidContent coverage and joining the dots in a way that creates a new article without just repeating the original piece.

UK editor Robert Andrews did and still does this brilliantly – as well as reporting the news, he uses his vast knowledge to adds analysis on the fly, creating a unique kind of news. The addition of opinion to paidContent's reporting elevates it beyond the many faceless grey websites that re-report press releases and the tired old 'he said, she said' processes of packaged news. Many journalists will balk at the suggestion that they should add informed opinion to their reporting – but paidContent is a B2B title and its purpose of B2B media is to tell executives what they need to know to make decisions every day.

I think it's unlikely I'll ever be a full-time reporter again, in the sense that I'd spend all my time writing news and features. The start-up I'm involved in now – Briefing Media – is all about sorting and intelligently tagging content across the web. We're commissioning experts to write comment and analysis pieces, but the bulk of the site is linking to other sources and making sense of the semantic relationships between issues, people, companies and sectors.

The most important thing is to add value – don't just report news. If reporters aren't adding any value – i.e. helping readers make decisions about their jobs – then they should ask why not. Who has moved where and who's having a row with whom might be interesting, but is it useful?

12 Science journalism

Sophie Schünemann

I believe the intellectual life of the whole of western society is being split into two polar groups ... at one pole we have the literary intellectuals ... at the other scientists ... Between the two a gulf of mutual incomprehension – sometimes ... hostility and dislike, but most of all lack of understanding.

(Snow, 1963: 11–12)

Grouping journalism with the humanities as Goldacre (2008: 207–8) has done, or even with the arts, as suggested by Hartz and Chappell (1997), it easily takes its place at the pole opposing the sciences. When surveyed, both journalists and scientists will frequently profess to the existence of Snow's gulf of miscomprehension (Hartz and Chappell, 1997; European Commission, 2007b). With '[s]cientists who don't speak English' and '[r]eporters who don't speak science' (Hartz and Chappell, 1997: 21–22) there are instances in which the two groups literally speak different languages – and that is only one of many barriers that block the flow of science communication in modern Anglo-American societies. Considering that the lay public receives most of its information about science and health from the news media (Nelkin, 1995: 67; House of Lords, 2000), implications of this corrupted flow are potentially severe.

The literature on the problem-ridden subject of scientists and journalists is already extensive and it continues to grow. A detailed examination of both the scientific and the journalistic viewpoints is given in early key texts on the topic by Friedman, Dunwoody and Rogers (1986), by Nelkin (1995) and by Hartz and Chapell (1997). More recent accounts are provided in a literature review by Weigold (2001), in the newly launched magazine *Science Journalism in Europe* published by and for science journalists and academics (Lehmkuhl, 2008), and in a 2007 survey of European scientists and media professionals by the European Commission (2007a, 2007b).

What scientists and journalists have in common

In some ways, this deep gulf between science and journalism is surprising, considering that the two professions traditionally share several significant characteristics.

Hartz and Chappell (1997: 13, 14) describe both scientists and journalists as 'highly motivated. Both are above average in intelligence, above average in education, and above all, freethinking'. They are 'data collectors who utilize their experience and insight to bring understanding and order out of uncertainty'. They are natural sceptics: 'As keen observers of inconsistency, journalists and scientists are equally good players at the game of "gotcha"'. Crucially, Salisbury (1997 cited in Allan, 2002: 85) also emphasises their shared 'devotion to discovering the truth'. This is the ideal. The current reality, however, especially with regard to journalistic practices, is rather different. Recent texts highlight an increasingly corporate mentality both in science and journalism. Coupled with the loss of journalistic scepticism which arises from the constraints of modern news culture, this mentality exacerbates the already existing differences in the norms and values of the two cultures.

The two cultures

'When we talk about the marriage of science and journalism, our dilemma is clear. Science is slow, patient, precise, careful, conservative and complicated. Journalism is hungry for deadlines and drama, fast, short, very imprecise at times' (Kathy Sawyer, 1997 cited in Hartz and Chappell, 1997). Herein lies the problem. Scientists are, necessarily, sticklers for detail (Salisbury, 1997 cited in Allan, 2002: 85; Goldacre, 2008: 221). Objectivity – in the form gleaned from 'tests that permit theoretically incompatible outcomes' – is key (Weigold, 2001). They see debate as a means to approach further towards the truth by working towards consensus. They consider peer review as a crucial step towards minimising errors and have developed a language of technical terms to enhance precision and clarity in their scientific discourse. Scientists operate on time scales of months or even years to complete and publish their research. So a scientific paper published a few months before will be far from old news for them (Dunwoody, 1986: 12; Nelkin, 1995: 165; Salisbury, 1997 cited in Allan, 2002: 85).

In contrast, reporters must adhere to a number of rigid deadlines every day (Weigold, 2001: 179). They must see the big picture rather than get caught up in details. Debate merely serves as dramatic element to their story, highlighting the conflict between two sides (Salisbury, 1997 cited in Allan, 2002: 85–86). They are after cutting-edge exciting research findings, no matter how uncertain (Weigold, 2001: 179). While researchers will generally consider their new discovery as a tiny piece in the big puzzle of science, for journalists, this tiny piece is the whole story (Weigold, 2001). Also, despite much debate about journalistic objectivity, journalism is essentially a subjective metier. In fact, some news organisations have replaced the concept of objectivity with that of 'fairness' (Hartz and Chappell, 1997: 17; Weigold, 2001). Showing their writing to others before publication is generally despised as impingement on editorial freedom. Lastly, scientific jargon, far from adding precision and clarity, makes much of the material virtually incomprehensible to them and to their readers (Salisbury, 1997 cited in Allan, 2002: 85–86; Weigold, 2001). Indeed, few journalists 'understand the scientific method, the dictates of peer review, the reasons for the caveats and linguistic precision scientists employ when speaking of their work' (Hartz and Chappell, 1997). Similarly, many scientists are not aware of, and definitely do not apply, the news values that are so intuitive to journalists (Dunwoody, 1986: 11; European Commission, 2007b).

Their motivations for communication differ too. Scientists communicate to educate, or to get public recognition and approval that will secure funding, while journalists are out to entertain, rather than educate, their audience with the news (Friedman, Dunwoody and Rogers, 1986: xii; Westm, 1986: 40, both cited in Weigold, 2001). Naturally, on an individual basis, many scientists and journalists 'have positive experiences with each other' (Friedman, Dunwoody and Rogers, 1986: xv) and there is always a danger of over-generalisation where criticism is applied. On the other hand, perhaps over-generalisations are necessary in order to awaken the big majority of news practitioners to the problems inherent to their standard practices – problems whose existence and wide-spread prevalence are apparent from the growing body of critical literature on the subject of science journalism, let alone from newspapers and news programmes themselves.

Bridging the gap?

To bridge the communicative gap, scientists frequently demand more specially trained science journalists, ideally with a background in science (European Commission, 2007a). Problematically, scientists appear to expect these specialist science reporters to then be equipped to have an (at least basic) understanding of any piece of science thrown at them. This is rather naïve, if not presumptuous, considering that scientists themselves are usually highly specialised within one science. Physicists, say, might be hard put to explain certain biological phenomena and vice versa.

Moreover, while it is true that much science is being covered by generalist reporters (Nelkin, 1995: 94), a lack of specialists might not actually be the problem. Hansen (1994), for example, interviewed 31 specialist science journalists working in the British national press. The finding that emerged most strongly from his interrogations was that even these long-term science, technology, medical, health and environmental reporters saw themselves as 'journalists first and specialists second'. Moreover, even if there are well-trained and conscientious science specialists with much expertise in the newsroom, they are frequently not listened to and passed over when it comes to covering the big science stories (Goldacre, 2008: 213–14, 290).

Science journalism is just journalism, after all

Science news is just one more piece of news (Gregory and Miller, 2000: 105–6; European Commission, 2007b). It is selected according to the same news values as any other news item, and the editor is the final 'gatekeeper' (Hartz and Chappell, 1997). The concept of news values was first introduced by social scientists Galtung and Ruge (1965) who identified ten main criteria for news selection: relevance, timeliness, simplification, predictability, unexpectedness, continuity, composition, élite people, élite nations and negativity (cited in Brighton and Foy, 2007: 7). In the survey of European media professionals,[1] 65 per cent of respondents stressed relevance to everyday life as the most important criterion, followed by novelty, which was seen as crucial by 42 per cent of respondents (European Commission, 2007b) and is equatable with Galtung and Ruge's timeliness.

These news values are engrained in journalistic thinking and practice, and stories that do not conform to them are highly unlikely to pass the editor. Editors choose which stories will be published and which dropped. They decide on the number and type of science stories passed on to the public. They make those choices and edit those stories according to their judgements about what will 'hook' the reader most (Nelkin, 1995: 108; Hartz and Chappell, 1997). For Goldacre (2008: 290–91) editors are a big part of the science journalistic problem. He blames them for maintaining the gulf between the two cultures, so famously coined by Snow (1963), by favouring all subjects, especially the humanities, over science as well as by favouring generalist reporters over science specialists when they do let a big science story through:

> My basic hypothesis is this: the people who run the media are humanities graduates with little understanding of science, who wear their ignorance as a badge of honour ... there is an attack implicit in all media coverage of science: in their choice of stories, and in the way they cover them, the media create a parody of science.
>
> (Goldacre, 2008: 207–8)

But even editors are powerless against the modern challenges that have crept into their workplace and the modern journalistic system.

The journalistic mill

These changes were most notably and recently revealed in Nick Davies' exposé *Flat Earth News* (2008). He commissioned a unique investigation into 'a sample of the stories running through the British media' during two randomly chosen weeks (Davies, 2008: 52). The results were sobering: even on the more prestigious nationals like the *Guardian*, *The Times*, the *Independent* and the *Daily Telegraph*, an average of 60 per cent of stories relied on wire-copy and/or PR material, only 12 per cent could be said to be generated solely by the reporter. In 70 per cent of wire-copy-based stories, facts were not verified before publication: 'the most respected media outlets in the country are routinely recycling unchecked second-hand material' but newspapers try to gloss over that fact. The researchers who analysed the story samples on Davies' behalf reported: 'We found many stories apparently written by one of the newspaper's own reporters that seem to have been cut and pasted from elsewhere' (Davies, 2008: 52–53).

Reporters hardly left their computers. One young journalist's working week consisted of 42.5 hours in the office and only three hours outside it. Reporters do not have the time to be critical, to check, let alone go see for themselves (Davies, 2008: 51–60; Hartz and Chappell, 1997), because they are expected to churn out eight to ten articles a day and to have them online ideally within five minutes of the story's breaking – journalism has turned into 'churnalism' (Davies, 2008: 59, 69–70). 'Within the lifetimes of journalists not yet middle-aged, there was a period when deadlines came only twice a day … in the newsrooms of today's all-news channels, deadlines are virtually continuous' (Hartz and Chappell, 1997). This is the 24-hour news culture.

Time constraints become particularly acute in science reporting because of the perceived complexity of the material the journalists need to digest for their readers (Nelkin, 1995: 117–18). The dire situation is neatly accentuated in the above-mentioned survey of European media professionals. More than half of respondents named '[unverified] or unsubstantiated information' received from the scientific community as posing a 'major challenge' or at least 'some challenge' to their work. The survey authors summarised: 'This is a key issue which prevents journalists from doing their job.' Surveyed journalists also complained that scientific information was not being 'presented in a "story format"' (European Commission, 2007b). One wonders what the interviewed journalists do consider part of their job. Even writing stories seems no longer to be included, let alone verifying and sub-stantiating claims or gathering and checking the facts – routines traditionally so integral a part of the journalist's job. The researchers commissioned by Davies (2008: 53) make this point very well:

> Taken together, these data portray a picture of journalism in which any meaningful independent journalistic activity by the press is the exception rather than the rule. We are not talking about investigative journalism here, but the everyday practices of news judgement, fact-checking, balance, criticising and interrogating sources, etc., that are, in theory, day-to-day journalism.

Day-to-day journalism has taken a drastic turn for the worse. The result is an inattentive, hyperactive press. Inattentive because it simply does not have the time to check on the veracity of what it prints. Hyperactive because it feels under continuous pressure to hype and sensationalise: hype is what sells, and selling is ever more important in a corporate-ruled press world (Davies, 2008: 60–69).

The scientific constructions of an inattentive, hyperactive press

In its inattentive hyperactivity, even the quality press appears to construct a scientific reality which is severely skewed from its – at least comparatively – objective original in the scientific literature. This is not done for malicious reasons. Rather it is the product of already questionable journalistic conventions further corrupted by the severe time restraints of modern news culture. Four key factors in the con-structive process are: the routine use of articles from peer-reviewed journals, an arbitrary selection of 'experts', the notion of journalistic 'balance' and the media's tendency to eliminate uncertainty.

Peer-reviewed journals

Greenberg (1997 cited in Allan, 2002: 83) describes peer-reviewed journals as 'the steadiest of science news sources' and his view appears representative of the journalistic community. In the survey of European media professionals (2007b), journals turned out to be the most frequently used source for scientific information – indicated by 62 per cent of respondents. Hartz and Chappell (1997), too, found that 62 to 70 per cent of respondents 'often' or 'sometimes' resorted to major medical journals for stories. Apparently, journalists look to these journals as a source of uncorrupted science – as opposed to that conveyed in press releases (Dunwoody, 1986: 5). Hansen's (1994) interview with science specialists of the British national press revealed that reporters saw no need for verifying the information taken from peer-reviewed journals. Frequently, they did not even call the paper's author, let alone other scientists, for statements. As the most-used journals, Hansen cites: '*Nature*, *Science*, *New Scientist*, the *British Medical Journal*, *The Lancet*, and the *New England Journal of Medicine*'. First, it must be noted that *New Scientist* is not a peer-reviewed journal. Secondly, and more generally, this apparently blind trust in the integrity of academic journals intimates a general ignorance of the dynamics of these journals and about the function that their editors ascribe to peer review. As Horton (2000), editor of *The Lancet*, puts it:

> The mistake ... is to have thought that peer review was any more than a crude means of discovering the acceptability – not the validity – of a new finding. Editors and scientists alike ... portray peer review to the public as a quasi-sacred process that helps to make science our most objective truth teller. But we know that the system of peer review is biased, unjust, unaccountable, incomplete, easily fixed, often insulting, usually ignorant, occasionally foolish, and frequently wrong.

Peer-reviewed journals are not the conveniently reliable sources journalists would have them be. Information gleaned from them must be checked lest inaccuracies in the scientific literature be spread and magnified in the popular press. Yet checking, if done at all, is accomplished by contacting authors or other scientists for quotes and information on a paper's findings or any other item of science news. This indicates another problematic journalistic source: scientists or those who claim to be such.

Authority figures and experts

Often, whom reporters appoint as 'authority' or 'expert' on a scientific matter is the result of an arbitrary process rather than an informed choice:

> How do the media work around their inability to deliver scientific evidence? Often they use authority figures, the very antithesis of what science is about, as if they were priests or politicians or parent figures ... There is a danger with authority-figure coverage, in the absence of real evidence, because it leaves the field wide open for questionable authority figures to waltz in.
>
> (Goldacre, 2008: 223)

Always under time pressure, journalists often resort to interviewing those who are easily, and quickly, available to them. These may not always be the most expert sources. Sometimes, this goes as far as asking opinions of people in the streets because they are 'more available as quotable sources than scientists in institutions' (Gregory and Miller, 2000: 125–26). Political activists, too, may be called upon to give their opinion on animal rights, nuclear power, environmental and similar issues, in the process being 'presented to the public as qualified experts on issues of science' (Tavris, 1986 cited in Weigold, 2001: 181–82). Tavris notes that this 'raises a problem of evidence over assertions. Reporters rarely know how sources know what they know, or what evidence the knowledge is based on, or why it differs from conventional wisdom' (Tavris, 1986 cited in Weigold, 2001: 181–82). The problem becomes even more severe when reporters present the anecdotal information gathered from these groups as actual evidence (Griffin, 1999: 228). Gregory and Miller (2000: 126) write:

> Communications scholar James Dearing suggests that reporting the views of people in the street with whom readers can identify can give unorthodox science credibility among non-scientists ... Dearing also suggests that the public are more likely to believe a maverick because the public make judgements on a broader range of criteria than scientists – including fear, superstition and gut reaction.

In this manner, the media offer a platform to '[amateur] and unorthodox scientists ... and even conventional scientists who have been unsuccessful in publishing their work in the peer-reviewed literature' (Gregory and Miller, 2000: 124). The public, judging by the big publicity of those minority views, will take them for the consensus. Hansen (1994) stresses that the science reporters he interviewed all had many contacts, with whom they had – over long periods of time – built up a relationship of trust. Here, at least, they can be relatively certain of the sources' credentials and expertise. But even these long-known and trustworthy sources 'do not necessarily represent the spectrum of opinion' (Nelkin, 1995: 122). Yet once an expert has been cited in the press, he is likely to be used repeatedly, and to speak on any number of topics that are at best tangential to his specialism. Frequently, such authority figures are scientific administrators rather than active researchers (Dunwoody, 1986: 7; Conrad, 1999). Both Travis (1986 cited in Weigold, 2001) and Goldacre (2008) bemoan the dangerous arbitrariness of the system: They think '[you] can pick a result from anywhere you like, and if it suits your agenda, then that's that: ... it just depends on who you ask, nothing really means anything' (Goldacre, 2008: 271).

Balance

The issue of arbitrary 'experts' and 'authorities' is intricately linked with the journalistic notion of 'balance'. Balance is created by pitching one scientist's opinion against another's, but without situating them in relation to the wider scientific context (Goldacre, 2008: 223). Journalists defend this practice as crucial to fairness and journalistic objectivity, arguing that they need to give both sides of the story (Davies, 2008: 131). Yet in reality, fairness is abandoned when they pitch a scientist speaking on behalf of the scientific consensus view against a maverick as like and like (Crisp, 1986; Dearing, 1995 both cited in Gregory and Miller, 2000: 126; Nelkin, 1995: 88; Weigold, 2001). Davies (2008: 112) heavily criticises this practice:

> In reality, what [media managers] generally promote is not objectivity at all. It's neutrality, which is a very different kind of beast. Neutrality requires the journalist to become invisible, to refrain deliberately (under threat of discipline) from expressing the judgements which are essential for journalism.

Davies (2008: 131–32) terms this practice 'the safety net rule', denoting the thus generated 'balance' as a farce intended solely to shield the reporter from any kind of accusation of taking sides – whether or not taking sides and being critical is appropriate in that case.[2] Curiously, four of the six examples Davies gives to illustrate this conventional yet cowardly journalistic behaviour are science stories.

Elimination of uncertainty

The compulsion to pitch voice against voice stands in paradoxical contrast to another journalistic urge: the elimination of all uncertainty from articles (Weiss and Singer, 1988; Fahnestock, 1986 both cited in Stocking, 1999: 24–25). Journalists, especially editors (Nelkin, 1995: 109), minimise ambiguities by not mentioning caveats of research studies, by using only a single source, by providing little context information about previous similar or contrary research, and by stressing the scientific product over the process (Stocking, 1999: 24–27). All these strategies simplify the story. Study draw-backs and limitations fall under the news desk. A single voice is given all authority. Scientific discoveries become isolated events without precursors or follow-ups. The product is extolled without mention of the complicated long-term process taken to arrive at it. Most dangerously, all scientific evidence is eliminated. Instead, the reader is presented only with the researchers' – possibly overenthusiastic – conclusions which he has to take at face value (Goldacre, 2008: 220–21). These strategies serve not only to dumb down the science (Goldacre, 2008: 220) but, importantly, they also save the reporter a lot of time. Even more crucially, they are the tools for exaggeration and hype. In extolling results while failing to say that the study was done on only a tiny sample, in turning a scientist's 'may be' into a confident 'is', in neglecting to refer back to another story last week that said exactly the opposite, the media unabashedly proclaim a strongly distorted version of the truth (also see Stocking, 1999: 24–27). Ironically, as Goldacre (2008: 220–21) notes:

> Nobody dumbs down the finance pages. I can barely understand most of the sports section. In the literature pull-out there are five-page-long essays which I find completely impenetrable, where the more Russian novelists you can rope in, the cleverer everyone thinks you are. I do not complain about this: I envy it.

It is interesting that science, of all subject areas, would be the one to be so stripped of its essence. The elimination of context from science articles has particular implications when it comes to health stories about new treatments, tests and products. The US website project HealthNewsReview.org assesses and marks health news coverage, alerting reporters to their marks. About two years and 500 articles into the project, continuous themes include reporters' failure to critically evaluate and report on costs, on the quality of the research evidence, on possible alternatives as well as on the complete scale of potential harms or benefits (Schwitzer, 2008).

Similarly, Moynihan *et al.* (2000) analysed the coverage of benefits and risks of medications in 180 newspaper articles and 27 television programmes in the US over the course of four years. They found that if benefits were at all quantitatively reported, they were mostly given only as relative benefits – which look a lot more impressive than absolute ones. Less than half indicated potential harm to patients. Ties of study authors to manufacturers of the researched drug, revealed in half of the academic papers, were mentioned in only 39 per cent of newspapers stories on these papers. Such practices, enhanced by the constant manic race against time, leave the door wide open for scientists and corporations keen to realise their own professional and commercial goals.

The scientific agenda

Culpability lies not alone with the media. Scientists may very well be pursuing their own agendas when communicating with the press – a venture that is easier than ever before if Davies' (2008) findings are anything to go by. The media have become vulnerable, especially to potentially doubtful material conveyed by wire copy and PR material. This is no different for science stories (Nelkin, 1995: 120–23). It might even be particularly true for specialist areas like science. As the health editor of *The Times*, Nigel Hawkes (cited in Davies, 2008: 59) noted:

> Almost everything is recycled from another source … Specialist writing is much easier, because the work is done by agencies and/or writers of press releases. Actually knowing enough to identify the stories is no longer important. The work has been deskilled.

This is exactly what the surveyed European reporters were asking for. The work is being done for them – as long as they don't care about accuracy or conflicts of interest. It seems any scientist, whether mainstream or maverick, wanting to make publicity for his research or even himself need only ask his press office to write something up and send it out to the various media (Russell, 1986 cited in Weigold, 2001; Gregory and Miller, 2000: 124).

Woloshin and Schwartz (2002) examined press releases sent out by nine high-profile academic journals, including the *British Medical Journal*, the *Journal of the American Medical Association* and *The Lancet*, over the course of six months. They found that seven of the journals routinely sent out press releases, following the same basic pattern: '[T]he journal editor or press office selects articles on the basis of perceived newsworthiness, and releases are written by press officers typically trained in communications.' Journal guidelines for the officers proscribed the length of the article but did not give instructions to point out study limitations or on how to present data. The examined press releases 'frequently presented data in exaggerated formats and failed to highlight study limitations or conflicts of interest'. Here, sensationalism begins before reporters even get their hands on the topic. Indeed, in some cases scientists may profit from sensationalist treatment of their research (Ransohoff and Ransohoff, 2001). Publicity in the mainstream press has been shown to also increase citations of their work in the scientific literature (Phillips *et al.*, 1991 cited in Ransohoff and Ransohoff, 2001) and public visibility is also commonly linked with a heightened chance of receiving research funding (Dunwoody and Scott, 1982 cited in Dunwoody, 1999: 74).

The media's vulnerability to such less-than-altruistic ploys from the scientific lines is amplified by the enormous trust that journalists place in the scientific community. In Hartz and Chappell's (1997) survey, 51 per cent of journalists professed 'a great deal of confidence in scientists', more so than in practitioners of the journalistic community. In Weiss and Singer's (1988 cited in Stocking, 1999: 25) analysis this trust went so far that a scientist's comment on his finding was usually accepted without question. Only rarely was a second opinion from another scientist sought. This kind of trust – which seems to make all double-checking unnecessary – also saves reporters the time needed to locate and interview other sources. Concurrently, it leaves scientists free to manipulate the journalistic community and highlights journalistic dependence on scientists (Gregory and Miller, 2000: 126). Science-related corporations are left free to exploit this dependency and trust by letting (well-paid) scientists do the work for them. Under the mantle of respectable science, they can then send their questionable press releases to media outlets, taking the process full-circle (Nelkin, 1995: 135; Moynihan and Cassels, 2005: 79–80).

Why it matters

Sadly, one cannot just leave scientists and journalists to muddle it out among themselves, because, ultimately, the affected party is the public. Once people leave school, the mass media become their main source of science information (Nelkin, 1995: 67; House of Lords, 2000). In its most practical form, this information should enable them to confidently navigate the world they live in and to make informed decisions (Eagly and Chaiken, 1993 cited in Griffin, 1999: 226). Lay members of the public consciously turn to the media where risks are concerned (Allan, 2002: 91), especially health risks (Freimuth *et al.*, 1987; Singer and Endreny, 1987 both cited in Griffin, 1999: 227; Nelkin, 1995: 68). Nelkin (1995: 68), in particular, illustrates this reliance on health information in the media well. She writes:

A National Cancer Institute Survey of how people become informed about ways to prevent cancer found that 63.3 percent get their information from magazines, 60 percent from newspapers, and 58.3 percent from television. Only 13 to 15 percent had talked to physicians about cancer prevention.

This public reliance places on the media the responsibility of '[sorting] empirical fact from junk science' when presenting their audience with different health-linked options (Freimuth *et al.*, 1987; Singer and Endreny, 1987 both cited in Griffin, 1999: 227).

Simultaneously, it places on them the power to construct their own reality of particular science issues because their daily work involves placing a frame onto the world. They choose the events, facts and actors they want to include within that frame and which are thus made known to their audience audience (Tuchman, 1978). Nelkin (1995) takes this idea of the frame from Hall (1979) and applies it specifically to the science media: 'Science writers ... [frame] social reality for their readers and [shape] the public consciousness about science-related events ... Their presentation of science news lays the foundation for personal attitudes and public actions' (Nelkin, 1995: 161). Similarly, Hornig Priest (1993 cited in Allan, 2002: 92–93) awards the media a key role in constructing risk, or risk perceptions, as they amplify selected points of view – typically 'those of established institutional news sources' – while letting other voices go unheard. Allan (2002: 95) emphasises the necessity to recognise that the taken-for-granted common sense reality of everyday life, and of media representations of daily life, is really a social construct that is strongly influenced by the media. Indeed, society

> can be grasped theoretically, empirically, and politically only if one starts from the premise that it is always a knowledge, media and information society at the same time – or, often enough as well, a society of non-knowledge and disinformation.
>
> (Beck, 2000 cited in Allan, 2002: 95)

Conclusion

To sum up, science journalism is the meeting point of two very different cultures. Although both scientists and journalists traditionally work towards the same goal, namely that of discovering the truth, they do so using very different practices and holding very different values. While science is deliberate, precise and reflective, journalism is fast, sometimes imprecise and keen on drama. These traditional dissimilarities are exacerbated by the increasingly corporate nature of both cultures, which gears them towards the pursuit of money rather than truth.

In journalism, money is most efficiently made by speeding up the writing process, at the expense of accuracy and veracity, to produce more stories, and by hyping those stories to lure in a bigger, sensation-hungry readership. That is, money is most efficiently made by an inattentive, hyperactive press.

Ambitious scientists and medico-scientific corporations, whether mainstream or maverick, can easily exploit this fast-paced news world to further their own goals. Whether they package their manipulated or enhanced research in press releases and PR material or convey it through a spokesperson in interviews, the press – with little time to verify the facts – is likely to faithfully and unquestioningly reproduce it for its readers.

It should again be noted here that the criticisms outlined in this chapter are, of course, generalisations. There are many capable science journalists who are aware of the pitfalls of their metier and do everything in their power to circumvent them. Blame lies not so much with individuals in the journalistic industry but rather with the increasingly corporate system that steadily reduces human resources as well as limiting the time available for any given assignment. It has been attempted here to point out the troubles with science reporting in order to raise awareness and, with that, take a first step towards addressing these troubles.

Notes

1 The survey did not state the size of the sample of media professionals. Several enquiries to the European Commission have not yet been answered at the time of submission for binding.
2 Davies (2008:133) explains further: 'The idea of balanced reporting has its roots in the most honourable of journalistic traditions. The convention grew from an era when hack journalists were willing to sell their editorial soul, to write partisan and distorted stories for the greater good of their wallets. In that context, it was a brave and necessary step for honest journalists to declare that they would show no favour, that they would be willing to tell the truth from all sides. Now, however, that context has changed, and the demand for balance has become a gateway through which spokesmen for the consensus are invited to enter our stories with their comments, regardless of whether or not they are false, distorted or propaganda. The honourable convention aimed at unearthing the facts has become a coward's compromise aimed at dispatching quick copy with which nobody will quarrel.'

Bibliography

Allan, S. (2002) *Media, Risk and Science*. Buckingham: Open University Press.

Brighton, P. and Foy, D. (2007) *News Values*. London: Sage Publications.

Conrad, P. (1999) 'Uses of Expertise: Sources, Quotes and Voice in the Reporting of Genetics in the News'. *Public Understanding of Science* 8: 285–302.

Davies, N. (2008) *Flat Earth News*. London: Chatto & Windus.

Dunwoody, S. (1986) 'The Scientist as Source'. In: Friedman S.M., Dunwoody, S. and Rogers, C.L. (eds.) *Scientists and Journalists: Reporting Science as News*. American Association for the Advancement of Science, pp. 3–16.

——(1999) 'Scientists, Journalists and the Meaning of Uncertainty'. In: Friedman S.M., Dunwoody, S. and Rogers C.L. (eds) *Communicating Uncertainty*. Mawah: Erlbaum, pp. 59–79.

European Commission (2007a) *European Research in the Media: The Researcher's Point of View* [online]. http://ec.europa.eu/research/conferences/2007/bcn2007/researchers_en.pdf [Accessed 7 June 2009].

——(2007b) *European Research in the Media: What Do Media Professionals Think?* [online]. http://ec.europa.eu/research/conferences/2007/bcn2007/journalists_en.pdf [Accessed 7 June 2009].

Friedman, S.M., Dunwoody, S. and Rogers, C.L. (eds) (1986) *Scientists and Journalists: Reporting Science as News*. American Association for the Advancement of Science.

Goldacre, B. (2008) *Bad Science*. London: Fourth Estate.

Gregory, J. and Miller, S. (2000) *Science in Public*. Cambridge: Basic Books.

Griffin, R.J. (1999) 'Using Systematic Thinking to Choose and Evaluate Evidence'. In: Friedman S.M., Dunwoody, S. and Rogers C.L. (eds) *Communicating Uncertainty*. Mawah: Erlbaum, pp. 225–48.

Hansen, A. (1994) 'Journalistic Practices and Science Reporting in the British Press'. *Public Understanding of Science* 3: 111–34.

Hartz, J. and Chappell, R. (1997) *Worlds Apart: How the Distance between Science and Journalism Threatens America's Future*. Nashville: First Amendment Centre.

Horton, R. (2000) 'Genetically Modified Food: Consternation, Confusion, and Crack-up'. *Medical Journal of Australia* 172: 148–49.

House of Lords (2000) 'Summary: Chapter 7'. *Science and Technology – Third Report* [online]. 23 February. www.publications.parliament.uk/pa/ld199900/ldselect/ldsctech/38/3801. htm [Accessed 13 June 2009].

Lehmkuhl, M. (ed.) (2008) *Science Journalism in Europe* 1. Bonn: Wissenschaftliche Pressekonferenz (WPK) e.V. & Dortmund University.

Moynihan, R., Bero, L., Ross-Degnan, D., Henry, D. (2000) 'Coverage by the news media of the benefits and risks of medications'. In *The New England Journal of Medicine* 342: 1645–50.

Moynihan, R. and Cassells, A. (2005) *Selling Sickness: How the World's Biggest Pharmaceutical Companies Are Turning Us All Into Patients*. New York: Avalon Publishing.

Nelkin, D. (1995) *Selling Science*. Revised edition. New York: WH Freeman and Company.

Ransohoff, D. F. and Ransohoff, R. M. (2001) 'Sensationalism in the Media: When Scientists and Journalists May Be Complicit Collaborators'. *Effective Clinical Practice* 4: 185–88.

Schwitzer, G. (2008) 'How Do US Journalists Cover Treatments, Tests, Products, and Procedures? An Evaluation of 500 Stories'. *PLoS Medicine* 5(5): 700–704.

Snow, C. P. (1963) *The Two Cultures: And a Second Look*. 2nd edn. Cambridge: Cambridge University Press.

Stocking, S. H. (1999) 'How Journalists Deal with Scientific Uncertainty'. In: Friedman S.M., Dunwoody, S. and Rogers, C.L. (eds.) *Communicating Uncertainty*. Mawah: Erlbaum, pp. 23–41.

Tuchman, G. (1978) *Making News: A Study in the Construction of Reality*. New York: The Free Press.

Weigold, M.F. (2001) 'Communicating Science: A Review of the Literature'. *Science Communication* 23(2): 164–93.

Woloshin, S. and Schwartz, L.M. (2002) 'Press Releases: Translating Research into News'. *Journal of the American Medical Association* 287(21): 2856–58.

13 Medical reporting

Robert Whitaker

When I first began covering medicine for a daily newspaper, back in 1989, I immediately felt that I had stumbled into unfamiliar journalistic terrain. The rules for doing the job well seemed quite different from when you report on politics, business, or general-assignment news. As a medical reporter, you interview physicians and researchers who are "experts" in their field – there is an implied deference in that word that is absent when you interview a politician or a business-person. You are then expected to get the expert to "explain" a medical finding and write about it in a manner that is "intelligible" and "interesting" to lay readers. It is almost as though a medical reporter is expected to put aside investigative reporting skills and instead become an able "translator" of information.

Here's how Thomas Linden, director of the Medical Journalism Program at the University of North Carolina, put it in an article published in 2003:

> To really own the medical beat, you need to know the subject matter. You don't need to be a scientist or a doctor, but you do need to understand how scientists think and be able to translate their jargon and their ideas into simple English.[1]

There is, of course, some truth in that recommendation. The medical reporter does need to become well versed in the subject matter, gain a working knowledge of statistics, and learn to explain complex biology and research findings in a clear, accurate manner. But that advice is incomplete. Medicine is not just a scientific enterprise, it is a business one too, and in order to report on that aspect of med-icine, a reporter needs to follow the usual advice. Don't trust everything you are told, follow the money, and do your best to dig up documents that reveal how this financial enterprise works. The medical journalist who writes about *science* and *business* – and reports on how the commercial forces influence the science – will provide readers with a much thorough understanding of this field.

The shadow cast by history

To fully understand the societal expectations that shape coverage of medicine today, we need to briefly revisit medicine's proud record of accomplishments during the first half of the twentieth century. This story of progress begins with the work of Robert Koch and Louis Pasteur, who proved in the 1870s that microbes caused infectious diseases. Their findings led German scientist Paul Ehrlich to conceive of finding "magic bullets" that could cure those diseases. In 1909, he synthesized a poison that could kill the microbe, *Spirocheta pallida*, which caused syphilis, and yet did not unduly harm the patient. "This was the magic bullet!" exulted science writer Paul de Kruif, in a 1926 bestseller. "And what a safe bullet!" The drug, Kruif added, produced "healing that could only be called Biblical."[2]

In 1935, Bayer chemical company provided medicine with its second miracle drug. Bayer discovered that sulfanilamide, which was a derivative of an old coal-tar compound, was fairly effective in eradicating staphylococcal and streptococcal infections. By that time, Alexander Fleming had already discovered penicillin, and during World War II, scientists in England and the United States developed methods for culturing bacteria-killing mold in large quantities, providing medicine with an even better antibiotic. Soon, pharmaceutical companies discovered other broad-acting antibiotics – streptomycin, Chloromycetin, and Aureomycin – that could cure pneumonia, scarlet fever, diphtheria, and a long list of other infectious diseases. "The age of healing miracles had come at last," wrote Louis Sutherland, in his book *Magic Bullets*.[3]

As the 1950s began, medicine could look back and count other successes as well. Pharmaceutical firms had developed improved anesthetics, sedatives, anti-histamines, and anticonvulsants, evidence of how scientists were getting better at synthesizing chemicals that acted on the central nervous system in helpful ways. In 1922, Eli Lilly had figured out how to extract the hormone insulin from the pancreas glands of slaughterhouse animals, and this provided doctors with an effective treatment for diabetes. Medicine was on a triumphant march, and in 1950, British scientist Sir Henry Dale, in a letter to the *British Medical Journal*, summed up this extraordinary moment in medicine's history:

> We who have been able to watch the beginning of this great movement may be glad and proud to have lived through such a time, and confident that an even wider and more majestic advance will be seen by those living through the fifty years now opening.[4]

The ink was barely dry on Dale's letter before Jonas Salk, on April 12, 1955, announced the successful results from his multinational trial of a polio vaccine for children. He was hailed as a "miracle worker," and a photo of this white-coated scientist graced the front pages of newspapers around the world. Moreover, when a television reporter asked Salk if he had patented his vaccine, he looked startled. "There is no patent. Could you patent the sun?" he replied. Salk was not just a miracle worker, but a selfless scientist too.

That is the past that provides a cultural context for reporting on medicine today. Reporters assigned to the beat are seen by society and by their editors as providing updates on a historically successful scientific enterprise, one populated by doctors devoted to improving medical care. Medical reporters tell of basic research that harbors hope for the future; of new discoveries being made of the biology of diseases; and of new and improved treatments that have been brought to market. Medical journalists labor under a long shadow cast by antibiotics and the white-coated figure of Jonas Salk.

Evolution of an unholy alliance

There is another history that medical reporters need to know, and it is the story of how the financial interests of physicians and pharmaceutical companies came to be aligned, at least in the United States. Although the financial interests of physicians and pharmaceutical companies in Canada and Europe may not be so closely aligned, much medical research originates in the United States, and thus reporters in other countries need to understand the financial forces at work in the U.S. The financial entanglements of medical researchers in the U.S. pose a problem for journalists everywhere reporting on the "progress of medicine."

In the early years of the twentieth century, the American Medical Association (AMA) set itself up as the organization that would help the American public distinguish good drugs from bad ones. Pharmaceutical companies did not have to prove to the federal government that its drugs were safe or effective, and so the AMA assumed the task of assessing these products. It set up a Council on Pharmacy and Chemistry to conduct tests of new agents, with the best drugs earning its "seal of approval." The AMA also published a "useful drugs" book each year, and its medical journals would not allow advertisements for any drug that had not passed its vetting process.

With this "watchdog" work, the AMA was both providing a valuable service to the public and furthering its members' financial interests. At that time, the public could go directly to a pharmacist to obtain a drug, and thus patients did not legally need a "prescription." But the AMA's drug evaluations provided patients with a good reason to visit a doctor. A physician, armed with the AMA's book of useful drugs, could prescribe an appropriate one. It was this knowledge, as opposed to any government-authorized prescribing power, that provided physicians with their value in the marketplace (in terms of providing access to medicines).

However, the selling of drugs in the United States began to change with the passage of the 1938 Food and Drug Cosmetics Act. The law required drug firms to prove to the Food and Drug Administration that their products were safe (they still did not have to prove that their drugs were helpful), and in its wake, the FDA began decreeing that certain medicines could be purchased only with a doctor's prescription. In 1951, Congress passed the Durham-Humphrey Amendment to the act, which decreed that most new drugs would be available by prescription only, and that prescriptions would be needed for refills too.

Physicians now enjoyed a very privileged place in American society. They controlled the public's access to antibiotics and other new medicines. In essence, they had become the retail vendors of these products, with pharmacists simply fulfilling their orders, and as vendors, they had financial reason to tout the wonders of their products. The better the new drugs were perceived to be, the more inclined the public would be to come to their offices to obtain a prescription. "It would appear that a physician's own market position is strongly influenced by his reputation for using the latest drugs," explained *Fortune* magazine.[5]

With the financial interests of the pharmaceutical industry and American physicians newly aligned, the AMA quickly abandoned its watchdog role. In 1952, it stopped publishing its yearly book on "useful drugs." Next, it began allowing advertisements in its journals for drugs that had not been approved by its Council on Pharmacy and Chemistry. In 1955, the AMA abandoned its famed "seal of acceptance" program. By 1957, it had cut the budget for its Council on Drugs to a paltry $75,000, which was understandable, given that it was no longer in the business of assessing the merits of these products. The AMA, in its relationship to the pharmaceutical industry, had "become what I would call sissy," confessed Harvard Medical School professor Maxwell Finland.[6]

Indeed, following the passage of the Durham-Humphrey Amendment, the American medical community began collaborating with the pharmaceutical industry to promote new drugs. In 1951, Smith Kline and French and the AMA began jointly producing a television program called *The March of Medicine*, which helped introduce Americans to the many "wonder" drugs that were coming to market. In addition, newspaper and magazine articles about new medications inevitably included testimonials from doctors touting their benefits. "Virtually all important drugs," explained *FDC reports*, an industry trade publication, receive "lavish praise by the medical profession on introduction."[7]

This new storytelling partnership proved to be a very profitable one for all parties involved. Drug industry revenues topped $1 billion in 1957, the pharmaceutical companies enjoying earnings that made them "the darlings of Wall Street," one writer observed. The AMA's revenues from drug advertisements in its journals rose from $2.5 million in 1950 to $10 million in 1960. And now that physicians controlled access to antibiotics and other prescription drugs, their incomes began to climb rapidly, doubling from 1950 to 1970 (after adjusting for inflation).

The co-opting of academic medicine

Even in the new financial environment wrought by the 1951 Durham-Humphrey Amendment, many academic physicians in the United States, in the following decades, did maintain their distance from pharmaceutical companies. They looked to the National Institutes of Health to fund their research efforts, and when pharmaceutical companies asked them to conduct trials of experimental drugs, they generally insisted on the right to help design the studies and to freely publish the study results. But during the 1980s, psychiatrists at academic medical schools began to accept money from drug companies to give speeches, and that practice, which is so corrosive to the honest dissemination of medical information, eventually spread to other disciplines as well.

Psychiatry's salesmen

In 1974, the American Psychiatric Association formed a task force to assess the importance of pharmaceutical support for its future. The answer was "very," and in 1980 that led the APA to institute a policy change of transformative importance. Previously, pharmaceutical companies had regularly put up fancy exhibits at the APA's annual meeting and paid for social events, but they hadn't been allowed to put on "scientific" talks. However, in 1980, the APA's board of directors voted to allow pharmaceutical companies to start sponsoring scientific symposiums at its annual meeting. The drug firms paid the APA a fee for this privilege, and soon the most well-attended events at its annual meeting were the industry-funded symposiums, which provided the attendees a sumptuous meal and featured presentations by a "panel of experts." The speakers were paid handsomely to give the talks, and the drug companies made certain that their presentations went off without a hitch. "These symposia are meticulously prepared with rehearsals before the meeting, and they have excellent audio-visual content," explained the APA's Melvin Sabshin.[8]

For pharmaceutical companies, the beauty of this arrangement was that they could use these academic doctors to build a market for their drugs (i.e., use them as salesmen), even while the doctors considered themselves "independent" and were presented to the public as such. And once this sleight-of-hand marketing door opened, the pharmaceutical companies exploited it to the maximum. They began paying academic psychiatrists to speak at conferences and continuing education programs throughout the year, and to serve as "advisors" and "consultants." The drug companies found multiple ways to funnel money to academic psychiatrists, whom they dubbed "thought leaders," and they found this practice so commercially useful that, during the 1990s, they offered money to virtually every academic psychiatrist in the United States. As a result, in 2000, when the *New England Journal of Medicine* tried to find an "expert" to write an editorial on depression, it "found very few who did not have financial ties to drug companies that make antidepressants."[9]

Thanks to a 2008 investigation by Iowa senator Charles Grassley, we now have some sense of the amount of pharmaceutical money flowing to psychiatry's "thought leaders." Here are a few examples:

- Between 2000 and 2007, Charles Nemeroff, who was chair of the psychiatry department at Emory Medical School in Atlanta, earned at least $2.8 million for his services to the pharmaceutical industry. GlaxoSmithKline paid him $960,000 to promote Paxil and Wellbutrin.[10]
- Frederick Goodwin, a former director of the National Institute of Mental Health, received $1.2 million from 2000 to 2008 as a member of GlaxoSmithKline's speaker bureau, primarily to promote mood stabilizers.[11]
- Forest Laboratories paid Jeffrey Bostic, a child psychiatrist at Massachusetts General Hospital in Boston, $750,000 from 1999 to 2006 to promote the prescribing of Celexa and Lexapro to children and adolescents.[12]

- Joseph Biederman, a child psychiatrist at Harvard Medical School, received $1.6 million from pharmaceutical companies for his various services from 2000 to 2007. Much of this money came from Janssen, the maker of an atypical antipsychotic that Biederman recommended as a treatment for juvenile bipolar disorder.[13]

As a result of this co-opting of American psychiatry, medical reporters in the United States today have a difficult time finding "experts" who will speak freely about the benefits and risks of psychiatric medications. In truth, when they interview psychiatrists from academic medical schools, they are likely to be speaking with physicians paid, in essence, to tell a positive story about the drugs.

The rest of academic medicine follows suit

Industry's co-opting of academic physicians in other disciplines in the United States is not as pronounced as it is in psychiatry. But it is a recognized problem, with the former editor-in-chief of the *New England Journal of Medicine*, Jerome Kassirer, observing in 2005 that thanks to "payoffs" from drug companies, "joining the ranks of academic medicine [today] can be a ticket to great wealth and privilege."[14] This larger corruption of American medicine, extending to nearly every discipline, was spurred on by two factors.

First, in 1980, Congress passed the Bayh-Dole Act, which allowed universities to patent discoveries from research sponsored by the National Institutes of Health, and to grant exclusive licenses to drug companies to commercialize those discoveries. When such deals were struck, the individual researchers and their institutions often retained an ownership stake in the product, and thus the Bayh-Dole Act transformed academic medicine into the entrepreneurial partner of the drug industry.

Second, in the late 1980s, the clinical trials industry in the United States changed. Up until that time, pharmaceutical companies primarily relied on academic doctors to conduct clinical trials of their new drugs, and since the supply of academic doctors was limited, these physicians had the upper hand in their negotiations with drug companies. They could insist on a fair degree of scientific independence as they conducted industry-funded trials. However, during the late 1980s, community physicians began to see their incomes curbed by the rise of health maintenance organizations, and in order to replace their lost earning power, many became interested in participating in multi-site clinical trials of new drugs. These physicians promised the drug companies they would recruit patients quickly, and leave study design and data analysis up to them. The supply of "clinical investigators" in the United States suddenly expanded, which provided the drug companies with a new leverage over academic physicians. They told the academic doctors that if they wanted to get industry "grants," they would have to become more "cooperative" and more "service oriented." The drug companies delivered this message at the same time that many academic physicians were finding it increasingly difficult to get funding from the National Institutes of Health, and so the academic doctors changed their tune. They would now work with the pharmaceutical companies in a much more "collaborative" manner.

The end result of these two developments – the passage of the Bayh-Dole Act and the transformation of the clinical testing of drugs in the United States – was that academic medicine, as the *New England Journal of Medicine* observed in a 2000 editorial, allowed itself to be bought. Physicians at prestigious medical schools, the journal explained,

> serve as consultants to companies whose products they are studying, join advisory boards and speakers' bureaus, enter into patent and royalty arrangements, agree to be the listed authors of articles ghostwritten by interested companies, promote drugs and devices at company-sponsored symposiums, and allow themselves to be plied with expensive gifts and trips to luxurious settings.[15]

Or as Kassirer wrote in his 2005 book, many academic doctors were now "on the take."

The challenge for reporters

It is easy to see why these two twin currents – the history of medical success in the past and the buying of academic physicians in the present – pose such a problem for medical journalists. The past successes of medicine prompt reporters to write stories that tell of progress in the field, with editors – and the public – expecting such news as well. However, the financial landscape is one that encourages the academic "experts" to tell an exaggerated – or even false – story of progress to reporters. This is a combustible mix that puts journalists into the position of writing stories that lead society astray, particularly in terms of the public's understanding of the risks and merits of new drugs (and other medical therapies). When academic physicians are shilling for a product, medical journalists can become a conduit for "misinformation," and in order to see an example of that, we can look at the stories that were written about atypical antipsychotics when they came to market in the 1990s.

Psychiatry's new miracle drugs

Thorazine, haloperidol, and other "first-generation" antipsychotics, which are often called "standard neuroleptics," work by powerfully blocking dopamine receptors in the brain. The first atypical antipsychotic, clozapine, was synthesized in the 1970s, and it was said to be "atypical" because it blocked receptors for serotonin, dopamine, and several other neurotransmitters. It acted more broadly on the brain than the old drugs did. While it showed much promise in clinical studies, it was found to cause agranulocytosis, a potentially fatal side effect, and in 1989, the U.S. Food and Drug Administration approved it only for patients who didn't respond to standard neuroleptics. Pharmaceutical companies then sought to develop "atypical" agents that would provide clozapine's benefits but without causing agranulocytosis, and in 1993, Janssen obtained approval for the first such drug, risperidone (marketed as Risperdal).

As the drug came to market, more than 20 reports appeared in the scientific literature attesting to its merits. Risperidone was said to be equal or superior to haloperidol in reducing positive symptoms (psychosis), and superior to haloperidol in improving negative symptoms (lack of emotion). Researchers reported that it reduced hospital stays, improved patients' ability to function socially, and reduced hostility. Best of all, the incidence of extrapyramidal symptoms with risperidone was said to be "equal to placebo."[16] This meant that risperidone didn't cause the Parkinsonian symptoms that the old standard neuroleptics did.

The media presented risperidone in even more glowing terms. This new drug, the *Washington Post* reported, "represents a glimmer of hope for a disease that until recently had been considered hopeless." Risperidone, it said, did not "cause sedation, blurred vision, impaired memory or muscle stiffness, side effects commonly associated with an earlier generation of antipsychotic drugs." George Simpson, a physician at the Medical College of Pennsylvania, told the *Post*: "The data is very convincing. It is a new hope, and at this moment it appears, like clozapine, to be different from all existing drugs."[17] The *New York Times*, quoting Richard Meibach, Janssen's clinical research director, reported that "no major side effects" had appeared in any of the 2,000-plus patients who had been in the clinical trials. The *Times* also provided its readers with a diagram of how risperidone worked. "Researchers," it said, think that drugs like risperidone "relieve schizophrenia symptoms by blocking excessive flows of serotonin or dopamine, or both."[18]

Psychiatry and medicine had clearly taken a great leap forward. The news was so positive that Janssen won the prestigious Prix Galien for its new drug, an international award touted as the pharmaceutical industry's Nobel Prize.

But the atypicals "revolution" was just getting underway. In 1996, Eli Lilly brought olanzapine to market, selling it as Zyprexa, and the academic physicians it had paid to conduct the trials hailed it as even better than risperidone. Olanzapine, they reported, worked in a more "comprehensive" manner than either risperidone or haloperidol. It was a well-tolerated agent that led to remarkable global improvement – it reduced positive symptoms, caused fewer motor side effects than either risperidone or haloperidol, and improved negative symptoms and cognitive function. It reduced hospital stays, prevented relapse, and was useful for treatment-resistant schizophrenia.[19]

Apparently, yet another step up the therapeutic ladder had been taken. Olanzapine, the *Wall Street Journal* announced, has "substantial advantages" over other current therapies. "Zyprexa is a wonderful drug for psychotic patients," said John Zajecka, at Rush Medical College in Chicago. Harvard Medical School's William Glazer told the *Wall Street Journal*: "The real world is finding that Zyprexa has fewer extrapyramidal side effects than Risperdal."[20] Stanford University psychiatrist Alan Schatzberg was even more enthusiastic in an interview with *The New York Times*: "It's a potential breakthrough of tremendous magnitude."[21] On and on it went, the glowing remarks piling up, and finally Laurie Flynn, executive director of the National Alliance for the Mentally Ill, put an exclamation point on the story: "These new drugs truly are a breakthrough. They mean we should finally be able to keep people out of the hospital, and it means that the long-term disability of schizophrenia can come to an end."[22]

Soon, AstraZeneca brought a third atypical, quetiapine, to market, and this time the media warmed to the idea that all of these new "atypicals" were markedly better than the old ones. The atypicals, *Parade* magazine told its readers, were "far safer and more effective in treating negative symptoms, such as difficulty in reasoning and speaking in an organized way."[23] The newer drugs, explained the *Chicago Tribune*, "are safer and more effective than older ones. They help people go to work."[24] Or as the *Los Angeles Times* put it: "It used to be that schizophrenics were given no hope of improving. But now, thanks to new drugs and commitment, they are moving back into society like never before."[25]

This was a story of progress that fit neatly into the larger history of medicine that had unfolded over the past 100 years. New wonder drugs for madness had arrived, which apparently put multiple neurotransmitter pathways back into "balance," and at last this old scourge could be tamed. Sales of the new atypicals soared, in the United States and abroad, and since they were touted as safe, American psychiatrists began prescribing them to people of all ages, including children, and for many off-label conditions, including bipolar disorder. In 2008, antipsychotic medications – a class of drugs that in the old days of Thorazine and Haldol had been seen as extremely problematic, useful only in severely ill patients – were the top revenue-producing class of drugs in the United States, ahead even of the popular cholesterol-lowing agents.

Government documents tell a different story

After the atypicals came to market, I reported on these new drugs in two journalistic forums. First, in a 1998 series I co-wrote for the *Boston Globe*, I told of how the scientific reports of the atypicals, which said that these drugs were so safe, failed to report that one in every 145 people given the drugs in the trials had *died*, often from suicide. I got this information through a freedom of information request to the FDA for its reviews of risperidone, olanzapine, and quetiapine. Next, in a 2002 book, *Mad in America*, I detailed how the FDA, in its review of the clinical trial results for the atypicals, did not find that the new drugs were safer or more effective than the old ones.

Janssen conducted two "well-controlled" trials that compared risperidone to haldol.[26] In the first one, which involved 523 patients at 26 sites in the United States and Canada, four doses of risperidone were compared to a 20-milligram dose of haloperidol. Janssen maintained that this study showed that risperidone, at an optimal dose of six milligrams daily, was superior to haloperidol, which was the conclusion published in medical journals. However, the FDA reviewers noted that Janssen had used a single, high dose of haloperidol for comparison, a dose that "may have exceeded the therapeutic window" for many patients, and thus the study was "incapable by virtue of its design of supporting any externally valid conclusion about the relative performance of haloperidol and Risperdal."

In the second study, which involved 1,557 patients in 15 foreign countries, Janssen compared five doses of risperidone to a 10-milligram dose of haloperidol. Janssen claimed that this study showed that its drug was "more effective than haloperidol in reducing symptoms of psychosis," but once again, FDA reviewers noted that the study was "incapable" of making any meaningful comparison between the two drugs. Janssen had compared multiple doses of its drug to one dose of haloperidol, and in order to honestly compare two drugs, an equal number of "equieffective" doses must be tested, as otherwise the study unfairly favors the drug that is given in multiple doses. Such trial design, the FDA reminded Janssen, is "a critical preliminary step to any valid comparison of their properties."

As for risperidone's safety profile, the trials had shown it to be a very problematic drug. Although *The New York Times* informed its readers that "no major side effects" had appeared in any of the 2,000 patients given the drugs, in fact 84 patients had experienced a "serious adverse event," which the FDA defined as a life-threatening event, or one that required hospitalization. Moreover, the incidence of adverse events in risperidone patients and haloperidol patients was roughly the same. Seventy-five percent of risperidone patients experienced at least one adverse event, compared to 79 percent of haloperidol patients. The public had also been led to believe that this new drug didn't cause extrapyramidal symptoms (EPS), but, in truth, even on a moderate dose of risperidone, 17 percent of the patients suffered this side effect, and at a higher dose, one-third of the patients did, which was about the same incidence of EPS seen in patients treated with a high dose of haloperidol. "It remains to be seen how risperidone compares with other antipsychotics with regard to EPS, as haloperidol is at the high end of the spectrum," the FDA concluded.

In its final letter of approval to Janssen, the FDA made explicit its conclusions about the relative merits of risperidone and haloperidol. Robert Temple, director of the FDA's Office of Drug Evaluation, told Janssen:

> We would consider any advertisement or promotion labeling for RISPERDAL false, misleading, or lacking fair balance under section 502 (a) and 502 (n) of the ACT if there is presentation of data that conveys the impression that risperidone is superior to haloperidol or any other marketed antipsychotic drug product with regard to safety or effectiveness.[27]

However – and this shows why it is so beneficial for pharmaceutical companies to hire academic physicians to be their "speakers" and "advisors" – the FDA can't control what physicians report in their medical articles or say to the press, and so Janssen's "thought leaders" continued to inform the public that risperidone had been shown to be better than haloperidol in the clinical trials. The academic physicians told a story that the FDA had explicitly banned from advertisements as false.

The FDA's review of olanzapine struck many of the same notes.[28] Eli Lilly's studies of its new drug were "biased against haloperidol" in much the same way than Janssen's had been. Multiple doses of olanzapine were compared to one dose of haloperidol, and the drugs were not compared at "equieffective" doses. In addition, many of the patients in the trials had previously taken haloperidol and had not responded well to it, and including such "bad responders," the FDA officials concluded, made it likely that results for haloperidol would be worse than normal, and thus help make olanzapine look superior by comparison. "The sample of patients used is an inappropriate choice" for comparison, they wrote. Eli Lilly's investigators, in their published reports in medical journals, had detailed the results from a large phase III trial, involving 1,996 patients, as evidence of olanzapine's benefits, but the FDA concluded that it was "fundamentally flawed" in its design, and thus "provides little useful efficacy data."

As for olanzapine's safety profile, of the 2,500 patients who received the drug in the trials, 20 died. Twelve killed themselves, and two of the remaining eight deaths, both from "aspiration pneumonia," were seen by FDA reviewers as possibly causally related to olanzapine. Twenty-two percent of the olanzapine patients suffered a "serious" adverse event, compared to 18 percent of the haloperidol patients. Two thirds of the olanzapine patients didn't successfully complete the trials. Weight gain was a common problem for olanzapine patients, and other common side effects included Parkinson's, akathisia, dystonia, hypotension, constipation, tachycardia, diabetic complications, seizures, increases in serum prolactin (which may cause leaking breasts and impotence), and liver abnormalities. This was a long list of vexing side effects, and the FDA even warned that given olanzapine's broad action on multiple receptor types, "no one should be surprised if, upon marketing, events of all kinds and severity not previously identified are reported in association with olanzapine's use."

The FDA reviews were quite clear: both Janssen and Eli Lilly had employed biased trial designs to make their new drugs look better than haloperidol, and those trials did not provide any evidence that atypicals were better than existing drugs. The FDA reviews of the clinical trial data made it clear that pharmaceutical companies and their "thought leaders" had told a false story in their scientific articles and to the press.

The Lancet asks a question

While FDA reviewers dismissed the clinical trials of risperidone and olanzapine as biased and flawed, approving the drugs only because they showed some degree of benefit over placebo in curbing psychotic symptoms, there remained the possibility that the new drugs, in properly designed trials, would still prove superior to haloperidol or one of the other older drugs. Three government-funded studies assessed that possibility. In a 2003 trial conducted by the U.S. Department of Veterans Affairs, which compared olanzapine to haloperidol, the researchers reported that "there were no significant differences between groups in study retention (compliance); positive, negative, or total symptoms of schizophrenia; quality of life; or extrapyramidal symptoms."[29] Two years later, in a study that compared a standard neuroleptic to four atypicals, the National Institute of Mental Health concluded there was no "significant differences in measures of effectiveness" between any of the drugs.[30] Finally, investigators funded by the British government announced that in 2006 and 2007 that they too had found that atypicals were no more effective than the old standard neuroleptics, and that, if anything, schizophrenia patients on the older drugs enjoyed "higher quality-adjusted life-years."[31]

These sobering results proved rather embarrassing to psychiatry. "The claims of superiority for the second generation agents were greatly exaggerated ... (they) are not the great breakthroughs in therapeutics they were once thought to be," confessed Jeffrey Lieberman, a professor of psychiatry at Columbia University Medical School, in 2007.[32] In 2009, *The Lancet*, in an article titled "the spurious advance of antipsychotic drug therapy," summed up the story in this way:

> As a group, (the atypicals) are no more efficacious, do not improve specific symptoms, have no clearly different side-effect profiles than the first-generation antipsychotics, and are less cost-effective. The spurious invention of the atypicals can now be regarded as invention only, cleverly manipulated by the drug industry for marketing purposes and only now being exposed. But how is that for nearly two decades we have, as some have put it, "been beguiled" into thinking that they were superior?[33]

There is an easy answer to that question. The pharmaceutical companies making these drugs paid academic psychiatrists to serve as their "thought leaders," and these psychiatrists signed off on trials that were biased by design, and then they hyped the results from those studies in the medical literature. And when these "experts" were interviewed by medical journalists, they upped the exaggeration another notch.

The challenge for medical journalists

In this essay, I have sought to make one basic point. Medical journalists, when they report on medical research, are writing about an endeavor that has produced great advances in the past, and will undoubtedly continue to produce future successes. That preps them to tell a story of progress. At the same time, industry's co-opting of academic medicine in the United States (and increasingly its co-opting of academic physicians in Europe and other parts of the world) is corrupting this endeavor. Trials are biased by design, results are spun, and ghostwritten articles populate the medical journals. While journalists covering medicine do need to report on advances in the field, they also need to report on the financial forces that are corrupting this scientific enterprise, and to find ways to check the veracity of what they are told by "experts."

This latter task, of course, can be approached in the usual ways: follow the money, read the published studies to see if the data supports the story being told by the "experts," and dig up documents from government sources and legal proceedings. The seasoned medical reporter today needs to both be an able "translator" of information and a dogged investigative journalist in order to do the job well.

Notes

1 T. Linden, "Learning to be a medical journalist," *Nieman Reports*, Summer 2003.
2 P. De Kruif, *Dr. Ehrlich's Magic Bullet* (New York: Pocket Books, 1940), 387.
3 L. Sutherland, *Magic Bullets* (Boston: Little, Brown and Company, 1956), 127.
4 T. Mahoney, *The Merchants of Life* (New York: Harper & Brothers, 1959), 14.
5 M. Mintz, *The Therapeutic Nightmare* (Boston: Houghton Mifflin, 1965), 166.
6 Ibid., 488.
7 Ibid., 59, 62.
8 M. Sabshin, *Changing American Psychiatry* (Washington, D.C.: American Psychiatric Publishing, Inc. 2008), 194.
9 M. Angel, "Is academic medicine for sale?" *New England Journal of Medicine* 342 (2000):1516–18.
10 J. Pereira, "Emory professor steps down," *Wall Street Journal*, December 23, 2008.
11 G. Harris, "Radio host has drug company ties," *New York Times*, November 22, 2008.
12 L. Kowalczyk, "US cites Boston psychiatrist in case vs. drug firm," *Boston Globe*, March 6, 2009.
13 G. Harris, "Researchers fail to reveal full drug pay," *New York Times*, June 8, 2008.
14 J. Kassirer, *On the Take* (New York: Oxford University Press, 2005), xiii.
15 Angel, ibid.
16 S. Marder, "Risperidone in the treatment of schizophrenia," *American Journal of Psychiatry* 151 (1994):825–35. G. Chouinard. "A Canadian multicenter placebo-controlled study of fixed doses of risperidone and haloperidol in the treatment of chronic schizophrenic patients," *Journal of Clinical Psychopharmacology* 13 (1993):25–40. For Janssen advertisement touting risperidone's EPS as being safe as a placebo, see *American Journal of Psychiatry* 151 (1994).
17 "New hope for schizophrenia," *Washington Post*, Feb. 16, 1993.
18 "Seeking safer treatments for schizophrenia," *New York Times*, January 15, 1992.
19 C. Beasley, "Efficacy of olanzapine," *Journal of Clinical Psychiatry* 58, supplement 10 (1997):7–12.
20 "Psychosis drug from Eli Lilly racks up gains," *Wall Street Journal*, April 14, 1998.
21 "A new drug for schizophrenia wins approval from the FDA," *New York Times*, October 2, 1996,
22 Ibid.
23 "Schizophrenia, close-up of the troubled brain," *Parade*, November 21, 1999.
24 "Mental illness aid," *Chicago Tribune*, June 4, 1999.
25 "Lives recovered," *Los Angeles Times*, January 30, 1996.
26 FDA reviews of risperidone data included reviews by Andrew Mosholder, May 11, 1993 and November 7, 1993; David Hoberman, April 20, 1993; and Thomas Laughren, December 20, 1993.
27 Approval letter from Robert Temple to Janssen Research Foundation, December 29, 1993.
28 FDA reviews of olanzapine data include reviews by Thomas Laughren on September 27, 1996; by Paul Andreason on July 29 and September 26, 1996; and by Paul Leber on August 18 and August 30, 1996.
29 R. Rosenheck, "Effectiveness and cost of olanzapine and haloperidol in the treatment of schizophrenia," *JAMA* 290 (2003):2693–2702.
30 J. Lieberman, "Effectiveness of antipsychotic drugs in patients with schizophrenia," *New England Journal of Medicine* (2005):1209–33. R. Rosenheck, "Cost-effectiveness of second-generation antipsychotics and perphenazine in a randomized trial of treatment for chronic schizophrenia," *American Journal of Psychiatry* 163 (2006):2080–89.
31 L. Davies, "Cost-effectiveness of first-v. second-generation antipsychotic drugs," *British Journal of Psychiatry* 191 (2007):14–22.
32 J. Lieberman, "Comparative effectiveness of antipsychotic drugs," *Archives of General Psychiatry* 63 (2006):1069–71.
33 P. Tyrer, "The spurious advance of antipsychotic drug therapy," *The Lancet* 373 (2009):4–5.

14 Legal affairs journalism

Richard Orange

It should go without saying that legal affairs as a specialist topic is distinct from court and crime reporting. It is simpler to establish clear blue water between legal affairs from crime reporting because criminal law forms only one element of law. Newspapers and broadcasters will have dedicated crime correspondents as well as court reporters. The distinction between legal affairs and court reporting is less clear cut, but both require particular skills, knowledge and expertise. Fundamentally, the task of the legal affairs correspondent is to explain how the law operates and why certain judgments have been reached. Comment and criticism come into play. Crime and court reporters have a different agenda and function.

Legal affairs embraces non-contentious relationships between individuals, companies or organisations, contentious civil litigation and criminal investigations/ prosecutions. The latter should be familiar territory for media students and trainee journalists. The police charge a suspect with a crime. There is a guilty or not guilty plea. There is a trial or a plea in mitigation. There is an acquittal or a sentence. Court reporting rules govern what information may be published at the time. Court reporters mainly regurgitate what is put before the courts. Legal affairs specialists are expected to offer educated and informed views on the law. That might be to comment on the progress of legislation (statute and common law) and to explain the respective rights, remedies and obstacles facing litigants and defendants (in the criminal and civil courts or tribunals). It may be to highlight discrepancies and absurdities in the legal system, to identify failings in the civil and family court procedure, or to take ministers to task over the scope and impact of legislative reforms.

One key difference between civil and criminal law is that once a suspect is charged with an offence it is taken as read that the matter will go to court (subject to the proviso that a suspect is not dealt with by way of police caution or that the Crown Prosecution Service drops the matter). However, civil law operates inside and outside court. The vast majority of actions are dealt with outside. About three per cent of claims filed to court and served on defendants/respondents actually proceed to trial. A number are abandoned or struck out for substantive or technical reasons, but the majority are settled by negotiation, arbitration or mediation. Contentious litigation tends to be dropped or settled out of sight and hearing of court reporters – regardless of merit or value or newsworthiness.

It is against that background that London national newspaper campaigns against 'secret justice' need to be set. The principle that cases may be settled by and subject to confidentiality clauses regardless of 'public interest' factors is not alien to the British legal system. Civil litigation is conducted between private parties, regardless of any 'public interest' flavour. Only a minority of cases get to trial. Any number are dealt with in judges' chambers, with limited press access. Fewer achieve the status of 'leading authorities', mainly because they clarify untested points of law or set out tests by which future claims may be resolved. These are often technical in nature and therefore of negligible interest to the tabloids.

However, civil proceedings are more complex, and outside the scope of most court reporting modules on media courses which have a heavy bias towards the magistrates, crown court and criminal appeal court procedures. The Woolf Reforms of the civil procedure system (CPR) in the late 1990s prompted a fundamental rewriting of the rules governing the treatment and disposal of claims – including libel and privacy actions. Law students are required to know their way around the CPR, in considerable detail. Compliance with the CPR is critical when it comes to determining which side pays the expensive court costs once the trial is over. This is an important issue as any publisher or broadcaster with experience of litigation will know. But few 'hackademics' will refer their students to the CPR on media training courses, and there is little scope for in-house training for employees.

There is also a lack of detailed legal training on university courses, not least because of demand. There are insufficient employment opportunities for legal affairs specialists. Only a handful of London-based titles employ dedicated reporters in the field. Solicitor Joshua Rozenberg (now with the *Guardian* and BBC, and previously with the *Daily Telegraph*), legal affairs editor Frances Gibb at *The Times* and qualified lawyer Mike Dodd at the Press Association, are highly regarded commentators and analysts. The mantle 'court reporter' would not sit well with their brief or range.

There are job opportunities in the trade press for newshounds with a taste for the subject. London-based publications such as *Legal Week*, *The Lawyer* and *The Law Society Gazette* provide an alternative opening for skilled reporters. However, these publications tend to tailor coverage at practitioners rather than 'lay readers', with an emphasis on executive profiles, key personnel changes and corporate affairs. Trade publications generally steer clear of 'investigative journalism' because publishers chase a niche advertising pool and are anxious to retain regular clients. It follows this chapter is a study of a specialism seriously under-represented in the mainstream media. This is freely acknowledged. The purpose is to highlight the consequences of entrusting 'legal affairs' to crime journalists, general reporters and court correspondents, without insisting or ensuring the writers are sufficiently trained to deal with the brief.

Dodd advises students and journalists with an interest in legal affairs to consider the one-year full-time or two-year part-time Graduate Diploma in Law course, after completing undergraduate media degrees. He said:

> If you are not a qualified lawyer and don't have a degree in law then it is good idea to take a course. You will understand contract, tort, criminal law, European Union law, English legal methods and the civil court rules.[1]

Gone are the days when journalists could rely on the watchful eye of the in-house lawyer. The legal and the publishing landscapes have changed. More journalists are self-employed, blog, tweet, self-publish and have limited access to in-house solicitors. Readers' online comments may be published without vetting. Litigation does not always follow publication. It need not matter that a media lawyer has approved an article for publication. Mistakes made by a reporter in the initial stages of an investigation can be scrutinised by the courts. Media training courses have not moved with the times. Journalism graduates get a piecemeal overview of 'media law'. Lectures and seminars may be taught either by legal academics or by non-legally qualified media tutors. Courses can be overly weighted towards production skills at the expense of academic study. The result is that too many editorial staff (at all levels) possess an inferior knowledge of the law than teenage undergraduates on LLB courses. Does this matter?

There are cautionary tales about the pitfalls of sending untrained journalists into court to cover hearings. One national London newspaper, the *Guardian*, got into trouble in February 2012 when a sports reporter attending a criminal trial of a prominent England football manager tweeted information that had not been made known to the jury. Dodd said:

> Sports journalists are used to people saying all sorts of things about each other and they just report it that way. But you need to have someone able to tell the difference between that situation and one where there a risk of a contempt of court. It (the *Guardian* tweet) was ridiculous. I have said to journalists: If you are going to cover criminal proceedings then leave it to the general news staff or check what you can and cannot write.

News reporters are expected to know the rules about reporting restrictions for criminal trials, and to keep a copy of McNae's *Essential Law for Journalists* (Hanna and Dodd, Oxford University Press, currently in 21st edition 2012) or Frances Quinn's *Law for Journalists* (Quinn, Longman Pearson, currently in 3rd edition 2011) to hand. But these texts are also thin on information about civil court proceedings. Joshua Rozenberg said:

> I do share a concern that if a reporter does not understand that what they are doing, or that they do not know the difference between the civil and criminal courts, then they are going to have problems. I speak to young producers in television who do not seem to grasp the differences. Another example is where journalists confuse the European Court of Justice with the European Court of Human Rights. We have also had examples of journalists getting Lord Justice Leveson's name wrong. He is not Lord Leveson. It is incorrect and the legal profession tends to notice these errors.

The theme of this chapter is that a lack of detailed knowledge of the civil court process does not appear to act as a disincentive to journalists and their editors. Newspapers appear to be more than ready to instruct non-legally qualified reporters to plunge into the unfamiliar world of civil law, and indulge in impassioned and colourful commentary on the rights and wrongs of litigation. There are horrors awaiting those who become entangled in disputes with neighbours, businesses, lawyers, administrators, landlords or tenants, insurance firms, health services, estate agents and local councils. A favourite ploy deployed by public sector PR staff is that people who sue the National Health Service, councils or their local police are diverting public funds from patients, social services and constabularies. All journalists need to do is identify what money is 'ring fenced' in annual budgets for future litigation actions and settlements to bust that line. Likewise, if newsdesks decide to cover judicial review hearings, employment appeals tribunals and county court applications then journalists despatched to hearings need to be adequately briefed about the function and remit of the respective courts. Hearings for applications for judicial review are distinct from full judicial review hearings. Outcomes and settlements need not result in one side 'winning' or 'losing' – which is a difficult concept for court reporters used to handling criminal trials. One of the purposes of a judicial review is to enable a judge to interpret and explain how the law applies to the different parties. A similar journalistic error may arise where disgruntled protestors threaten to 'judicially review' a controversial action by a local authority, only to have the claim rejected at either first or second stage. It does not mean that the judge has given permission for the council to (for example) sell off playing fields to a housing developer. It means the council has acted within its powers but that does not mean that the protestors have 'lost' their campaign. Another common mistake on the part of newsdesks and inexperienced reporters is to assume that the procedure by which a domestic court may refer a question about European Union regulations to the European Court of Justice, means that the hearing is being transferred to Brussels. A legally-trained journalist should know that the ECJ's role here is to provide guidance on an area of uncertainty to the domestic court – and that the advice need not be binding on the 'local' court.

Where do (or where should) journalists obtain reliable information? One source is the Internet. Official sites provide extensive judicial interpretation of the common law, access to Law Commission reports and authoritative statute texts. Journalists are well advised to trawl subscription sites carrying commentaries on current topics, including critiques of Ministry of Justice proposals, Parliamentary bills and judicial/tribunal decisions, penned by barristers and solicitors. Many of these sites use technical language and are heavily referenced in case law with limited explanations for the lay-reader. Legal affairs correspondents may well know the meaning of 'tracing' in relation to trust property but general reporters not. They are also unlikely to gain an understanding of legal affairs by sitting in court to listen to cases. Rozenberg agrees that a court reporter's job is 'simply to report what is said in court very neutrally and not to include so much background or interpretation' whereas the dedicated legal affairs specialist's job 'is to explain why these things matter'. He advises media students and reporters to follow practitioners' blogs.

The reason there are not so many legal affairs journalists in the mainstream media is that newspapers are simply cutting back. They think there is more copy to be gained from crime and home affairs. But this trend has been more than compensated for by the rise of bloggers – and here I mean barristers and solicitors who are blogging.

Dodd said:

> One of the things a journalist must be able to do is get through data and get to the relevant information quickly. They then need to make sense of it. If they can't then they need to know where to get clarity. A reporter can ask the in-house specialist on the lawyer.

The free-to-use British and Irish legal database (www.bailii.org) can be a useful research resource for a specialist or non-specialist reporter. Dodd said:

> I would look at Bailii if I was after a particular case. If it is a story about family law then you can find many judgments by Lord Justice Munby which explain the law step by step. You can see what you are dealing with. I have read a number of judgments online which are crystal clear and do make a lot of sense. The judgments are not necessarily written for lawyers but for the general public, and explain why decisions are made.

Much of the law is non-contentious. Take trusts, wills and probate, where the courts seldom adjudicate. The media want stories dealing with wealthy families in inheritance disputes or local authorities grabbing homes off elderly relatives who had intended to leave properties to children. Newsdesks happily assign these stories to general news reporters, rather than specialist freelance writers. Similarly newsdesks will focus on the exceptional stories involving employment law and tribunals, involving 'six figure' compensation payouts to employees, without highlighting the limitations on payouts available to the vast majority of successful claimants. These rare compensation payouts are awarded for discrimination actions brought by high-earning employees. Other types of claims are limited to a statutory maximum of just over £12,000. Workers made redundant can expect the biggest payout to be capped to just over £400 for each year in service. Legally-trained reporters with background knowledge of employment rights would be able to deliver more balanced, accurate and trustworthy copy.

Practitioners deal with claims in tort. Journalists should be most familiar with defamation and privacy. But these are only two of the torts. Legal affairs specialists require a wider understanding of forms of remedy against civil negligence or non-criminal malicious harm (such as medical mistreatment or psychological injury directly resulting from a wrongdoing). These stories are often newsworthy. Compensation claims from families and victims of the Hillsborough and Bradford soccer disasters, the Herald of Free Enterprise and Kings Cross tube fire tragedies made headlines. So too did media coverage of a growing 'compensation culture' accompanied with dire warnings of 'floodgates' opening to claimants and lawyers with dubious and avaricious motives. It is curious that editorial departments are willing to take an inconsistent approach, sympathising or vilifying victims, rebuking 'excessive' or 'meagre' damages, castigating the scope or demanding widening of entitlements of those classes of victims to compensation. Rozenberg recognises that newspapers tailor coverage to suit their readers' sensibilities. 'All newspapers do this. Papers like the *Mail* and *Telegraph* have a fair idea (or at least they think they have a fair idea) of what their readers think. They will provide stories on that basis.' Dodd said:

> Journalists need to bear in mind that people may have axes to grind. If Mr A tells you he has won his case on such-and-such a basis, then it is important to ask his lawyer or better still go off and get a copy of the judgment. Then read it very carefully. Often there will be something that Mr A does not like and won't want you to know or report. You can't write about the law from the basis of complete ignorance. This does not mean that you need to be a lawyer to work as a legal correspondent. It is not necessary to know the law inside out. However, you need a good understanding of the law and legal issues. You have to be aware that there are all sorts of differences in terms of how the law operates. You may be writing about aspects of the law which you are not aware about. If you are writing about a dispute between neighbours over a garden fence then all sorts of things can come out of it including County Court hearings. There are different rules about how contracts operate. Even European Union law might come into play in some stories.

Law students are required to learn the strict time limits affecting people's rights to file a claim in court, in relation to contracts, physical or mental injuries caused by someone's negligence, appeals against County Court judgments, bankruptcy petitions, landlord notices to quit tenancies, employment discrimination actions, and libel claims. Some 'windows of opportunity' are open for a few weeks, while others remain 'live' for several years. Journalists covering employment tribunal hearings will encounter judges having to dismiss perfectly reasonable claims on the basis that claimants have missed the three-month deadline. Lawyers who fail to file claims for clients in time risk being sued for negligence. Closer to home, employment rights and contract deals can be problematic for in-house and freelance journalists.

A rule of thumb is that employers will exploit staff on the basis that employees will use regional and national media firms for their own career ends. Staff turnover rates in editorial departments are high and it is well known that salary rises are best achieved by job hopping. So there is little incentive for editors to put their reporters through intensive legal training. Practical and financial considerations limit the scope for CPD (continuous professional development) training. Is it really necessary (employers argue) for journalists to know about 'the law' in depth, when they can just as easily get on the phone to an 'expert' or the in-house media lawyer? The employer enjoys an unequal bargaining position over the employee.

Some media companies axing editorial staff persist in engaging in questionable conduct, imposing onerous and unenforceable 'restraint of trade' clauses in return for enhanced payoffs. These deals include contract clauses in which a departing journalist agrees not to work as a reporter within a 50-mile radius of the office and not to apply for reporting jobs elsewhere in publishing group. The employee is told that these terms and conditions are covered by a gagging clause, so s/he is bound by confidentiality. The in-house lawyer acts for the employer, not for the employee, and must not act for both parties. In any event, even if the lawyer advises the client to take certain steps (see below), it is up to the client to act on that advice or to ignore it. The employee is cast adrift. Journalists with the LLB would know employment law obliges firms offering such deals of their obligation under employment law to advise employees to take independent legal advice first (and to pay for it). Students would also know that contract law forbids restraint clauses which stop people from working in an area without very good reasons, or attempt to stifle competition. In the case of journalists, such clauses may affront Article 10 of the Human Rights Act. Journalists unfamiliar with the law are more likely to accept such deals at face value, not appreciating the contract terms are unenforceable in courts and are not worth the paper they are printed on.

One example amongst many illustrates the problems which arise due to the media's failure to deploy dedicated legal affairs correspondents to high-profile cases. The Madeleine McCann case brought several newsworthy elements together. A child abduction with the hallmarks of a sex crime, a respectable middle-class couple as victims prepared to 'play' the daily press conference routine, a fearful crime in a holiday resort popular with British families, an investigation led by a 'foreign' police force (the underlying theme being the need for specialist child abduction officers from the UK to take charge of the inquiry), and (thanks to either a straightforward misrepresentation or ignorance concerning the Portuguese legal system) the finger of suspicion unfairly pointing at the parents.

Crime correspondents and general news reporters got the wrong end of the stick when the McCanns were called in for questioning and were assigned the formal status of 'Arguido'. Although the *Guardian* online site reported the correct meaning of the term (more than a witness but not an indication at that stage that a person was to be charged with a crime) much of the British media failed to give an adequate explanation of 'Arguido' status in terms of the equivalent UK procedure. 'Arguido' is a formal process which the police are obliged to follow if (as in the UK under the Police and Criminal Evidence Act) they suspect a person may be guilty of a crime (but the suspected offence is not made public prior to any charge) because it provides the individual with certain right (i.e., to legal representation and to the right to silence).

British newspapers (notably the *Daily Star* and *Daily Express*) misrepresented the McCanns' position and incorrectly translated 'Arguido' as 'Prime Suspect', which was incorrect. Since Portuguese law is based on the inquisitorial system (as opposed to the UK's adversarial system) Algarve police were restricted in the amount of information that could be released to the media. In seeking to overcome these 'hurdles', newsdesks and journalists risked undermining the investigation.

There were unofficial briefings and leaks, and regurgitated accounts of the investigation published in the Portuguese media. All lacked any privilege against a defamation action. Headlines alluding to the McCanns' 'guilt' were false, libellous, malicious (in the strict legal sense of being blasé to the truth) and lacking a legitimate public interest factor.

Reporters, newsdesks and sub-editors also failed to draw appropriate parallels with UK criminal investigation procedure in child abduction cases. In every instance involving a missing child, where the perpetrator is unidentified, police are trained and obliged to regard immediate relatives including parents and siblings as both witnesses and potential suspects, and the priority is to eliminate them from inquiries as soon as practical. On occasion the police will wheel relatives of a missing person in front of a press conference in order to observe their reactions and responses to journalists' questions, and compare the replies with statements made in police interviews. This practice is familiar to news organisations. Had parallel events occurred in Great Yarmouth, Norfolk police would have been compelled to question the parents under caution. Those individuals would have received the standard Miranda warning, with a right to legal representation and the right to silence. The adage 'never let the facts get in the way of a good story' appeared to prevail.

Since the Miranda and Arguido interviews are designed to provide legal safeguards for both police and witness/suspects, and to ensure proper procedures are followed in the event of a charge and a trial, it was nonsensical for the media to demand those safeguards to be annulled after interview. This may have been an attempt by certain media interests to shift the blame of careless reporting back onto the police. Many national newspapers and broadcasters attempted to 'make something' of the fact that the Portuguese police had omitted to 'revoke' the McCanns' 'Arguido status' – another misunderstanding of the procedure.

The British media's fundamental mistake was to assume that the Portuguese police action in affording the McCanns with 'Arguido' status was prejudicial in itself. In fact it was no different to the procedure applied in any child abduction case in the UK and other jurisdictions. A Miranda warning issued prior to a formal police interview cannot be 'annulled' because to do so would be a breach of procedure under the Police and Criminal Evidence Act. A legally informed and trained journalist should have spotted the error in the McCann coverage and the consequent risk of defamation proceedings. In any event, Express Newspapers had to publish prominent front page apologies to the McCanns and pay substantial libel damages. This publisher was not the only wrongdoer.

High-profile claims against businesses either focus on the impact on investors and shareholders or the general public. An example of the former is the coverage on both sides of the Atlantic regarding BP litigation in the wake of the Gulf of Mexico oil spill disaster. In the UK it was generally centred on the company's woes, at the expense of more sympathetic coverage of victims (people and businesses dependant on the tourism industry). An example of the latter is where the story is geared in the opposite way, sometimes with little reference to the corporate impact (e.g., the *Concordia* cruise ship disaster). The focus was on families, interviews with survivors, criticism of management and safety, and pressure for quick answers and rapid justice. The effects on share prices were confined to the financial columns.

When the media picks up the 'compensation culture' theme from politicians and other commentators, the 'victims' tend to be corporate bodies. The *Concordia* story was not portrayed in this manner but other incidents involving large-scale casualties have attracted coverage unfavourable to people seeking financial settlements from companies and organisations alleged to have been culpable or negligent. This theme received added media attention when the Princess Royal used a speech to suggest that too many claims for 'nervous shock' were a consequence of a lack of 'moral fortitude' on the part of victims. Distinguished judges, including Lord Justice Denning, have delivered stern warnings about 'floodgates' opening unless the barriers were put in place to prevent a 'tide' of claimants surging forward with their compensation claims.

Law students encounter these issues in tort exams. Typically there is a car crash. A bystander is hurt, but on the way to hospital the ambulance takes a corner too quickly and the patient suffers further injuries, or in the operating theatre a surgeon tries out a new treatment technique which goes wrong. The patient's aunt arrives at the hospital with a next-door neighbour and both are traumatised by the events. The student has to work out whether the motorist is responsible for all of the mishaps, and whether the aunt and neighbour can claim compensation from the driver and/or the hospital for their resulting depression. In the case of real disasters, such as the Hillsborough and Bradford football catastrophes, the media generally fail to explain where, how and why the courts draw the compensation line. Furthermore, newspapers do not highlight instances where claims that would succeed in Germany, France, Italy or Poland (where tort claims are subject to a civil code) are rejected by judges in England, Wales and Scotland (where claims are determined on judicial interpretation of the common law). In the case of the *Concordia*, there are likely to be many compensation claims for non-physical, 'nervous shock' injuries. Those considering action could include the crew, passengers, rescuers (police, local people, firefighters, coastguards), families of the bereaved, friends of the bereaved, husbands, wives, intended husbands and wives, boyfriends and girlfriends, ex-boyfriends and former girlfriends, next-door neighbours of the victims, work colleagues of the injured and deceased, and former work colleagues. All those lives were touched and affected, but the English-speaking courts have whittled the list down to a handful of worthy claimants.

The same judges have also demanded positive proof of entitlement to compensation from those with a genuine bond of 'love and affection' with the victim or were in close proximity to the incident or arrived on the scene or at the hospital soon afterwards. Courts are also reluctant to hold a 'wrongdoer' responsible for any unconnected mishaps suffered by a victim. This is why it is always a story for the media when a motorist is seen to 'get off lightly' for a mistake which triggers a series of events. The challenge for the specialist legal affairs journalist is to 'lift the lid' on the way that judges balance access to justice, with justice and culpability.

On one hand the popular press rails against litigants and their lawyers who fire off claims against businesses, traders and employers, on the reasonable assumption that most will settle out of court to avoid hassle, expense and bad publicity. Some in the media protest against gagging clauses which prevent claimants who settle out of court from 'telling their story'. At the same time, newspapers are prepared to use gagging clauses to prevent former employees setting up in competition. It is a shared 'news value' among journalists that officials, teachers, bosses and managers generally have something to hide. The antidote is not necessarily publicity ahead of a civil hearing or confidential settlement. The London press and journalism websites built up a furore over a recent change in law to protect the identities of teachers accused of misconduct. These anonymity orders may be lifted once police charge suspects, but not during the investigation. Some journalists and editors claimed the law had tilted in favour of paedophilic or violent teachers, arguing the 'guilty' would resign and go quietly to another school, cloaked in a conspiracy of silence.

These journalists did not appear to consider the flip-side. Teachers occasionally face malicious allegations from pupils and unwarranted abuse on social network sites. The suggestion that schools and local education authorities were in any position to frustrate an independent police enquiry into a serious allegation was without any foundation or precedent. We appear to have been here before. Providing teachers with anonymity is not opening the 'floodgates' to 'secret justice', because the anonymity is stripped away when the suspect attends court, and – as we have learned from Portugal – it is dangerous and irresponsible to suggest that 'Arguido' means 'prime suspect'.

If you are unsure whether you want to be a court reporter, a crime writer, an investigative journalist or a legal affairs correspondent, here are some rhetorical questions to consider in your university seminars or professional training workshops.

- Do we report the outcome of court proceedings and rely on lawyers, relatives and interested parties to embellish coverage with diametrically-opposed comment, or should legal affairs correspondents provide a reasoned and informed overview?
- Do we campaign for a change in the law to remedy unfair or unjust laws and decisions, or wait for judicial reform groups and politicians to raise issues (which may or may not prove newsworthy)? Should legal affairs correspondents play a role in exposing 'miscarriages of justice', or leave that work to dedicated investigative reporters?
- Do we explain why the criminal courts impose what may be regarded as 'lenient sentences', by reference to sentencing guidelines, budget constraints on crown prosecutions, admissions of guilt by defendants and mitigation by advocates, or the consequences of successful 'plea bargaining' between defence and prosecution before trial?
- Do we inform readers how these problems are dealt with in different parts of the world, or highlight disparities within the UK? What lessons are to be drawn from overseas in allowing cameras in court? Will the media provide an

accurate and reassuring or distorted and voyeuristic view of the judicial process? How should legal affairs correspondents react?

- Do we agree or disagree that the public interest is best served by encouraging opposing sides to reach (confidential) out-of-court settlements in civil litigation, to avoid expensive and time-consuming trials? Or must 'justice be seen to be done' at any price, thereby foisting the principle of the 'loser paying' onto one of the parties?
- Do we bow to any pressure to report the work of the criminal and civil courts in terms that reinforce or pander to our readers' interests and prejudices?
- Or do we report legal affairs in ways that may challenge or affront our readers' views and assumptions, since the purpose of 'public service' journalism is to educate and enlighten?

Note

1 Comments attributed to Mike Dodd and Joshua Rozenberg were from interviews with the author in May 2012.

15 Travel journalism

Tim Hannigan

Andrew Beatty, in his book on Java *A Shadow Falls*, writes:

> We are all travellers now, all tellers of tales. In novelty there is a routine, and with today's frictionless travel, an easy familiarity with the exotic. Yet in the best travel writing the steady eye, the alert ear, catches more: a detail that suggests the whole, a turn of phrase that opens up hidden lives. To fix the moving world in words is a strange and remarkable art.

Travel writing might well be the oldest form of journalism. Its basic formula – *I came, I saw, I wrote* – is essentially journalistic, but it is one that predates the invention of newspapers, magazines, and indeed 'journalists' by many centuries. The book of 'travels', in which the writer ventures to foreign lands and records his impressions and encounters there, is a form which stretches back beyond the birth of mass media, beyond the inception of European empire, beyond the invention of the modern 'novel' (often pinpointed as the publication of *Robinson Crusoe* in 1719), past the thirteenth-century launch of the *Travels* of Marco Polo, and all the way to the writing desks of Herodotus and the other reporters of the ancient world.

This, then, is a specialist genre with *serious* antecedents. Given this, and despite travel writing's reputation as lying at the softer end of the journalistic spectrum, it is perhaps unsurprising that it is a form that strays into deeply contentious territory, and which encounters daunting critical issues out there in the theoretical wilderness.

The beaten track: forms and formulas

What exactly is 'travel writing'? In the most basic sense it is simply any non-fiction writing which takes 'place' as its central subject matter. However, in the twenty-first century the great gamut of travel writing can be broken down into three main subsets.

At the top of the pile is 'travel literature', published in book form and spanning a spectrum from the light-footed anecdotes of Bill Bryson, to the highbrow impressions of Colin Thubron. Much of this travel literature – particularly that which focuses on a specific theme within a place – can certainly be regarded as journalism, or reportage, but it is not the stock in trade of the average jobbing travel writer; such a person will work in one of the remaining subsets of the genre, the first of which is guidebooks.

The guidebook industry is enormous, and the list of specialist publishers is a long one, stretching far beyond the big beasts of *Lonely Planet*, *Rough Guide*, and *AA*. This is where many professional travel writers make their principal living, but although introductions and boxed texts involve a good deal of 'colour' writing, the fact that most publishers turn out updated reissues of the same books every couple of years, means that in practice guidebook writing often amounts mainly to an assemblage of prices and opening hours. This, then, is the least 'journalistic' branch of travel writing.

The final subset is certainly journalistic, and it is what most people think of when they hear the term 'travel journalism': the writing of travel articles for newspapers, magazines and websites.

Unlike 'travel literature', 'travel journalism' is intrinsically linked to the global tourism industry. The places described almost always have some established form as tourist destinations, and the article generally deals with somewhere that the reader might actually want to visit ('travel literature', on the other hand, may well tackle places that the reader has absolutely no intention of going to – a war zone, for example). The features in supplements and magazines very rarely make a place sound bad.

But there is another, tighter connection between travel journalism and the tourism industry: advertising. Take a look at the features in glossy travel magazines like *Wanderlust*, *Condé Nast Traveller* and *Sunday Times Travel*, then take a look at the adverts wrapped around them: a feature on a Kenyan safari will often be flanked by adverts for operators offering Kenyan safaris; a piece on trekking in Nepal will be dappled with adverts for trekking agencies specialising in the Himalayas. This helps to explain why the same destinations are covered again and again. A freelancer may have produced a fascinating article on independent hiking in Azerbaijan with flawless accompanying photos, but a travel magazine would probably prefer to take a piece on Kenyan safaris: they'll find it easier to sell the advertising space.

It may seem counterintuitive, but often travel journalists do best when they focus on the places that have been covered a thousand times before.

***

Travel articles come in various shapes and sizes. There are short fillers, usually 500 words or fewer; there are 'destination profiles' focusing on an individual city or region, and usually organised in a format similar to that used in guidebooks. There are 'list' features – run-downs of the 'ten best', and so on (these are usually written without anyone leaving the office, or necessarily ever having been to any of the places mentioned). For certain publications – particularly inflight magazines and the advertising free-sheets circulated in tourist destinations – there are pieces that are indistinguishable from brochure puffs. And there are features on specialist travel, often for specialist publications – surf travel, food travel, mountaineering and so on.

But the typical travel feature – the central piece in a newspaper travel supplement, or one of the three or four 'main features' in a magazine – sticks to a tight formula. Despite the fact that in theory travel writing has no boundaries, and that 'everything can potentially be included which the traveller/writer sees fit' (Korte, 2000: 5), it generally journeys along a very well-beaten track.

The formula goes as follows:

- Length ranges from 1000 to 2500 words.
- The feature is structured as a first-person narrative, with the impressions and experiences of the writer paramount.
- One of those impressions or experiences – a dramatic or particularly colourful one – will be used for the intro (and will often be followed by a 'flashback' to introduce the destination and the background of the journey described).
- Either past or present tense can be used (for strictly linear narratives many writers choose the present to create more drive; but if there are extensive flashbacks and narrative sidesteps, then the past is much more practical).
- A brief potted history of the destination will be included in the narrative, probably tied to a description of the writer's visit to a monument or historic site; some light cultural background will be included in the same fashion.
- Ideally the narrative will feature some encounters with local people, and possibly some brief quotes. Usual journalistic practice for interviews will likely be dispensed with, however: unless the 'local' is someone other travellers might actively seek out, or read of elsewhere – a professional guide, or a tourism official for example – only a first name is given, and in practice the quote may not be strictly verbatim. The encounter will invariably be positive, and will ideally be connected to something of direct interest to tourists: a craftsman making prized souvenirs would be a prime candidate for a brief and cheerful encounter.
- Throughout the feature as much 'colour' as possible will be described – the sights, the sounds, the smells – to convey the exotic image and atmosphere of the place.
- The feature will end with a neat narrative close – in most cases the writer's own departure.

This, clearly, is journalism with a tendency to travel deep into the territory of the cliché. But the formula works, and – as with those endless features on Kenyan safaris – it sells.

The key critical theoretical issues around travel writing do not involve its tired structures or tendency to repeat itself; they focus instead on its relationship with its subject matter. For although a weekend travel supplement may include a few articles on domestic destinations, the great bulk of travel writing deals with foreign places, and the foreign people who inhabit them. Travel writing is all about encounters with 'the Other', and therein lies the rub …

Us and them: othering

In its most pared down, psychological context 'the Other' is simply the opposite of 'the Self' – everyone who isn't *you* is *other*. But in discussions of sociology and media theory both the Self and the Other are expanded. The Self becomes *us*, and 'the Us' represents a national or cultural mainstream, 'a relative commonality of outlook and values that the media believes exists in its target audience' (Sonwalker, in Allan, 2005: 264).

The Other then, is any individual or group lying beyond the frontiers of that mainstream, and the grammatically ugly term 'othering' refers to the process by which that 'otherness' is portrayed, emphasised and exaggerated – by highlighting (or inventing) the things about the Other that make him different from 'us'. Dominant theories about the purpose of othering – both psychological and sociological – can be summed up in the line from the French philosopher Emmanuel Levinas: 'the self is only possible through the recognition of the Other'. To have a sense of 'me' I need a sense of 'you'; to have a sense of 'us' we need a sense of 'them'.

Most studies of othering focus on cases where the Other is portrayed in an overtly negative fashion; travel journalism meanwhile, as previously mentioned, is typified by exuberantly positive portrayals of its subject matter. However, the most obviously, instantly identifiable Other is that which is somehow foreign. The foreign people that a travel writer encounters and features in his articles – the guides, the artisans, the 'friendly locals' – are unmistakably the Other, no matter how warmly they are described.

According to the Polish journalist and travel writer Ryszard Kapuściński, every foreigner we meet 'consists of two beings whom it is often difficult to separate'. On the first level the foreigner is, of course, a unique individual, but 'The other being, who overlaps and is interwoven with the first, is a person as a bearer of racial features, and as a bearer of beliefs and convictions' (Kapuściński, 2008: 14). In short the individual foreigner is a representative of his race, nationality or culture. Very often that is exactly how a travel writer uses him, and given the narrow scope, tight formulas and repetitive nature of travel articles, there is a decided tendency for the writer to choose as a representative someone who conforms closely to touristic stereotypes about the destination being described. A travel article about Spain is much more likely to feature as a representative of the 'Spanish Other' a bullfighter or a flamenco guitarist than a computer programmer or a refuse collector.

This tendency to plump for reductive stereotypes in depictions of the inhabitants of tourist destinations is in itself an interesting and thorny matter, but it is when travel writing ventures beyond 'the West' and into the developing, postcolonial world – as it often does in its endless search for 'the exotic' – that it encounters still more complex critical issues.

All the world's a stage: Orientalism

Traditionally 'Orientalism' was taken to mean the academic study of 'Oriental' (i.e., Asian, or Middle-Eastern) subjects. But the literary theorist Edward Said – who published his hugely influential book on the subject, *Orientalism*, in 1978 – expanded the term to encompass *all* 'Western' approaches to 'the Orient', from art and literature to political policy, and of course, travel writing.

This 'Orient' (which in Said's discussions encompassed the 'Islamic world' as well as East Asia, and which could very readily be expanded still further to encompass the entire 'non-Western' world, including its African and South American components), as viewed by Westerners in the colonial era, was largely an imagined entity, and the principal purpose – intentional or otherwise – of the vast, overarching scope of Orientalism was to highlight Western dominance and cultural superiority over the inferior and barbarous Oriental Other. For Said, throughout the period of European colonialism and beyond, Orientalism functioned as 'a western style for dominating, restructuring, and having authority over the Orient' (Said, 1978: 203). Travel writing was one of the key props of this 'western style'.

The age of empire was a boom time for travel writers. Dozens of books of travels – the majority of which involved a Western writer journeying through a colonial possession of his own or another European country – appeared each year. The distinction between travel *journalism* and travel *literature* was much less obvious then than it is today (despite the long history of the travel book, serious literary travel writing, with its inventive approaches to narrative structure and style, did not really emerge on a large scale until the mid-twentieth century, and only truly took flight in the 1970s with the rise to prominence of writers like Bruce Chatwin, Patrick Leigh Fermor and Paul Theroux). The travel books of the day were thoroughly journalistic: the writer simply visited a colonial possession, recorded its exotic scenes, noted down details of encounters with local people, perhaps interviewed a few native chiefs and a few European administrators, and perhaps passed comment on the efficiencies or otherwise of the system of government, and then went home and published what was usually little more than a polished journal.

These nineteenth-century travel writers were rarely equipped with skills in the local languages, and rarely had deep background knowledge of the places they wrote about. Their depictions of 'the Orient' were 'not quite ignorant, not quite informed' (Said, 1978: 55), and in this, as well as in their wider approaches, they were almost indistinguishable from the average twenty-first-century travel journalist flying into Cairo or Kathmandu on a magazine assignment.

The following description of the market in Leh in northern India from the Victorian journalist E.F. Knight, with a few of the less politically correct terms excised, would make a fine intro for a modern travel feature on Ladakh:

> [T]here is such a motley collection of types and various costumes, and such a babel of different languages, as it would not be easy to find elsewhere. Savage Tartars in sheepskins, and other outlandish men, jostle with the elegant Hindoo merchant from the cities of Central India, and the turbulent Mussulman Pathan scowls at the imperturbable idolaters from the Celestial Empire.
>
> (Knight, 1894: 178)

Of course, many would suggest that Said's arguments about Orientalism are no longer applicable, given that the age of European empire has passed. The West has no further need to 'have authority over the Orient', and while any decent travel journalist would still be eager to convey the exotic bustle of an Indian bazaar, he would have no interest in portraying its participants as 'savages' or 'idolaters'. Indeed, does not the previously discussed fact that the vast majority of travel journalism is obliged to be entirely positive about its subject matter make such discussions of nefarious Orientalism redundant? Unfortunately not.

Being positive is no defence, for it has frequently been pointed out that many nineteenth-century Orientalists, particularly the academics, were themselves openly admiring of their subject. As Ziauddin Sardar explains, the fact that Orientalism can appear admiring, 'does not mean that it cannot, at the same time, be obsessed with the Other in a way that the Other found denigrating, even in its admiring form. A paedophile admires and reveres a child even before he denigrates and deprecates it!' (Sardar, 1999: 71).

This is where travel journalism often finds itself irrefutably implicated. In its enduring craving for 'colour' it forms part of a 'positive' discourse on the foreign Other essentially unchanged since the nineteenth century, in which the non-Western world is a place of 'exotic, sinful, sexual delights all wrapped up in an ancient, mystical and mysterious tradition' (Sardar, 1999: 6). An admiring, reverential travel article about India, where the Indian Other is represented entirely by saffron-clad holy-men and photogenic peasants is surely somewhat denigrating to the country's enormous Anglophone middle class.

The very existence of that Anglophone middle class in a non-Western country might in itself suggest that the old issues of Orientalism may finally be beginning to give way: huge numbers of wealthy Indians, Chinese and other non-Westerners now wing their way around the world as tourists, and consume travel journalism. But a glance at travel articles in magazines published from Dubai to Delhi, from Shanghai to Singapore, reveals the same familiar stereotypical representations of the exotic Other. If therefore, in discussions of travel writing, Said's concept of 'the Orient' can be expanded to include the entire non-Western world, then perhaps his concept of 'the West' can be equally expanded to encompass the entire global elite with the disposable income to travel (in some respects this expansion could also have been applied in the past: medieval Arab and Chinese travellers like Ibn Battuta discussed the places they visited, especially in India, in the same unmistakably Orientalist tones as their European contemporaries, such as Marco Polo. The Other is the Other, no matter what your point of departure; you just need to have the money to travel).

***

But if, in the twenty-first century, the West (or the travelling global elite) is no longer actively, politically engaged in trying to have 'authority over the Orient', is it actually a problem if travel journalism continues to form part of an on-going Orientalist discourse? The answer is probably yes, because while Orientalism may no longer be tied to a grand colonial project, its denigrating, deprecating aspect endures – and no one enjoys being denigrated.

Wilfred Thesiger, one of the most celebrated twentieth-century travel writers – and the very epitome of the Orientalist who 'admires and reveres' even as he 'denigrates and deprecates' – wrote of Sudan in 1959 that 'fifty years earlier a great part of Africa had been unexplored. But since then travellers, missionaries, traders, and administrators had penetrated nearly everywhere. This was one of the last corners that remained unknown' (Thesiger, 1959: 29). Something is implicit here: Thesiger has no need to spell out who his 'penetrating travellers' are, or where they come from; that this particular corner of Africa was hardly 'unknown' to the people who already lived there is irrelevant to him.

This same inference is prevalent in much modern travel journalism about 'exotic' places. Within the restrictive confines of the need to write about 'elite destinations' the contrary quest for the 'authentic' is endless, and 'off the beaten track' is the most well-worn of all travel clichés. All of this contains an unwritten suggestion of ownership, turning the destination primarily into a playground for the visitor in which the identity of the permanent inhabitants is obliterated, reduced to nothing more than local colour, reductive representatives of an exotic culture. But while a remote valley in the Atlas Mountains may be thoroughly 'off the beaten track' for a visiting travel journalist and his readers, it is less so for the Moroccans who live and work there.

For Edward Said, the West's imagining of the Orient

> is a stage on which the whole East is confined. On this stage will appear figures whose role it is to represent the larger whole from which they emanate. The Orient then seems to be, not an unlimited extension beyond the European world, but rather a closed field, a theatrical stage affixed to Europe.
>
> (Said, 1978: 63)

The typical travel article, tackling a non-Western destination, is simply a one-act performance on that stage; the local people who feature in it are simply actors playing the well-rehearsed role of the Other, decided for them by the writer.

Syed Manzurul Islam (1996), writing of Marco Polo, describes '"the speaking subject" whose monologue gives the world its map'. When he describes the foreign people he encounters 'Marco Polo only needs to speak of the others because [he] is doing all the talking'.

The polished formula of the modern travel feature with its organised first-person narrative automatically places the writer at its centre as 'the speaking subject'. And though 'the others' – the market traders and masseuses, the happy hoteliers and hospitable villagers – may be given a few lines to speak, they do not get to choose them.

Truth and friction: the demands of narrative

Travel writing has had a complex relationship with 'truth' for a very long time. There are scholars who have devoted their entire careers to proving that Marco Polo never went to Xanadu. More recently, in the 1970s and 1980s, Bruce Chatwin committed flagrant immigration offenses on the frontier between fiction and non-fiction. No one, least of all the author, really knew whether his most famous book, *The Songlines*, should be classed as a novel or a travel book.

Chatwin is a particularly extreme example, but as 'a re-creation of a journey' any kind of narrative travelogue, including an article, 'has an element of fictionality despite the fact that it normally claims to be and is read as a "true" account' (Korte, 2000: 180).

Anyone who has written professionally about travel will be hypersensitive to the fabrications of others: the professional, agency-hired guides disguised as chance-met 'local companions'; the unmentioned break in the journey when the writer left the country and went home; the chunk of guidebook-gleaned history thrust into the mouth of an invented English-speaking stranger on a bus, and above all the cutting and pasting of chronology, the placing of things in an order other than that in which they actually happened.

Outright invention is probably more common in travel literature than in travel journalism. But the tight formula of the travel feature, with its need for a sharp intro and a neat ending means that travel journalists may well rearrange events for the sake of narrative. What happens on Day Three in the article, might actually have happened on Day One on the ground.

How much this matters is a subject of debate. 'Truth' is generally a sacred totem of journalism, and journalists who make things up are usually – and rightly – condemned. Rearranging the order of events, however, is arguably not actually to lie, and given that travel writing is 'entertainment' as well as 'journalism', many would choose to excuse it. But the problem lies in the crossing of that threshold. Travel writing is perhaps the form of journalism most conducive to laziness. A competent travel journalist can fly in to Marrakesh, check into a hotel, go and have a coffee, have lunch, visit a couple of ancient monuments, buy a souvenir, have dinner, and fly home the next morning. He already has material for a perfectly respectable travel article.

But if the re-jigging of chronology is accepted as standard practice, then the temptation to invent a quote from a friendly local must also be great – especially if the local only needs to be a Moroccan metalworker called Mohamed, and all he needs to say is 'I learnt this craft from my father, my son will learn it from me' …

In the terms of the othering and Orientalism discussed above, however, to do this would be to commit a monumental crime. If the travel journalist actually *invents* his representative of the Other, then the first half of that duel personality described by Kapuściński – that in which the foreigner is a unique individual – is entirely erased. The 'friendly local' exists *only* as a representative of his race, nation and culture – and one invented by an outsider at that. This, surely, is a prime example of 'dominating, restructuring, and having authority' over an exotic subject.

That any travel journalist who does occasionally invent quotes in this way would probably regard himself as guilty of no greater offence than laziness is not the point.

Facing the challenge

Many travel journalists are probably unaware of the ideological hornets' nest they are poking when they put pen to paper on the subject of a far-off land. If the critical issues were pointed out to them they would likely react defensively, dismissively, or in horror, for the arguments outlined above suggest that travel writing is irredeemable. Its formulas are rigid, and given its subject matter and the inherent cultural and national disconnect between the writer and his human subjects, an element of othering is inevitable. Meanwhile, the intrinsic link between travel journalism and tourism creates certain inflexible demands: people travel specifically to encounter something *different*; they leave home to experience the exotic, to meet with the Other (although the encounters may be superficial, packaged and sanitised).

Travel journalism, then, *must* accentuate the exotic colour in the seething souks of the non-Western world; it *must* give cameos to those local people who are manifestly different from 'us'. A travel feature on Marrakesh that entirely eschews its medieval mosques and markets, that deals only with its air-con shopping malls and office blocks, and which features only a cast of Moroccan doctors, lawyers and engineers with jeans, iPhones and a penchant for American fast food, will be a very hard sell for a freelance travel journalist.

So what – if anything – can such a travel journalist do, if he or she is aware and concerned about the issues?

The first and most obvious measure, of course, is *never* to invent quotes from the representative Other, and, if the needs of the narrative formula demand a chronological rearrangement, to be constantly alert to the ideological dangers that lie beyond the threshold of absolute truth. The second step is to guard against the laziness that travel writing so readily invites – both on the ground and on the page.

Hidebound by its repetitive structures, travel journalism is rife with cliché, and every travel journalist has their own stock of them. In travel features the same 'pungent aromas', 'bustling markets' and 'hospitable locals' appear everywhere from Bali to Bogota. The clichés are clichés because they are perfectly effective of course, but the conscientious writer should strive for something more – the detail that really *does* suggest the whole. What *exactly* does that 'pungent aroma' smell like? In what precise *way* are the locals so hospitable?

And it is in its encounters with the Other, the inhabitants of the foreign land, that travel journalism needs to make the most effort. The strictures of the form – and the perfectly natural demands of tourists – mean that refuse collectors and computer programmers will never rank above tribesmen and artisans in the cast of characters who appear in travel features, but a good, energetic writer should seek out, not merely the representative sound-bite, but 'the concrete detail of human experience' (Said, 1981: xxxi). They should remember the twofold identity of the Other described by Kapuściński, and attempt, wherever possible, to pay attention to the first part, in which the foreigner is a unique individual, as well as to the second in which they take a representative role.

Of course, like their Victorian predecessors, few travel writers will have the extensive language skills – or indeed the time – to make deep anthropological investigations into the world of the villagers and craftsmen they meet, but within the limitations they can still seek out that 'turn of phrase that opens up hidden lives'.

For even with its formulaic structure, even bowing to the demands of advertising, and even when traversing a well-trodden track through an elite destination, the best travel writing *can* still be something more; it can uncover authentic colour that goes beyond the generic 'exotic', and give a compassionate glimpse that reveals the essential humanity of the Other. To do that is indeed to practice 'a strange and remarkable art'.

Bibliography and references

Allan, Stuart. *Journalism: Critical Issues*. Maidenhead: Oxford University Press, 2005.

Beatty, Andrew. *A Shadow Falls: in the Heart of Java*. London: Faber & Faber, 2009. Preface (p. ix).

Chatwin, Bruce. *The Songlines*. Australia: Franklin Press, 1986.

da Pisa, Rustichello. *The Travels of Marco Polo*. Genoa: Circa 1290.

Defoe, Daniel. *The Life and Surprising Adventures of Robinson Crusoe of York, Mariner*. London, 1719.

Islam, Syed Mazurul. *The Ethics of Travel: From Marco Polo To Kafka*. Manchester: Manchester University Press, 1996.

Kapuściński, Ryszard. *The Other*. London: Verso, 2008.

Knight, Edward Frederick. *Where Three Empires Meet: A Narrative of Recent Travel in: Kashmir, Western Tibet, Gilgit, and the Adjoining Countries*. London: Longmans, Green, and Co., 1894.

Korte, Barbarba. *English Travel Writing: From Pilgrimages to Postcolonial Explorations*. Basingstoke: Macmillan, 2000 (digital edition 2003, first published in Germany 1996).

Levinas, Emmanuel. *Le Temps et l'autre Presses* Paris: Universitaire de France, 1983.

Said, Edward W. *Orientalism*. New York: Random House, 1978.

Said, Edward W. *Covering Islam*. London: Routledge, 1981.

Sardar, Ziauddin. *Orientalism*. Oxford: Oxford University Press, 1999.

Thesiger, Wilfred. *Arabian Sands*. London: Longmans Green, 1959.

16 War reporting

Mark Nicholls

Introduction

There are few reporting assignments to compare with being on the frontline of a war zone with a military unit. It is exciting, exhilarating and also dangerous. For more than two decades, western forces, particularly British and US troops, have been in constant action deployed in war zones, primarily in Iraq and Afghanistan. There has never been a busier time to be a defence correspondent and experience at first hand the challenges faced by soldiers, air force personnel and Royal Navy crews in the face of a hostile foe.

Yet to be able to function effectively in such an environment and to deliver relevant and meaningful reports to an audience/readership takes an enormous amount of care and preparation. To be a successful defence correspondent or war reporter requires physical and mental preparation combined with the acquired knowledge and experience that will enable a journalist to perform to the best of their ability and be able to report the story with balance, depth and maturity.

But it goes far beyond reporting from the raw edge of the military theatre. There are stories back home: from the training of the troops or air crew; the survival of a base that may be under threat of closure from defence cuts, and the wider impact of its loss on that community; policy decisions; and the basic groundwork of contact building and getting to know the units that you may link up with in the future. Above all, there is the human story – tales of courage and survival in the face of danger and adversity and the harrowing toll of serious injury and death on the troops, the units, and the families and loved ones left behind. There is a need for honest, accurate, factual reporting combined with humanity, understanding and sensitivity. This all comes under the remit of a defence correspondent.

Knowledge, history, opportunity

Military units are acutely aware of their history: the battles and campaigns they have been involved in; significant victories and anniversaries; and returns to countries where their predecessors fought. Regiments may merge or change their names, RAF squadrons are disbanded and then reformed or change aircraft or their base, and personnel move on from one station to another as they are deployed on various postings. But the thread of past deeds runs as a constant through the history of the regiment, ship or squadron.

It is this history and ancestry that the defence correspondent must absorb. It shows that you are serious about your subject, that you do appreciate the importance of, and know, the history of these military units. But in addition, it provides fantastic opportunities for new angles, stories and features you may otherwise miss as that history is recalled, remembered or even recreated.

An example is that of the Royal Air Force's 617 Squadron of Lancaster bombers – The Dambusters – which under Wing Commander Guy Gibson's leadership gained fame for carrying out the daring raids on the dams that powered Germany's wartime industries in 1943 at the height of World War II. On the 60th anniversary of the formation of the squadron, as offensive operations were under way during the Iraq War of 2003, the RAF deployed a new weapon in a combat scenario for the first time – the Storm Shadow missile. The aircraft chosen for the first deployment of this weapon was a two-seater ground attack Tornado GR4 from 617 Squadron. The anniversary, the significance of the squadron and the link with the past, added an extra dimension to the story.

But the knowledge required to be an effective defence correspondent reaches far beyond the historical context. The defence correspondent needs to be aware of the rank structures within the Army, the Royal Air Force and the Royal Navy: what the role of a Squadron Leader or a Wing Commander is; how many soldiers are in a Battalion or an Army company; where a Lieutenant Commander and Sub-lieutenant fit into the structure aboard a warship; and also the critical role that Regimental Sergeant Majors, Petty Officers and Warrant Officers play in the realm between officers and the basic soldier, sailor and airman.

Much of this experience can be gleaned from basic research, but it is crucial to enhance it by spending time with the units, seeing where and how the different tiers work together and the subtleties within that. The more time a defence correspondent spends at an RAF station or on an army base, the better equipped they will be to respond when away on assignment with the personnel in a combat zone having gained a better understanding of how the military works.

Equally, a degree of familiarity with the equipment they use and the terrain they operate under enhances that knowledge further. If you have flown in an RAF Tornado or Jaguar warplane, landed on the deck of a Type 23 frigate aboard a Lynx helicopter, ridden in a Challenger Tank or stood beside the Captain on the bridge of a British warship, it adds an extra dimension to your knowledge and the articles you write. You are aware of the confined space an RAF pilot operates in; just how difficult it is to put the Lynx safely down on a flight deck in choppy seas, or the awesome power of a tank and its capabilities. As a defence correspondent, you need to add this extra dimension to your own personal 'armoury' to enable you to portray the role of the service personnel in a way that is meaningful and relevant to a broader, often non-military, readership.

There are political and geographical aspects to be aware of too; the backdrop to a conflict (such as the debate over Weapons of Mass Destruction – WMD – ahead of the Iraq War) or that the decision to send coalition troops into Afghanistan could be viewed as the latest in a long line of deployments to that rugged, inhospitable, nation stretching back almost two centuries to the 1st Afghan War (1839–42), the 2nd Afghan War (1878–80) or 3rd Afghan War (1919).

But above all, whatever you report and wherever you report from, never forget the unique journalistic dimension you can bring to a scenario. Use your eyes, ears, taste and sense of smell to bring that scene to life with the words that are your most important tool – just make sure you have the background knowledge and awareness at hand to do that to the best of your ability.

Frontline reporting

Reporting from the frontline is the ultimate experience for a defence correspondent, it is what we enter the speciality subject to do – to experience what personnel from the Army, RAF and Royal Navy endure in a combat zone. For the reporter it is hugely rewarding to send despatches back from the frontline to an audience in a home area and it is a role that sustains a long tradition of reporting stretching back to the correspondents who travelled to the Crimea or to South Africa during the Boer War with the British Army.

A point worth making at this stage is that it could also be argued that there is a subtle difference between a defence correspondent and a war reporter, with one specialising in broader defence issues while the other travels from one combat zone to another reporting conflict wherever it occurs around the world. However, those parameters may become blurred and cross over as the role evolves and is shaped by the individual journalist's approach.

Correspondents have been present at points of conflict throughout history. In recent times, they were there during the Falklands War of 1982, and where the British military has seen action since; in the Gulf War of 1991, the Balkans in the late 1990s and in the first decade of the twenty-first century in Iraq and Afghanistan alongside US forces. Today, for a UK-based correspondent, that is likely to see deployment to Afghanistan where British forces have focused much of their efforts since the September 11 attacks of 2001. The RAF has seen almost constant service in these theatres. In the aftermath of the first Gulf War, British jets – often in an unreported role – flew for a number of years over the skies of Iraq, enforcing the so-called no-fly zones. Jaguars patrolled northern Iraq from the Turkish airbase at Incirlik, while Tornados flew from the Kuwait airbase at Ali Al Salem over southern Iraq to protect the Marsh Arabs from the persecution of Saddam Hussein, virtually up to the outbreak of the second Gulf conflict. It was also from Ali Al Salem that British Tornado jets were to launch their attacks on Baghdad in March 2003.

It was the Iraq War of 2003 which heralded a major turning point in war reporting, where British and American military used the concept of embedding journalists with military units on a mass scale for the first time – but more of that later.

For the middle years of the first decade of this century, British and American forces, along with some other western allies, were embroiled in post-conflict Iraq. Against this backdrop, the Taliban had regrouped and re-established new strongholds across Afghanistan, despite being removed from power late in 2001.

That in turn saw US and British forces deployed to the country in ever-increasing numbers as the Taliban became a deadly enemy. British troops were primarily deployed in Helmand province in the south of the country, often facing the Taliban in close combat to such an extent that it has not been unusual to report British soldiers using bayonets rather than bullets against the enemy.

For the defence correspondent on assignment to Afghanistan, this has provided an opportunity to report from the stronghold of Camp Bastion, the air base at Kandahar, Kabul and other locations but also be deployed to northern Helmand to the green zone around places such as Sangin and Kajaki, though in the last three or four years the danger levels for correspondents and troops has increased significantly with the Taliban using IEDs (improvised explosive devices) to deadly effect against British soldiers, killing and maiming many. Journalists travelling with those soldiers face the same level of threat and danger. For those reporters who want to experience frontline reporting, that underlines the importance of thorough preparation.

Be prepared

For journalists accompanying soldiers to some of the more dangerous frontline postings, thorough preparation is crucial. That comes with awareness and experience and it is advisable where possible to let your combat experience evolve and build up to postings where there is a potential serious risk by gaining knowledge of accompanying troops: try to go on training missions with them ahead of deployment, or restrict your coverage on a first assignment to a safer location. But once you are ready and confident enough to accompany troops further up country and closer to the frontline, and have the opportunity to do so with a specific unit, ensure that you are mentally and physically prepared for whatever may lie ahead. You need to be fit, agile and able to respond to dangerous situations and not be a burden to a group of men who may be lean and battle-hardened, able to sense danger and deal with it. You also need to be mentally prepared; you may witness serious and even fatal injuries, you may be under attack and there is always the risk that you will be injured yourself. That is something that you – and those closest to you at home – must address before you head off on such a deployment. In addition, you need to make sure that you are adequately insured; not only through your company but also check the terms and conditions of your personal insurance policies before you decide to venture out on the frontline.

Often, the defence correspondent will be working in very basic conditions, usually with no desk, possibly with inadequate lighting and intermittent power. Do not be afraid to speak to other defence correspondents for advice on what they experienced on a specific deployment as what they tell you will be invaluable and will help you prepare for what you may expect.

It is also advisable to ensure you have had any relevant training. The military can offer advice and at times may even provide training, and there are also independent organisations that can offer survival and combat courses. You may, or may not, decide these are necessary and much will depend on the budgeting limitations of the organisation sending you on such a deployment, though they will clearly have a duty of care for your overall wellbeing.

Ahead of offering British journalists the opportunity to embed with UK air, land and sea units during the War with Iraq of 2003, the MoD organised specific training for journalists. This included a briefing on prisoner-of-war training in the event a correspondent was detained, plus a more practical and highly relevant two-day NBC (Nuclear, Biological and Chemical) course with the threat of chemical weapon attacks from Iraq considered high at that time. Along with all military personnel deployed in the Iraq theatre, embedded correspondents were issued with full protective NBC suits and gas masks.

Apart from specialist equipment, defence correspondents need to have the correct type of clothing, footwear and ancillary gear that will ensure that they have whatever is needed to sustain themselves alongside troops. There is always the likelihood that going out on patrol on the frontline could be a deployment that can last for days in open and hostile countryside.

Never forget why you are there – to get the story home – and a key part of that preparation is ensuring that you have the necessary equipment to gather and write the story as you see it and then be able to transmit that story at a time that is safe to do so, without hindering the operational element of the troops' deployment or compromising operational security. When out on the ground with troops, or at a military base when embedded with troops, any transmission needs to be conducted in a way that will not leave other personnel exposed. Your equipment needs to be modern, robust and reliable.

Responsible reporting is crucial. It is no exaggeration to suggest that lives are at stake. Inaccuracies, misinterpretations and a mistimed article can have implications. It is also important to be aware of operational security and that any communication you make from a conflict zone – either by mobile phone, satellite phone, or email – could be intercepted by hostile forces. Also, be alert and ready to think on your feet during communications. I remember doing a live interview with a local radio station in England from an RAF base in northern Kuwait in 2003 at a time that RAF Tornado jets were flying daily combat missions over Iraq when the presenter suddenly asked: 'and can you tell our listeners what the RAF will be doing later today?' I could imagine any Iraqis monitoring the conversation suddenly pricking up their ears and awaiting the answer. It was a case of keep calm, keep talking, but don't answer the question and focus on what has happened and not what will or may happen.

Defence correspondents should have an understanding of the Ministry of Defence Green Book, which is a document produced in consultation with editors and press and broadcasting organisations as a general guide to the procedures that the MoD will adopt in working with the media throughout the full spectrum of military operations. It covers the practical arrangements for enabling correspondents to report on operations, including the MoD's plans for representative numbers of correspondents to accompany British Forces and sets out what editors can expect from the MoD and what the MoD seeks from the media. Issues of operational security and what may and may not be disclosed are detailed.

Military operations are far from 9–5, so be prepared for long days and with time zone differences and often extended night-time deadlines in Europe when there is a war on, it can mean that the defence correspondent can at times be working round-the-clock. The work can be tiring but it is of significant importance and an over-riding sense of achievement for the defence correspondent is that they were there, and did the job well.

Embedding

Embedding is a subject that has polarised debate over conflict coverage in the last decade. First used on a major scale by the US and British military in the Iraq War of 2003, being embedded with specific units has now became the main way journalists cover military conflict.

Its harshest critics frown upon it, suggesting its ethics are controversial, with 'un-embedded' journalism associated with independence and courage. They suggest that the disadvantage of embedding is that you are no longer impartial, that journalists report everything from one particular angle, spoon-fed information about the course of a war by the military and at very worst, the journalist can 'go native' and align themselves too closely with the military unit that they are with. A further criticism is that embedding leads to more conflicts being reported primarily from a military rather than a broader humanitarian perspective. These are valid observations and any journalist who embeds with a military unit needs to be acutely aware of them.

While academics may sit back in their armchairs and criticise the purity of war reporting when delivered through an embed system, they seem to overlook that under the current climate, accompanying armies in the field is usually the only way of finding out what they are doing. However, while not necessarily regarding themselves as being embedded in the past, writers have often attached themselves to military units in the field over years either for safety or because it was simply where the story was. There is also little alternative in the modern conflict because organisations such as al Qaeda and the Taliban potentially target foreign journalists as hostages. There is extreme danger in operating independently in states such as Afghanistan.

Renowned Irish journalist Patrick Cockburn, the *Independent*'s Middle East correspondent, summed up the position in an article in his newspaper in November 2010. He said:

> I used to get a certain amount of undeserved applause at book festivals by being introduced as a writer 'who has never been embedded', as if I had been abstaining from unnatural vice. Embedding obviously leads to bias, but many journalists are smart enough to rumble military propaganda and wishful thinking, and not to regurgitate these in undiluted form.

However, he warns that the 'most damaging effect of "embedding" is to soften the brutality of any military occupation and underplay hostile local response to it'. That reflects my view too. I believe that experienced reporters will have a natural instinct over what feels right and which information they are comfortable in sharing with their readers and how they interpret and relay that information. They will temper their copy accordingly, as well as making the context clear and that they are embedded with a military unit.

While an independent war correspondent will not appear to have any of those restrictions, they will also only see a snapshot of the wider scenario – because at times they will be limited to specific locations because of the risks of travelling from one destination to another through hostile territory.

The other reality is that these are grim times for the media, particularly the regional press in the UK. Where embedding has a clear advantage, particularly for the regional press which does not have the budgets to travel independently and hire private security protection, is that it gives unique access to a unit whether it is heading across Iraq towards Basra, on patrol in northern Helmand province, or based with squadrons of RAF Tornado jets flying bombing and reconnaissance missions over Baghdad and other parts of Iraq. The alternative to embedding is usually the prospect of not covering these conflicts at all. All of this, inevitably, places the onus on the integrity of an individual defence correspondent to produce balanced, accurate copy.

The needs of the regional defence correspondent, and his publication, may also differ from those with a national/international audience. Whereas national media are portraying the conflict from a national/international perspective, regional media are often looking at covering it through the eyes of the unit they are embedded with, simply because a regiment or certain RAF squadrons are based within the publication's circulation area and recruits personnel from that area. The troops may, a few years' previous, have been pupils at local schools, for example. That, however, should not mean that the reporting from the regional media is dumbed down to the level of 'local boy on the frontline' coverage, which unfortunately it can be at times. What is still required is a mature, experienced, informed and authoritative approach to reporting that combines the relevance to the publication with a national and international outlook on a par with the type of informed reporting offered by national and international media. In many cases it can often be better as the regional journalist will usually be better informed about the activities of a specific unit having built up a long-term relationship with it and its key personnel.

When it works well, what embedding does is offer journalists the opportunity to report the activities of a specific unit at close quarters with real-time access to personnel, often in perilous and tense scenarios.

Whether an embedding is successful depends on a wide range of factors and many of them can be dictated by chance and the outlook of individual, influential and powerful personalities. If you are embedded with a military unit where the commanding officer is anti-media, it can become very difficult. There were cases of media units embedded with military units during the 2003 Iraq War that were effectively neutralised – they were taken to a location and 'locked down' for long periods with nothing to report or write about and limited facilities to transmit any story they may have come across.

There were, however, many highly successful embeds where journalists virtually had 'access all areas' and the opportunity to interview personnel from every level; from senior officers down to private soldiers on the frontline; to pilots about to embark on high-risk bombing missions to ground crew involved in re-arming and refuelling aircraft; or reservists who often felt that they were at the bottom of the 'pecking order' when it came to equipment and living conditions. It was not all positive coverage either but in several cases there was a very mature attitude from the military that as long as the reporting was fair, accurate and balanced and did not compromise operational security, then it could be reported with little (or in many cases) no censorship or interference whatsoever.

What helped lead to this position was trust and familiarity and those embeds that tended to be most successful were those where defence correspondents already had an effective working relationship with the units they were embedded with. I was embedded in northern Kuwait with Tornado squadrons from RAF Marham in Norfolk and had spent a lot of time with them – before and after the Iraq War of 2003. I knew key individuals across all ranks and had covered the build up to their deployment, flew with them on occasions and was there at the RAF station for the return after the war. It is this continuity that is important and facilitates access and leads to informative briefings and also assistance and support with transmission of stories and pictures. There were, of course, difficult moments particularly when a Tornado aircraft was shot down in a well-documented 'friendly fire' incident involving an American defensive Patriot Missile but this was handled with maturity, sensitivity and transparency on all sides and that was the result of established trust and familiarity.

Embedding offers unparalleled access. You can talk to a private soldier moments after he has been under fire in a Taliban ambush or to RAF ground crew about the complexities of re-arming an aircraft or waiting for their warplane to return, uncertain if it will come back. One of the most memorable personal experiences for me was being able to interview the pilot and navigator of the first British Tornado to take off as the bombing of Baghdad started in late March 2003 and gauge feelings and emotions, and then two hours later speak to the same air crew as they climbed from their cockpit after they safely returned from a successful bombing mission over Baghdad. That produced a graphic eyewitness account of the mission and what the Iraqi capital under attack looked like from the air, leading to a 3am front page lead article and background interview back in the UK. The ability and opportunity to report that, comes only from embedding.

Similarly, patrolling around Sangin with A Company of the 1st Battalion Royal Anglian Regiment on September 11 – a poignant date which the Taliban may have used for an attack – is not an opportunity that readily arises apart from being an embed. Walking the narrow alleys and through isolated villages had a heightened sense of tension, particularly as the Battalion had already lost nine soldiers killed in action at that point and six of its soldiers were later to be awarded the Military Cross.

One of the aims of embedding is to allow journalists to cover the activities of military personnel on deployment 'as it is' rather than a sanitised version of the

Army, Navy or RAF on deployment and the reports that reflected best on media outlets and military units were those that were unhindered by over-restrictive military guardians, the ones where senior officers allowed writers to tell the story as it was. Being embedded meant experiencing the dangers, hardships and living conditions of the military; it meant describing how it really was to live out in the desert overnight with an unseen enemy close by; it meant living among the inadequate sanitation of an air base trying to cope with twice the number of personnel it was designed for; and feeling the tension of air raids where there was no indication whether the missile flying towards you had a chemical warhead. It meant leaping out of bed five times during the night – often at 3am – and dragging on gas mask/respirator and a full chemical suit and dashing to the air raid shelters, cramped and tense until the all clear was sounded, or carrying your gasmask wherever you went because of the supposed threat of WMD. But it means that for a defence correspondent, every second and every minute of every day has the potential to provide interesting, exciting and well-written copy.

It is important that any reporting from an embed situation is placed in context, that the correspondent is based with a military unit and is seeing only one part of that conflict. There is a responsibility on news editors in newsrooms or studios back in the UK or US to incorporate the correspondent's report into the wider context of the conflict, perhaps dovetailing it with reports from journalists operating independently to give the reader or viewer a wider, more considered picture.

In some areas of the military and Ministry of Defence, there was confusion over what was good news and bad news, what was pro- and anti-military. At the time of the Iraq War of 2003 the British newspaper the *Daily Mirror* adopted an unwavering anti-war stance. This was perceived by some in the armed forces as being anti-military, which was not the position of the newspaper. When the war was over, the Ministry of Defence conducted an exercise which 'assessed' every story produced on the war, particularly those from embeds in order to decide what was 'good news' and what was 'bad news'. It seemed oblivious to the fact that what may have been bad news for one audience was good news for another. Take the example of journalists highlighting difficulties with military post getting through to frontline troops. This was 'bad news' from the MoD perspective but 'good news' from that of the frontline troops as it highlighted the issue and led to a rapid solution. What tends to be overlooked is that most journalists do not do good news and bad news – they just do news and let the reader decide.

Embedding is undoubtedly the safest avenue for defence correspondents to cover frontline activities but because they are so conspicuous in their blue helmets and body armour, they are easily identifiable. As embedding means journalists see, feel and experience what frontline troops go through, it means they are equally exposed to the dangers, which as we have seen with the deaths of journalists in combat zones, remain very real.

At the time of writing, journalists continue to be embedded with military units in Afghanistan – often for several weeks at a time – providing gripping copy and producing stories that would not otherwise come to the attention of readers back home in the UK. What embedding does is offer unrivalled opportunities for

eye-witness war reporting. It is for the defence correspondent to seize those opportunities and produce accurate, impartial and interesting reports.

Beyond the frontline

The role of the defence correspondent reaches back far beyond the frontline and
into the communities in which military personnel live and are stationed. It covers
the impact their presence and that of the base they operate from, has on a specific
area. A military base, often with 2,000–3,000 personnel in situ plus their families
and dependants, has a huge economic impact on a community. It generates wealth,
employment for suppliers and support staff, and sees millions of pounds spent
locally every year within a relatively small radius. Any change to that can have
far-reaching consequences for a community. With every round of defence cuts,
any proposal to scale back on installations raises serious concerns and this is where the
defence correspondent can adopt a particularly partisan approach – campaigning
for an RAF station or army base to be kept open and remain active within a community. Far from being of benefit to the military and service personnel – many of
whom move to different postings every two to three years – this is more for the
long-term economic stability of a local community and its citizens. Being aware of
the political nature of these decisions enables the defence correspondent to offer a
particular insight into the implications, combining the economic and political aspects
with defence issues to produce in-depth analytical pieces written with knowledge,
confidence and authority that go beyond straightforward news reporting.

Stories may not always be positive and when it comes to issues of procurement
and achieving best value for money for the taxpayer, the Ministry of Defence and
the military does not have a great track record. It falls to the defence correspondent
to explore these issues, often in a way that may not always be palatable to the
MoD but that remains an important part of the role in providing fair, accurate
and balanced coverage of the activities of the armed forces.

With every deployment, there are homecomings and reunions as personnel
return to their home base after a deployment that can often mean they have been
away from their family and friends for up to six months. In the last few years, the
public has become more aware, and generally more supportive, of the activities of
the military. Homecoming parades, for example, attract wide coverage and often
bring town centres to a standstill as a battalion or squadron marches through
on their return from a frontline deployment. The fact that so many people now
turn out for these events is a direct result of media interest and coverage; it is not
so long ago that such parades hardly attracted any public attention. The media
has played a massive part in highlighting military deployments and informed
reporting from defence correspondents has underpinned that. Likewise, acts of
bravery are recognised with regular awards for gallantry, which are events the
correspondent should endeavour to attend as they offer the opportunity to interview the recipients and also gain a clear insight into the events surrounding the
incident and act of courage that led to the award. In addition, the media has
been staunch supporters of military charities such as Help for Heroes.

That goes to underline that behind every deployment, every act of bravery and every confrontation with the enemy is a human story to be told. Sometimes they are harrowing and emotional, of soldier's families coming to terms with grief over the death of a loved one in action or a family member with horrific life-changing injuries sustained after being caught in an explosion; but stories of recovery and of rehabilitation too. This is one of the human faces of war, one that also falls to the defence correspondent to cover and where the knowledge and experience gained from the role – often from frontline assignments – can help with coverage that is sensitive.

Fulfilling, challenging ... and a privilege

The role of defence correspondent remains as challenging as it is rewarding, with exciting and interesting assignments combined with an undeniable degree of risk. Being sent to a combat zone truly follows the journalistic ethos of 'going to where the story is' – to see for oneself what is really happening and then to report on it. There are few roles that combine all elements of journalism in such a way, making this one of the most fulfilling of all specialist reporting positions. There is a burden of responsibility that accompanies the role as the correspondent endeavours to offer independent accounts in a sphere of reporting where there are so many conflicting interests and also where it has often been remarked that 'truth is the first casualty of war'. But to be a defence correspondent, with its challenges, dangers and responsibility, is also a great privilege.

17 Wine journalism

Geoff Adams

Introduction

The causality dilemma 'which came first, the chicken or the egg', which has tantalised mankind since time immemorial, can very much be applied to that rare breed of professional journalist who specialises in writing or broadcasting on the subject of wine.

So, which did come first? The trained journalist who later on discovers a passion for wine, then specialises in wine writing, or the life-long wine buff who accidentally falls into journalism through writing a small weekly or monthly column at the request of, say, a local newspaper or regional magazine, or guesting on a regular slot for a local radio station?

Rather than dwell on the dilemma, it is useful to understand that in the world of wine journalism, both species of journalist exist, and co-exist together comfortably.

You will usually find the journalistically untrained life-long wine buff freelancing for various authoritative specialist consumer wine magazines, consumer wine books and specialist publications aimed at professionals working in the industry. Many also contribute to online publications or have their own websites or blogs. These freelancers bring to the table with them a vast wealth of knowledge, often gathered over a lifetime, and their depth of knowledge concerning their own particular specialist area within the subject – for example, a specific region or wine producing country – can often be greater than those who actually work within that specialist area of the industry.

Conversely, trained journalists who are latecomers to wine are often found working in-house at the various consumer wine magazines and book publishers, and also within specialist wine industry magazines, as either writers and/or editors. They apply their journalism skills to the editing of work done by freelancers, and also to writing the bulk of the content for their publication, making sure all copy is tailored to their publication's particular readership. To write effectively in-house for a specialist wine publication requires a good working knowledge of the subject, and importantly the ability to turn out articles with sound copy; but although working in-house requires a sound all-round grasp of the subject, it does not require the journalist to possess a bottomless depth of knowledge in all areas of the industry equivalent to that which a specialist of a particular field can bring to the publication on his specialist subject.

Either way, one thing is for certain, any budding wine writer or broadcaster must enjoy a passion for wine! And as with almost any specialist subject, if you do not possess this passion, a deep interest in and appreciation of wine, it would be a mistake to try to specialise in the subject.

Reviewer or critic?

For those who enjoy tasting and appreciating wine and are interested in the subject, but are not familiar with the concept of critiquing wine, to understand what is involved a good comparison can be found in arts reporting.

For instance, like reviewing or critiquing any of the arts – literature, paintings, photography, stage plays or film – reviewing or critiquing wine requires a similar mindset, though obviously different human senses, including of course taste and smell, come into play. In fact it is helpful to understand that many winemakers, especially those small producers who specialise in making high quality wines of individual character – in many cases boutique winemakers – consider themselves artists of a sort.

Campbell Titchener (2005: 11–12), in the third edition of his book *Reviewing The Arts*, touches upon the distinctions that are found between the trained journalist and untrained critic; and the point he makes regarding arts review journalists can be applied to wine journalism: 'A critic is primarily a critic, but a reviewer is a generalist,' he says.

> [T]hose who review for a living often begin their careers on small newspapers ... Critics may have taken this path or may have come from the Arts. An ongoing argument deals with whether it is easier to teach an artist journalism or a journalist an art.
>
> (Titchener 2005: 12)

He goes on to say that reviewers are normally found to have come from a background of journalism, whereas critics are usually found to have entered journalism through writing about their specialist art. The same can be said for the subject of wine.

As with arts journalism, both types of wine journalist – the reviewer and the critic – exist. A critic writes subjectively about the product – in other words the wine itself – while reviewers write objectively about the subject of wine.

The primary job of the wine critic is to aim his writing at the consumer and those who care passionately about the wine and the story behind it. Reviewers often write for the non-involved reader, for instance those people whose work involves the marketing of big wine brands or maybe those in the financial side of the industry, so they do not require the tasting expertise of the critic.

I have attended press visits to vineyards and wineries where there has been a mixture of journalists – critics whose journalism skills are basically self-taught, and reviewers, usually highly trained journalists who are new to the subject of wine (usually in-house employees of specialist wine publications). The latter, I'm afraid, have without exception always found themselves lost, left behind, rummaging around for something to say, eventually resorting to passing only the biased views of the producers of the wines they taste on to the reader. Inevitably their articles are almost always hardly worth reading, except to note the staggering lack of eruditeness contained within.

Therefore, unless an article being written about wine does not touch upon the taste of a wine, it is the critic – the life-long wine buff with his depth of knowledge and experience, or alternatively the journalist, who has enough passion about wine to teach themselves or gain an education on the subject – who holds a distinct advantage over the reviewer who has little or no tasting experience and relies solely on his journalism training and skills to write his articles.

In the case of specialist wine journalism, the best and most successful journalists are the ones who are versatile enough to act as both reviewer and critic when the matter of quality or character of a wine forms part of any article or feature, which more often than not, it does.

As in the case of arts reporting – film critiquing for instance – reading or listening to a good critique of a film can be almost as enjoyable as watching the film itself. The same can be applied to wine. It can be almost as interesting to read a good article about a wine and its background as to taste it.

The best of both worlds

The rarest and most successful of all breeds within specialist wine journalism are those consummate experts on the subject who also possess the talent to write and/or broadcast entertainingly. Good examples of successful writers such as this are British authors Jancis Robinson and Hugh Johnson, and in the USA there is Robert Parker. And of course there is UK-based broadcaster and writer Oz Clarke, whose books rank as best sellers and whose various television series dedicated to wine are watched by huge audiences worldwide. Inclusion of a producer's wine in their books or programmes – especially Parker's – can make a huge difference in the global sales figures and selling price of that wine. These wine writers and broadcasters tend not to specialise in one single area of wine but are relative experts in the whole field. Some have gained the professional qualification of Master of Wine (MW), a very difficult qualification within the industry to attain. However, even these distinguished writers and broadcasters, who are at the very top of the wine writing/broadcasting tree, engage specialist freelancers to contribute to passages of their books where their expertise might not be as strong as in others. Hugh Johnson's *Pocket Wine Book*, for instance, is these days written almost exclusively by freelancers.

To be a successful and well-published wine writer the breadth and depth of your general knowledge of the subject must equal or rise above that of producers, sommeliers, retailers and others in the industry, as it is often they who will make up your readership. They will expect that, in general, you will have as great or greater knowledge of the subject and industry, as a whole, than they – although inevitably in some of the more technical aspects of their particular area of the industry they will have the advantage of a more intricate working knowledge than you. And should you choose to specialise in a particular area of wine writing, for instance a particular region, your depth of knowledge will be expected to be as great, if not greater, than those who work at the sharp end in that particular area of the industry.

A good wine journalist must be able to decide for themselves which wines stand out from the crowded category of mediocre, whether – and importantly why – they are good or bad, and which wines to include and which wines to leave out of their coverage. They must be able to talk authoritatively about the wines, the regions, the grape varieties, the vineyards (soil, orientation, microclimates, etc.), the vintage, production methods and how these affect the wines, plus myriad other complexities involved in the subject. This all comes with the experience of tasting vast quantities of wine, studying the subject, visiting the regions, wineries and vineyards, and importantly mixing and talking with producers and others involved in the industry, as well as other wine journalists and writers/broadcasters.

The senses

In order to be able to comment on an individual wine, you will need to be able to see it, smell it and taste it.

Those of us who have an acute sense of smell and taste have an advantage over the rest. If these two senses are dull or lacking in you, then it may be that wine is the wrong subject for you to choose as your speciality in journalism. If these senses are good, they can be honed and trained to recognise all the characteristics of the various grapes, production methods, for instance whether a wine has been cellared in oak barrels or not, the characteristics of the vineyard – for instance the type of soil the vines are cultivated in – and even the climate where the grapes have been grown. In other words, your senses of sight, smell and taste can be trained to analyse the glass of wine in front of you, to blind taste wine and determine what it is made from, how it's made and where it comes from. When you participate as a judge in any wine competition sponsored by the *Organisation Internationale de la Vigne et du Vin* (OIV), you will be expected to taste blind, with usually only the vintage of the wines being tasted revealed to you.

When I began tasting wine in the 1970s with my father at the age of fourteen, I honed my senses on some of the most graceful wines of Bordeaux, Burgundy, Champagne, not to mention the rest of France, Italy (especially Tuscany) and other regions of importance at that time. However, those wines were relatively affordable then – today's prices for the same wines, even the younger vintages, are to say the least, astronomical. Unfortunately for most students and newcomers to wine tasting, this rules out the purchase of individual bottles of these legendary wines for self-training.

It is pointless trying to educate your palate on mass-produced cheap wines that taste the same wherever in the world they are made. However, the good news is that since the 1970s, many new world wine producing regions such as New Zealand, South Africa, Australia and even some of the lesser old world regions such as the south-west of France, are producing affordable wines of great individuality and character, which can be used to train the eye, nose and palate. If you want to train your own senses using wines you purchase yourself, then to guide you through the process I highly recommend Michael Broadbent's *Pocket Guide To Winetasting* (Mitchell Beazley in association with Christie's Wine Publications).

Good introduction and training courses in wine and spirit tasting are provided by the Wine & Spirit Education Trust. Their prospectus ranges from a level one foundation certificate course for beginners to their level five Honours Diploma: 'an individual research project that enables students to develop skills in research, evaluation and analysis in a wine and spirit related subject of their choice' (see www.wset.co.uk).

In the end, whichever pathway you choose to gain experience in tasting wine, it is the old adage 'practice makes perfect' THAT must remain the mantra for all budding or indeed practising wine journalists, no matter how much experience they have under their belts.

Writing styles

The number of opportunities in broadcast for specialist wine journalists is infinitesimally small.

Almost all wine journalists work either in print or online. The bulk of wine journalism consists of what, basically, is feature writing for specialist trade and specialist consumer magazines, myriad generalist magazines, local and national newspapers, websites and specialist wine books. Like any other type of feature writing, a wine writer must tailor his articles to the writing style of the publication.

For instance, the editor of UK-based specialist drinks industry magazine *Drinks International*, Christian Davis, requires both his in-house and freelance writers to adhere to a specific in-house style, which involves writing exclusively in the third person with all opinions expressed emanating from those interviewed rather than from the writer: '[I]n other words the reviewer's approach, reporting different opinions and letting the readers make up their own minds,' says Davis.

> Whereas the leading consumer specialist wine magazine Decanter might prefer a first person approach, with plenty of personal critique and observation – in other words the critic who bases their writing or his or her opinion. I see it as, basically, the difference between journalism – reporting different opinions and letting the reader make up their own minds – and being a [critic] who gives his or her opinion.

Getting started

There are two well-worn pathways to becoming a wine writer. There is the obvious route of applying for a job with one of the specialist publications, which I will not touch upon in this chapter.

The other pathway is to make your name in the freelance world. To do this it helps to be recognised as an authority in at least one particular area of the subject, for instance a specific wine producing region or country, or maybe an area of production such as biodynamic winemaking.

As with every other field of writing getting your first article published in a 'serious' publication is the most difficult part of getting started. Once you have been published by one of the recognised publications, under your own by-line, others will be more willing to publish your work. You can, of course, raise your own profile by creating a blog, or even a website containing your work. If your website or blog gains popularity or repute, the editors of the mainstream publications might discover you – especially if you make them aware of your work by emailing them the link to your website or blog.

However, if you are able to write and self-publish a book on – for instance – your specialist area, and send a perfect bound paperback, or casewrap hardbound copy, whichever you think best suits your style of book, to the editors of the publications you are targeting for work, this can produce two very beneficial spinoffs. Your book will often get a mention within the magazine, newspaper, or other chosen publication – therefore raising the profile of the book and hopefully its sales – and your name will be highlighted before the editor as a published authority on your particular specialist area. This often leads to an editor being far more amenable to publishing your work in his publication, and sometimes just sending the book with a follow-up phone call or email requesting a mention for your book in their publication can lead to an editor commissioning an article from you based on the content of your book. Always remember, editors are constantly searching for something, or someone, new.

Self-publishing a book

It is easy and cheap to self-publish a book in this day and age. You do not need to engage with a publishing company to have a book published. With the correct software or online service, such as lulu.com, a book can be written and typeset at home on your PC, your cover designed by you, including ISBN, your book(s) ordered and then delivered within a matter of days. You can order a single copy or small quantities of your own self-published book. Although ordering your book in small quantities from an online service means each single copy will work out more expensive per copy than ordering copies of your book in bulk, the advantage is the initial expenditure to have your book made and sent to you – looking exactly how you would like it to look on the shelves of a book shop, with it not looking at all out of place alongside books published by major publishing houses – is relatively small. Also, these online services often offer small percentage discounts based on the number of books ordered.

However, if you are fortunate enough to require copies of your book numbering thousands rather than tens or hundreds, printing firms such as Cox and Wyman (UK-based) will print off your ready typeset book for a minimal price per copy, with further large discounts for run-ons of 500 copies or more. However, Cox and Wyman, for instance, have a minimum order of 2,000 copies, so be prepared to foot a hefty bill to pay for a large number of books in the first instance – and there is also the question of storage.

Should you wish to sell your self-published book yourself, the most difficult hurdle to overcome is distribution. Finding shelf space for your book is hugely time-consuming and often results in failure. However, it can be done on an individual shop-by-shop basis. The most powerful vehicle for sales of self-published books is now undoubtedly the internet. Websites such as Amazon.com and indeed lulu.com provide a good presence on the market for any self-published book.

Professional bodies

As with any type of journalism, or indeed any profession, wine writing has its own professional bodies. Two of the most important are the UK-based – but nevertheless internationally represented in its membership – *Circle of Wine Writers* (CWW) and the *Federation International de Journalistes en Vin* (FIJEV), which is regulated by French law. Both are well worth the small membership fee in services, support and news, and both are essential tools for making and maintaining contacts in the profession, as well as within the wine industry itself. Obtaining membership of either or both these organisations also gives your CV an impressive hallmark of professionalism which editors who work within this specialised area of journalism will recognise. To join either of these bodies, you must be able to prove that you have been published.

Merchant and other press and professional tastings

Being a member of these professional bodies will, importantly, also help you to be invited to the numerous supermarket and wine merchant press tastings plus other such events that occur throughout the year. Many of the wine merchants in the UK use the CWW membership list to send out invitations, which can otherwise be very difficult to obtain.

Wine merchant press tastings are an invaluable way of building up your portfolio of wine tasting notes, which are the essential tool for any wine critic. Most supermarket and merchant press tastings give you the opportunity of tasting the bulk of the interesting wines on their lists with a view to recommending some in your articles. They also provide an invaluable networking tool within this specialist area of journalism.

There are also many regional and international wine exhibitions – such as the London International Wine Fair, Vinitaly and Vinexpo in France – which are useful for wine writers to attend. These gatherings attract producers either from the region or from the different wine producing countries of the world, and collect them under 'one roof'. They are especially useful should you wish to, say, specialise in one particular region and taste as many wines as possible from a particular region, all gathered at the one location rather than travel from vineyard to vineyard and winery to winery in a particular region, which is both time consuming and expensive. However, should you wish to write about a producer, per se, there is really no substitute for visiting the vineyard and winery!

Often, with the vast number of wines available to taste at these press gatherings, it is important to limit yourself to the wines that you think will be of interest to your readers. For instance, if your palate is only capable of fully understanding around 80 wines over the course of one day – as mine is – without becoming overtired and jaded, it is a pointless exercise trying to taste the full 200 or however many wines that are on display. You should pick and choose – for instance, if you are writing for a small local newspaper, your readers will probably be more interested in wines that retail for around £7 a bottle than £70. But if you are writing for, say, *Decanter* magazine, your readers will be very interested in your opinion on certain wines in the £70 price range – so you should select your wines carefully to suit your audience. When tasting large numbers of wines, to get the best from your palate, it is advisable to start with the top end lighter white wines, working downwards in quality and value, then move on to the fuller bodied wines, working in the same order. Then move on to the top end lighter bodied reds in the same way as the whites, finishing off with the bottom end full-bodied reds. This gives your palate the chance to appreciate the nuances of the lighter wines before the senses become dulled by exposure to the heavier styles of wine. Sweet wines must always be tasted last. The dulling of the palate in this way also plays quite a large part in the reason why so many of the wines that do well in competition are bigger and heftier in style   and winemakers will often target some of their fuller-bodied wines at wine competitions for precisely this reason. In fact, within the industry, certain wines are actually known as 'competition wines'. Having a winning wine in a competition can often have a significant influence upon the success of that wine both in marketing and sales.

International wine competition judging

Sometimes international wine exhibitions have wine competitions attached to them – for example Vinitaly. However, many of the major international wine competitions are standalone events. Should you attend as a judge, most will fly you out to the location where the event is being held, or pay your travel expenses for you. And you will always be accommodated in luxurious hotels and be exposed to the finest local restaurants and cuisine. Being invited to judge at these competitions is very good for your profile and CV, and will often enable you to taste wines of the host region as part of a group, with other writers, winemakers and others connected with the industry.

As a wine journalist, to apply to be invited to join a panel of judges at one or more of these competitions it is almost essential you are first published in one of the mainstream publications, or are a member of one of the recognised professional bodies.

Conclusion

Wine journalism, like all types of journalism, is fractured into many different strands.

For those few who reach the top of the tree it can be well paid; but for those who work piecemeal, although individual jobs can in themselves be reasonably lucrative it can be difficult to commission a sufficient amount of work within this speciality alone to make a good living. When first starting out in wine journalism it is important that a budding wine writer has other forms of journalistic work or another source of income to fall back on, which will sustain them through the initial process of becoming established.

Like many other areas of specialist journalism, wine journalism is strewn with many opposing viewpoints and opinions – it is important for the individual wine journalist to form their own opinions, take a view and be able to defend their view with clarity and most importantly, eruditeness.

The wine industry as a whole also contains, geographically, neighbouring nations which hold politically opposing positions. For instance, the winemakers of the Bekaa valley in Lebanon and the Israeli winemakers of the Golan Heights are near neighbours, but their countries have often seen conflict with each other, and feelings often run high between the two groups of winemakers. Both regions make wonderful wine and in my view the producers and wine of both countries should be treated equally and with a fairness that respects the individuality of the producers over and above the political landscape. Therefore the wine journalist, although there is no reason why he should not include an unbiased view of regional politics in his work, must rise above the political problems of any region and concentrate on his unbiased coverage of the product and what lies behind it – in other words the wine, the story and individuals.

Finding a niche as an authoritative voice on the subject of wine is becoming increasingly difficult, in large part because of the internet. Some professional writers feel that they are being squeezed out of the market by 'the static' of online amateurs. The internet has given a voice to the whole world, with everyone who wants to voice an opinion, erudite or not, having access to this gateway to the world. With the vast amount of opinion and amateur writing that is forthcoming on the internet on the subject of wine, you might think your voice will be drowned out. However, as with any other type of journalism, if you can place your work in the recognised, more 'serious' publications – whether in print or online – your voice will inevitably rise above the rest and you will become known and respected as an authority within the field.

Above all if you apply comprehensiveness, consistency, accuracy and fairness as another of your mantras, you will find the more you become known and recognised as an erudite reviewer and/or critic within this specialist area of journalism, the more keenly your opinion and work will be sought after by editors and producers of 'serious' specialist and mainstream print and broadcast media.

Bibliography

Titchener, C. B. (2005) *Reviewing The Arts*. 3rd edn New Jersey, London: Lawrence Erlbaum Associates.

Directory of useful websites

Sports

Associated Press Sports Editors – http://apsportseditors.org
Employment guide – http://globalsportsjobs.com
Horse Racing – www.hwpa.org
Message boards – www.sportsjournalists.com
Snack Media Guide – http://thefootballjournalist.com
Soccer Writing – www.footballjournalism.co.uk
The Road to Sports Journalism – http://haydenpackwood.wordpress.com
The Sports Journalists Association – www.sportsjournalists.co.uk
USA national sports journalism center – http://sportsjournalism.org
USA sports reporting tips – http://sportsfieldguide.com/sports

Business

BBC Business Journalism Guide – www.bbc.co.uk/journalism/briefing/business/reporting-business
History of Business Journalism – www.bizjournalismhistory.org
Institute for Economic Affairs – www.iea.org.uk
Reuters handbook – http://handbook.reuters.com/index.php/Main_Page
Reynolds Center for Business Journalism – http://businessjournalism.org
The Wincott Foundation – www.wincott.co.uk/main.htm

Politics and international affairs

Centre for Investigative Journalism – www.tcij.org
Iain Dale – www.iaindale.com
John Snow – http://blogs.channel4.com/snowblog
Journalists Toolbox – www.journaliststoolbox.org/archive/electionspolitics
Michael White – www.guardian.co.uk/profile/michaelwhite+politics/blog
Paul Staines (Guido Fawkes) – http://order-order.com
Society of Professional Journalists – www.spj.org
10 Downing Street – www.number10.gov.uk

Crime

British Crime Survey (Home Office) – http://homeoffice.gov.uk/science-research/research-statistics/crime/crime-statistics/british-crime-survey
Institute for Justice and Journalism – www.justicejournalism.org
Journalism Center on Children and Families – www.journalismcenter.org
Organised Crime and Corruption Reporting Project – www.reportingproject.net/occrp

Environmental journalism

End of the Line – http://endoftheline.com
International Federation of Environmental Journalists – www.ijej.org
IPCC – www.ipcc.ch
Society of Environmental Journalists – www.sej.org
World Environmental Organisation – http://world.org

Motoring

Guild of Motoring Writers – www.gomw.co.uk/information/show/pagename/journalism

Fashion

Business of Fashion – www.businessoffashion.com
FashionNet – www.fashion.net
Fashion Stylist – www.fashion-stylist.net
Style Factory – http://thestylefactory.co.uk
StyleFirst – http://stylefirst.co.uk/academy

Food

Guild of Food Writers – www.gfw.co.uk
International Food, Wine and Travel Writers Association – http://ifwtwa.org
New Zealand Guild of Food Writers – www.foodwriters.org.nz

Music

Ask the Indie Professor – www.guardian.co.uk/music/series/ask-the-indie-professor
Collapseboard – www.collapseboard.com
NME – www.nme.com
Pitchfork – http://pitchfork.com
Rockfeedback – www.rockfeedback.com
Rock's Back Pages – www.rocksbackpages.com

Media

Centre for Investigative Journalism – www.tcij.org
Journalism – www.journalism.co.uk
Media Week – www.mediaweek.co.uk
Online Journalism – http://onlinejournalismblog.com
Press Gazette – www.pressgazette.co.uk

Science

African Federation of Science Journalists – www.africansciencejournalists.com
Association of British Science Writers – www.absw.org.uk
British Science Association articles – www.britishscienceassociation.org
Council for the Advancement of Science Writing – http://casw.org

Science and Development Network – www.scidev.net
World Federation of Science Journalists – www.wfsj.org

Medical

European Health Journalism (Coventry University) – www.europeanhealthjournalism.com
Free Medical Journals – www.freemedicaljournals.com/index.htm
Guild of Health Writers – www.healthwriters.com
Health News Review – www.healthnewsreview.org
Medical Journalists Association – www.mjauk.org
Medical Journalism USA – www.europeanhealthjournalism.com

Legal affairs

British and Irish Legal Information – www.bailii.org
Journalism Resources – http://cubreporters.org/legal_journalism.html
Joshua Rozenberg – www.rozenberg.net
Legal Cheek – www.legalcheek.com
UK Statutes – www.hmso.gov.uk

Travel

Australian Society of Travel Writers – www.astw.org.au
British Guild of Travel Writers – www.bgtw.org
Global Travel Writers – www.globaltravelwriters.com
International Food, Wine and Travel Writers Association – http://ifwtwa.org
International Society for Travel Writing – http://istw-travel.org/resources.html
North American Travel Journalists Association – www.natja.org
Outdoor Writers and Photographers Guild – www.owpg.org.uk
Travel Association of Canada – www.travelmedia.ca
Travel Journalists Guild – www.tjgonline.com

War reporting

War and Media Network – www.warandmedia.org/index.htm

Wine

Academy of Wine Communications – http://academyofwine.org/awc
Circle of Wine Writers – www.winewriters.org
International Food, Wine and Travel Writers Association – http://ifwtwa.org

Index

abstract/distant issues 62
abuse of power 8
academic journals 139, 142–43
academic medicine 150–53
academic study 69–70, 77, 85, 87, 92, 107–12, 117–22, 161–62
accountability 33, 52, 55–56
accuracy 26–27, 51, 53–55, 61, 142, 144, 147, 164, 187–88, 200
activists 60, 66, 140
Adams, S. 107–8
Adams, T. 104
added value 133
adversarial journalism 60, 66
advertising 79–83, 90–92, 97, 99, 103, 156, 161, 172, 180
Afghan War 181, 183–84, 186
Age 12
agencies 4, 6, 21, 23–24
agenda control 34
aggregation 133
Agha-Soltan, Neda 51
al Qaeda 186
alerts 126–27
Ali, Rafat 133
Allan, S. 135, 139, 143–44
Allan, Stuart 174
AllThingsD 127
Almassi, Hannah 86–93
Altagamma 85
Amazon.com 198
Amed, I. 83
American Medical Association 149–50
American Psychiatric Association 151
analytical approach 21, 27, 190
Anderson, Alison 60
Anderson, B. 109, 118

Andrews, Robert 133
Angeletti, N. 80
Anglo-American model 50–58
animal welfare issues 96
annual rhythms 125
anonymity orders 169
AnOther Magazine 81
apologies publishing 167
apps 81, 83
Arguido status 166–67
arranging interviews 125–26
arts reporting 193–94
Asian tsunami 2005 51
Asos 81, 83
assassinations 57
Associated Press 50–51, 53–54, 56
Association of Motoring Writers Groups 75
Association of Publishing Agencies 83
AstraZeneca 155
Atherton, Michael 19
Atkinson, Ron 17
Atomic Energy Authority 64
Atton, C. 114, 120–22
atypical antipsychotics 153–58
audience appeal 53, 62, 77, 79, 81, 83, 110, 114, 165, 179, 193, 199
Australian Open, 2012 12
authenticity 84, 114
authority issues 102–5, 113–14, 119, 139–41, 200
Auto Express 71
Autocar 71, 73–74, 77
automotive journalism 69–77
Automotive Journalists Association of Canada 75
Autosport International 73
awards 66–67, 76–77, 125, 190

B2B journalism 3, 23, 25, 75, 86, 124, 133, 192
balance 8, 30, 42, 64, 91, 140–41, 164, 187–88
banal journalism 54–57
Bangs, Lester 113
banking crisis 20, 26
Barber, L. 91
Barnado's study 44
Barnett, S. 35
Battuta, Ibn 176
Baudrillard, Jean 118
Bayer 148
Bayh-Dole Act 152–53
BBC 6, 25–27, 30, 56, 66, 69, 71, 100, 103, 131, 161
Bear Sterns 20
Beatty, Andrew 171
Bedard, Patrick 69
Belfast Telegraph 24
Bell, David 97, 100–101
Benson, R. 97
Berners-Lee, Tim, Sir 6
Bhopal disaster 66
Bhoyrul, Anil 26
biannual magazines 81
bias 72, 139, 186, 194
Biederman, Joseph 152
Big Four news agencies 50–51
Billig, M. 54
biodiversity 64–65, 67
Birmingham Post 24
Blair, Tony 30, 33–36
blogs/bloggers 11, 14, 27, 52, 79, 83, 88, 103, 114, 121, 127, 132; high profile 53; journalist 55, 86, 93, 126, 131, 133, 197; media 130–31; microblogging 53–54, 84–85; photography 89–90; political 33; practitioner 163–64
Bloomberg 23–24, 26
Blumenthal, Heston 101
book publishing 14, 172, 197–98
Bostic, Jeffrey 151
Boston Globe 155
Bourdieu, Pierre 97–98, 101, 114
Bow Street Runners 45–46, 48
Boyd-Barrett, O. 50–51, 56
BP Gulf disaster 61–63, 167
Bradford stadium disaster 164, 168
brand magazines 81–82, 100
branding 19, 91, 103, 113
Brants, Kees 36
Brazil Olympics, 2016 13–14
breaking news 54–55

Brennan, Marc 111–13
brevity 126
Briefing Media 133
Briffa, Dr John 102
Brillat-Savarin, Anthelme 98
British Airways 25–26
British and Irish legal database 164
British Cycling 16
British Fashion Council 81
British Leyland 74
British Medical Journal 9, 139, 142, 148
Britten, A. 110
Broadbent, Michael 196
Brown, D. 97
Brown, Gordon 33–34
Browne Review 120
Brownlee, S. 73
Bryanboy 83–84
Bryson, Bill 171
Burchill, Julie 113
business journalism 20–28
Business Life 25
business readership 24–25
Business Week 21
BusinessDesk.com 27
Buying Cars 77

campaign groups 60
campaigning journalism 74
Campbell, Alastair 32–37
cancer prevention reporting 143–44
CAR 71, 75, 77
Car and Driver 69
car testing 72–76
carbon emissions 62–65
Cardiff School of Journalism 6
Carson, Rachel 62
Cartner-Morley, Jess 79–80, 82–83, 85, 88, 90–92
Cassels, A. 143
Caterer & Hotelkeeper 100
catwalk shows 87–88
CCTV footage 44
celebrity 43, 79–80, 87–88, 97, 100–104, 124
Centre for Investigative Journalism 2, 7
Chalaby, J. 50, 56
Chappell, R. 134–39, 143
Chartered Institute of Journalists 75
Chat 86
Chatwin, Bruce 175, 177–78
chequebook journalism 47
Chesney, Kellow 41
Chibnall, Steve 40, 45
Chicago Tribune 155

children news value 44
Chilean miners rescue 2010 54
Christgau, Robert 121
chronological rearrangement 178
Churchill, Winston 30, 50
Ciancio, A. 85
Circle of Wine Writers 198
citizen journalism 11, 51–53, 56, 83–84,
    103, 121
City Slickers column, *Mirror* 26
civil law 160–63
civil liberties 45, 48
clarity 13, 120, 135–36, 147, 200
Clark, Sam 96
Clarke, Oz 194
Clarkson, Jeremy 69
class issues 97–99
cliché 173, 177, 179
climate change 60–65
clinical trials 152, 154–58
Clover, Charles 66
Cockburn, Patrick 186
Cockerell, M. 35
Coddington, Grace 85
codes of conduct 26, 75
Cohen, A. 56–57
Cohen, Stanley 40–41
collaborative knowledge production 52
Collin, Robert 74
colonialism 174–76
combat zones 183–84, 191
commerce-editorial content mix 83, 91
commodification 118
Company 81, 86
compensation stories 164–65, 168–69
competition wines 199
composition of the media 12
Concordia cruise ship disaster 167–68
confidentiality 161, 166
conflicts of interest 142–43
Conrad, P. 140
consensus 140–41
consequences of inaccuracy 143–44
conservative ideology 44
consumer journalism 3, 74, 100, 102, 119,
    192, 196
consumerism 15–16, 114
contacts/sources: cultivation of 6–7, 12,
    17–18, 22, 35, 74, 127–28, 130–31,
    140; independence from 7, 18, 20–21,
    26–27, 35, 61, 64–65, 72, 82, 124;
    reliability judgements 139–43
contempt of court 162
content-production skills 71

contextualisation 112, 117–18, 141–42,
    189
continuity 188
contract law 166
convergence of specialisms 97
cookery columns 100–101, 103
Copping, N. 89
copy approval arrangements 18
Cordero, R. 81
corporate mentality 135, 145
corruption 48, 72–73, 152–53, 157–58
Cosmopolitan 81
Coulson, Andy 35–36
counterculture press 114
County Court hearings 165
court reporting 160–63, 169
Cox and Wyman 197
crash tests 74
creative sector 124
credibility 8–9, 61–62, 81, 83, 90, 92, 140
credit crunch 20
crime reporting 39–48, 160–62, 166–67,
    169
Crimewatch 46–47
criminal law 160
Cropley, Steve 70, 72, 77
crowd sourcing 121
Crown Prosecution Service 160
cultural change 79
cultural hegemony 50
cultural proximity 43, 56–57
Cumberford, Robert 69
Curran, James 32
customer magazines 81
cyberspace 11
cynicism 36, 48

Daily Express 1, 166
Daily Mail 8, 24, 165
Daily Mirror 26, 189
Daily Star 166
Daily Telegraph 5, 60, 63, 66–67, 82–84,
    137, 161
Daimler 71
Dale, Henry, Sir 148
Dale, Iain 33
dangers 184, 189, 191
Daniels, Jeff 69, 74
data-driven journalism 6–7
David, Elizabeth 101
Davies, Nick 2, 6, 137–38, 141–42
Davis, A. 31
Davis, Christian 196
Deacon, Giles 80

deadlines 28, 87, 93, 138
Dearing, James 140–41
death of audience 52
Decanter 196, 199
defence correspondents 181, 183–85,
    190–91
definition of specialist 2, 5
democracy 48
Department of Culture, Media and Sport
    124, 128
deskilling 142
destination profiles 172
deviance 39, 41, 43–44, 57
D&G 2010 catwalk show 84
diary events 125–26
Dickens, Charles 30
distortion 40, 43–44, 141
DIY culture 114
Djokovic, Novak 12–13, 17
D'Monte, Darryl 66
Dodd, Mike 161–62, 164–65
Dore, Garance 84
dot.com boom 22
Dow Jones 23–24, 26
Doyle, G. 22
dramatisation 41, 43
Drapers 82
Drinks International 196
DrownedInSound.com 107–8, 114, 121
dumbing down 9–10, 141–42, 187
Dunne, Peter Finlay 8
Dunton incident 39
Dunwoody, S. 134–36, 139–40, 143
Durham-Humphrey Amendment 149–50

Earth Summits 59
economic pressures 107–8, 115; *The
    Economist* 21, 24–25
editors 7, 137, 141
education 9, 22, 108
Edwards, Richard 5
Ehrlich, Paul 148
Elbo.ws 121
electric cars 71
Eliot, P. 51
email alerts 126–27
Emap 25
embedded journalists 183, 185–90
emotional elements 111–12
employer-employee relations 165–66
employment prospects 3–4, 11–13, 24, 66;
    alternative routes 14–17, 25; decreasing
    opportunities 15–16, 161; getting
    started 69, 75, 85–86, 121, 196–97

engagement 109–10, 113, 116, 122
Enron exposé 22
entrance exams 24
environmental concerns 76
environmental journalism 59–67
equipment for war reporting 185
Esquire 83
ethical issues 5, 8, 18, 21, 26, 46, 48, 55,
    71–72, 75, 90–92, 186
EuroNCAP test programme 74
European Commission 134, 136–38
European Community 64
European Court of Human Rights 162
European Court of Justice 162–63
European Union 26
European Union law 165
Eurosport 16
Evening Standard 24, 101, 103
events planning 81–82, 90, 125–26
everyday routines 12, 23, 86–90, 93,
    125–27, 137–38
Evo 71
exaggeration 42, 44, 141, 143
exclusivity of lobby journalists 31–32, 37
expansion of sectors 1, 11, 16, 21, 32,
    59–60, 79
experience 109–11, 116, 118
expertise 16–17, 24, 59, 61–62, 67, 69–71,
    90, 121, 165, 181–83, 194–95, 200
experts 139–40, 147, 151–52, 158

fabrications 178–79
Fabulous 82; *The Face* 85
Facebook 14, 51, 79, 84–85, 130
Facehunter 89
fact checking 5, 137–40, 142–43, 145, 165
fairness 135, 141, 188, 200
Falklands War 183
Fantastic Man 81, 86
fanzines 114, 121
fascination with crime 39–40
fashion journalism 79–93
fashion spreads 89–90
Fawkes, Guido 33
Fearnley-Whittingstall, Hugh 101
Federation International de Journalistes en
    Vin 198
Federer, Roger 17
Ferguson, Alex, Sir 17
Ferguson, Priscilla Parkhurst 98
Fermor, Patrick Leigh 175
Ferrari 73
festivals 110, 125
Fielding, Henry and John 46

fields concept 97–98
financial interests 149–50, 158, 194
financial journalism 20–28, 141
financial press 124
Financial Services Authority 26
Financial Times 24
Finland, Maxwell 150
Finnan, S. 88
Flat Earth News 2, 6, 137
Fleming, Alexander 148
Flink, J. J. 71–72
fluidity of production/consumption 51–52
fly on the wall documentaries 44
Flynn, Laurie 154
following the money 19–20, 147, 158
following the story 14, 191
Food and Drug Administration 149,
    153–57
food journalism 96–105
food production issues 96, 102, 104
Forbes magazine 21
Forde, E. 113, 120–22
foreign correspondents 50–51
Foreign Office 32
Forest Laboratories 151
formulaic writing 40, 138, 173, 178–80
Fortune 21–22, 150
framing of news 56–57
Franklin, Bob 35
free magazines 81–82, 100, 172
freelance work 2, 4–6, 23, 85, 162, 192,
    194, 196
Freeman, Hadley 92
Friedman, S. M. 134, 136
Friends of the Earth 60, 64
Frith, Simon 110, 113, 115, 117,
    120–22
frontline reporting 183–84
FT.com 22, 27
Fugger newsletters 20

Gaber, I. 35–36
gagging clauses 169
Galliano, John 80; *The Garden* 105
garotting scare 41
Garval, M. 99
gastrochick 103
gastronomes 98, 101, 104
gatekeepers 51, 53–55, 109, 111, 114,
    119–21, 136
gender issues 91–92, 97–99, 101, 104
General Electric 21
general reporting 2–3, 22, 69, 136–37,
    161, 164, 166

generational gap 84, 111, 115–16, 121;
    The Gentlewoman 81
geographical proximity 43
George, Lloyd 33
Germany 47
Gevinson, Tavi 83
ghost writing 14, 158
Gibb, Frances 161
Gibson, Guy 182
gifts and hospitality 26, 72, 91, 125, 153, 199
GigaOM 127
Giggs, Ryan 17
Gill, A. A. 101
Gillett, Charlie 121
Gillmor, Dan 103
Glamour 81, 86
GlaxoSmithKline 151
Glazer, William 154
global perspectives 50, 53, 55, 65–66
Goldacre, B. 134–37, 139–41
Golding, P. 51, 56
Good Food 103
Good Housekeeping 99
Goodwin, Frederick 151
Goodwood Festival of Speed 73
Google News 27, 126–27
Gourmet Good Food 100
government documents 155–58
government ministries/departments 60,
    64–65, 149, 153–57, 163, 185, 189–90
graduate schemes 15
Gramophone 115
Grand, Katie 85
Grant, Amanda 101
Grassley, Charles 151
Grazia 81, 86–93
Great British Food 100
greedygourmet 103
Green Book (MoD) 185
Green, L. 83
Green Party 59
Greenpeace 60
greenwash stories 60–61
Gregory, J. 136, 140–43
Grey-Yambao, Bryan 83
Griffin, R. J. 140, 143–44
Grigson, Jane 101, 104
Grimod de la Reynière, Alexandre 98–99;
    The Grocer 99
Guardian 1, 6; automotive 70; business 24;
    environment 59, 63; fashion 79–80,
    85–86; food 96, 101, 103; legal affairs
    161–62, 166; media 127, 132; music 110;
    politics 32, 36; science 137; sports 15

Guild of Motoring Writers 70, 75–76
Gulf Wars 183

hacking scandal 35, 37
Hales, Mark 69
Halliday, Josh 132
Hammond, Richard 69
Hanke, Robert 101–2
Hanna, M. 80
Hansen, A. 136, 139–40
Hare Krishna dairy story 96
Harper's Bazaar 80
Harrods 83
Hartz, J. 134–39, 143
Hatfield, Greg 22
Hawkes, Nigel 142
Haymarket Media Group 25, 70, 77
health information reporting 143–44
HealthNewsReview.org 142
Hebdige, Dick 113
Heffernan, Richard 33
Help for Heroes 190
Hencke, D. 36
Henley committee 108
high street store press days 88
high-end fashion glossies 80–81
higher education 69–70, 77, 85, 92, 108–9
Hillsborough stadium disaster 164, 168
Hilton, Perez 53
hip hop 119
Hipwell, James 26
historical perspectives 20–22, 30–33,
    39–40, 45–46, 71, 80, 97–99, 147–50,
    171, 181–83
H&M 80
Hollows, Joanne 100–101
homecoming parades 190
Hootsuite 127
horizontal media 51; *The Horseless
    Age* 71
Horton, R. 139
Hoskyns, Barney 112–14, 117–18, 120
house styles 196
Huffington, Arianna 53; *The Huffington
    Post* 53
Hughes, K. 97
Human Rights Act 166
humanitarian perspective 186, 191
Hurt, John 102
Hussein, Saddam 183
Hutchison, Julia 83
hype 138, 141, 144, 158; The Hype
    Machine 121
hyperspecialization 121

IASPM 108–9
Icke, David 59
i-D 85
idea production 90
ideological issues 62, 66, 114
Iliffe, William Isaac 71
imagined communities 109, 111, 118
inattentive press 138, 144
Incisive 25
independence 55–56, 186–87, 191; from
    advertisers 90–91; from contacts/
    sources 7, 18, 20–21, 26–27, 35, 61, 64,
    72, 82, 124
Independent 32, 137, 186
Independent on Sunday 60
in-depth features 129
India 66
individual voice 12–13
individualism news value 42, 48
industry conferences 125
industry press offices 73–74
inflight magazines 172
influence of the media 9, 20, 25–26, 36,
    40–41, 46, 66
Ingham, Bernard 32–34
Inglis, I. 107, 115–16
in-house journalism 5–6, 192, 196
in-house lawyers 162, 164–66
Inside Soap 86
insider dealing 26
insider positions 37
Institute of Public Policy Research 86
insurance 184
intellectual property 52, 55
interactivity 51–52, 79, 102
interdependency 30–31, 35–36, 57, 72
international audiences 52–53
International Federation of Environmental
    Journalists 66
International Federation of Music
    Journalists 109
international journalism 50–58
International Motor Press Association 75
internet 15, 23, 33, 50–51, 55,
    57, 163
internships 24, 86, 93
interpersonal communication 53
intuition 67
investigative approach 2, 21–22, 47, 62,
    74, 147, 155, 158, 165, 169
Ipsos MORI 62–63
Iraq War 34–35, 52, 57, 181–83, 185–87,
    189
Islam, Syed Manzurul 177

J Brand 81
Jack of all trades approach 2–3, 5, 8–9
Jaguar 76
James, Martin 117–18
Jamie Magazine 100
Janssen 152, 154–57
Jewkes, Yvonne 40–45
job security 66
John Lewis Edition 81
Johnson, Dr. Samuel 1, 9–10
Johnson, Hugh 194
Journal Media 86
Journal of the American Medical Association 142
Journalism 2.0 50–52, 54, 116
judicial review hearings 163
juvenile offenders 44–45

Kane, Christopher 80, 84
Kansara, Vikram Alexei 83
Kapuściński, Ryszard 174, 178–79
Kassirer, Jerome 152
Kawamura, Y. 87
Kelly affair 34
Kerrang! 110, 115–16
Kings Cross tube fire 164
Kiss, Jemima 127, 130, 132
Knight, E. F. 175
Koch, Robert 148
Kompany, Vincent 14
Korte, Barbara 173, 178
Kovach, B. 52, 55–56
Kruif, Paul de 148
Kuper, Simon 14

labour mobility 85
Lady's Magazine 80
Lagerfeld, Karl 80
Laing, Dave 110, 112–13, 121
Lamb, Liz 86; *The Lancet* 139, 142, 158
Langmead, Jeremy 83
launch events 71–72
Law Commission 163; *The Law Society Gazette* 161
Lawson, Nigella 101; *The Lawyer* 161
laziness 178–79
Lean, Geoffrey 60, 64
learning on the job 3, 5, 15, 22, 28, 69, 75, 77, 86, 93
legal affairs journalism 160–70
Legal Week 161
legitimacy 57
Lehman Brothers 20
Lehmkuhl, M. 134

Leterme, Yves 57
Levinas, Emmanuel 174
Levine, Irving R. 22
Lewin, K. 51
Lewis, Alan 110
Lewis, Juliette 96
Lewis, Martin 22
Lewis, Tania 103
libel damages 167
Liberty London Girl 83
Lieberman, Jeffrey 158
lifestyle 101–4, 110
Lilly, Eli 148, 154, 157
Linden, Thomas 147
line of sight approach 53–54, 58
LinkedIn 27, 130
list features 172
literary-scientific polarity 134–37
live reporting 126
LLB courses 162, 166
lobby system 31–37
local papers 3, 9, 15, 77
local radio 15
Lockerbie bombing 57
Loffelholz, M. 51, 53
London College of Fashion 85–86
London International Wine Fair 198
London Olympics 2012 12
London-centricity 101–2
Look 84–86, 88
Los Angeles Times 155
Love Magazine 81, 85; lulu.com 197–98
LVMH Moet Hennessy 80
Lyst 84

Mabey, Richard 61
MacFadyen, Gavin 2
Madden, Lawrie 19
magazines 1–2, 25, 27, 80–82, 89, 100, 172
magic bullets stories 148
Maguire, Kevin 35
Mail on Sunday 24, 82
mailing lists 130
Maillard, Arnaud 16
Major, John 32
Manchester Guardian 1, 11
Manchester United 17
Mandelson, P. 35; *The March of Medicine* 150
Marcus, Griel 113, 121
Marie Claire 81, 104
Marks 67
McCartney, Stella 80

McCrystal, D. 22
McKay, J. 81
McLuhan, M. 55
McQueen, Alexander 80
McRobbie, A. 82, 85
McRobbie, Angela 91
meaning making 52–53, 55, 57, 109–12, 116, 120
media developments 79
media law 22, 47, 69, 162
media management strategies 33–35, 60
media reporting 124–33
media-political process 34
medical journals 139, 155
medical reporting 147–58
MedPage Today 8
Meibach, Richard 154
Melody Maker 110, 113, 117–19, 121
Mennell, Stephen 98–99, 104
Mercedes-Benz 74
metamusic 112–13
Metro 9
Metropolitan Police 46
Metykova, M. 52–53
Michael, George 43
microgenres 121
military perspective 181–82, 186, 190–91
Millbrook Proving Ground 73
Miller, S. 136, 140–43
Milligan, L. 84
minority views 14, 140
miracle worker stories 148
Miranda warnings 167
Mitchell, Joni 111
mobile devices 16, 27
Mojo 110, 116, 119
monetising 16, 82–83
mood boards 89
Moon landings 57
moral panic 40–46
morality tales 60
Morely, Paul 121
Morley, Elliott 5
Moses, L. 83
Moss, Kate 43
Motor Industry Research Association 73
Motor 73–74
Motor Press Guild 75
Motoring Correspondens' Circle 75
Moynihan, R. 142–43
MP3 118
MPs expenses scandal 5, 35–37
MSN News 27
mugging 40–41

multimedia approaches 25–26, 90, 101, 116, 131–32
Murdock, G. 56
Murray, Andy 17
music journalism 107–22
Music Standards Grant 108
MySpace 83, 103, 130

Nadal, Rafael 12–13, 17
naming and shaming 45
narrative 177–78
Nast, Condé 80, 83
National Crime Statistics 42
national identity 54
National Institutes of Health (US) 152, 157
National News Agency 54
national newspapers 23
Nature 139
nature conservation 65
Naylor, Laura 84
NBC 22
Needell, Tiff 69–70
Nelkin, D. 134–38, 140–44
Nemeroff, Charles 151
Net-a-Porter 83
networking 17, 54, 75–76, 84–85, 103, 198
neutrality 30, 141, 163
Neveu, E. 97
new angles 129
New England Journal of Medicine 139, 151–53
New Labour 34
New Look 80
New Scientist 139
New York Herald 20
New York Post 21
New York Times 20, 53, 84, 154, 156
Newcastle chronicle 86
news agencies 21, 23–24, 50–52, 54–56
News Chronicle 1
News Corporation 24
news management systems 32
News of the World 35, 37, 82
news values 40–45, 50, 56–57, 136–37, 169
newsgathering 50, 55, 73, 87, 127–29
Newsnight 32, 66
newspapers 12, 30, 82, 87, 100, 102 *see also individual papers*
newsrooms 23, 56
newsworthiness 56–57, 63, 124, 127–29, 137, 164, 166
NGOs 60

Niblock, S. 97
niche magazines 74–75
niche topics 1, 14, 21, 53, 200
Nichols, Mel 77
NME 107–8, 110, 112–13, 115–17, 119, 121
Noakes, A. 70
Northern Rock 26
novelty 40–41, 57, 97, 99, 103–4, 128, 137, 171
Noyes, Alexander 20
NUJ 4, 22, 26, 110
nutritional issues 98, 102

Obama, Barack 57
objectivity 8, 20, 26–27, 52, 54, 91, 114, 135, 138–39, 141, 193
Oborne, P. 34
O'Brien, L. 112, 114, 119–20
Observer 24, 59–60, 100, 102, 104–5
O'Connell, Dominic 27–28
Ofcom 26, 128
off-the-record briefings 31–33, 35
olanzapine 154, 156–57
Oliva, A. 80
online journalism 16, 25, 56, 82–83, 92, 100, 102–5, 107–9, 111, 121, 126, 133
operational security 185, 188
opinion 54–55
Organisation Internationale de la Vigne et du Vin 195–96
Orientalism 174–78
otherness 173–74, 176–80
outsider positions 39, 41, 44
over-fishing 67
Oxford Media Conference 125

paedophilia stories 44, 169
paidContent 126, 133
paparazzi 88
Parade 155
parish constables 45
Parke, Beth 66
Parker, R. 100, 194
Parkin, David 27
parliamentary debates 30–31
Parliamentary Press Gallery 31–33, 35–37
parrot reporting 8–9, 15, 20, 26, 35, 72–73, 91, 137, 194
participatory journalism 102–3
partisan writing 30
Pasteur, Louis 148
Patten, John 6
Patterson, Jane 35

Paulussen, S. 102
pay and conditions 22–23, 28, 86, 93, 199–200
Pearce, L. 73
Pearson 24
Pebble Beach Concours 73
Peck, Peggy 8
peer review 135–36, 139
Penman, Ian 121
performativity 113
periodicals 1–2, 9
peripheral openings 17
personalisation 41, 113
pharmaceutical industry 148–54, 156–58
photography 72, 81, 84, 87–90, 93
Pinault-Printemps-Redoute 80
Pinterest 84
Pitchfork 114, 121
planning and preparation 125–26, 181, 184–86
Polan, B. 82
Police and Criminal Evidence Act 167
police-press relationship 45–48
political elements 140, 200
political journalism 30–37
politician-journalist relationship 35–37
pollution 63
Polo, Marco 176–77
Polyvore.com 84
Pope, Albert A. 71
populist model 44–45
Porter, Charlie 86
Porter, D. 20
portfolio careers 11, 116
Portuguese legal system 166–67
positivity 92
practitioner-theorist divide 109–13, 117–19, 121–22
predictability 42
press advisors 33
Press Association 24, 54, 161
Press Complaints Commission 26, 128
press conferences 166–67
Press Gazette 131, 133
press launches 71–73
press releases 142–44
press wine tastings 198–99
pressure 28, 81, 132
pressure groups 60–61
Preston, Robert 25–26
Prime Minister's Official Spokesman 33–35
Private Eye 25
privatisation 21

productivity demands 72
progress stories 148–49, 153, 155, 158
protest campaigns 163
proximity news value 43, 56–57
psychiatry 151–58
public and private spheres 99
public interest 30, 40, 46–48, 62, 99, 161, 167
public relations 8, 21–22, 26–28, 32, 36, 56, 69, 73–75, 85–93, 137, 142–45, 163
public sector 163
publish and be damned principle 56
Puchan, H. 74
punditry 18–19
Punk 117

Q 110, 116
qualifications 2, 61, 69–70, 77, 85, 92, 161, 194, 196; The Quietus 121
Quinn, Frances 162
quotes pieces 15

race issues 40–41
radio 21, 25, 30–31, 35, 66
Rafter, K. 37
Ransohoff, D. F. 71
recession 20
recruitment 24
recycled news 54–55, 137, 142
Red 86
Reed Business Information 25
Reed, Paula 81
reform, calls for 36
regional press 187
regulation 26, 48, 55
relevance 137
report reading 126
reporting practices and standards 50
reporting restrictions 162
research 87, 149–50, 154, 164, 182
resources 5
responsibility 185, 191
restaurant reviews 100–103
Reuters 21, 23, 26, 50–51, 56
reviews/criticism 115, 117, 122, 193–94, 196
Reynolds Centre for Business Journalism 7
Reynolds, S. 115, 118–21
Reynolds, Simon 113
Richemont 80
Rickey, Melanie 93
risk news value 42, 144
risperidone 154–56
Robinson, Jancis 194

Rochdale Advertiser 69
Rocksbackpages (RBP) 117
Rogers, C. L. 134, 136
Rogers, E. M. 51
Roitfeld, Carine 85, 91
rolling news 51, 55, 138
Rooney, Wayne 12, 18
Roots 115
Rosen, J. 52
Rosenstiel, T. 52, 55–56
Ross, F. 32
Ross, Karen 35, 37
Roy, R. 86
Royal Television Society 125
Rozenberg, Joshua 161–64
RSPB 64, 67
RSS feeds 53, 127, 131
runway shows 87–88

Sabshin, Melvin 151
Said, Edward 174–77, 179
Salk, Jonas 148–49
Salomon Brothers 23
Sanders, K. 80
Sardar, Ziauddin 176
Sawyer, Kathy 135
scepticism 36, 62–64, 135
Schatzberg, Alan 154
Schechter, D. 20
Scherer, D. 89
Schuman, Scott 84, 89; The Sartorialist 84, 89
Schwartz, L. M. 142
Schwitzer, G. 142
Science 139
science journalism 134–45
scientific agenda 142–43
scientific knowledge: lacking in mainstream media 61
Scotsman 24, 32
Scott, C. P. 11
seasonality 125
secrecy ethos 32, 35
secret justice stories 47, 161, 169
self-censorship 124
Selfridges 81
self-taught journalism 193–94
SEMA 73
sensationalism 44, 138, 143–44; the senses 195–96, 199
Setright, L. J. K. 69
sex news value 43
Seymour Ure, C. 33
Shoemaker, P. 56–57

shopping online 83
Shulman, Alexandra 91
significance 57
simplification 41–42, 141–42, 147, 158
Simpson, George 154
Singer, J. B. 51–53, 55
Sitwell, William 100
Sky Ride events 16
Sky TV 17
Slater, Nigel 104–5
Slattery, Jon 131
Smash Hits 118
Smith, Delia 101
Smith, Patrick 126–27, 130, 133
Snow, C. P. 134, 137
Soames, G. 85
Sochi Winter Olympics, 2014 13
social media 33, 130–31
social responsibility 36, 46
Society of Editors 125
Society of Environmental Journalists 66
Society of Motor Manufacturers and
    Traders 76
software packages 7
soundbites 54, 179
Sounds 110, 117, 121
sources *see* contacts/sources
specialisation (other professions) 3, 136,
    140
specialist media 17, 25, 172, 192, 196
Speciality Food Magazine 99–100
spectacle 43; *The Spectator* 66, 101
speed 51, 53–55, 57, 84, 87, 144
Spektor, Regina 111
spin doctors 32, 36
sponsorship 151
sports reporting 11–19, 162
Spotify 111
staff turnover rates 165
Standen, Dirk 79, 83
star columnists 18–19
statistics interpretation 22, 40, 42,
    125–26
status of specialisms 80, 91
Stead, W. T. 43
stereotypes 174, 176–77
Steward, George 33
Stocking, S. H. 141, 143
Stone, Chris 15
street style 88–89, 93
Streetpeeper 89
student labour 4, 24, 86, 93
Sturmey, Henry 71
Style 82

Style Hunter 93
style over substance 34
Style Rookie 83
Style.com 79, 83
stylists 85–87
subcultures 112, 114
subjectivity 8, 135, 193
subliminal effect 54–55
sub-specialisms 74–75, 192, 194
Sun 43, 69, 82
Sunday Telegraph 24
Sunday Times 66, 69, 82; *The Sunday Times*
    1, 24, 26–28, 101
Sunday Times Travel 172
Super Bowl 12
supermarket magazines 81, 100
supplements 1, 21, 82, 96, 100, 102,
    172–73
survival courses 184
Sutherland, Louis 148
Syed, Matthew 19
Sykes, Rosie 96
symposia 151

Talbot, M. 118
Taliban 183–84, 186, 188
Taste 100
taste cultivation 98–99, 101–2
tastemakers 114, 120
Tatler 80–81, 83
Taylor, S. 71
TechCrunch 127
technical language 163
technology 13, 15, 27, 31–32, 51–54,
    76, 92, 102–4, 131–33 *see also* blogs/
    bloggers; internet; online journalism
Telegraph 5, 24, 27, 30, 36, 100, 165
telephone hotlines 47
Temple, Robert 156
terrorist attacks 51, 57
Tesco 81
Tesco Magazine 100
testing drugs 149–50, 152–53,
    156–58
Tett, G. 20
Thatcher, Margaret 21, 32–34
theming 89
Theroux, Paul 175
Thesiger, Wilfred 176–77
ThisisLondon.co.uk 103
Thompson, Hunter S. 54
thought leaders 151, 156–58
threshold news value 41–42
Thubron, Colin 171

Thurman, Neil 103
time constraints 56, 135, 138, 140,
    142–43, 145, 165, 186
The Times 19, 24, 27, 30, 53, 100–101,
    137, 142, 161
timing 87–88, 128
Titchener, Campbell 193
titillation news value 43
Ton, Tommy 89
Top Gear 69, 71
Topshop 80
torts 164, 168
tourism industry 172, 179
trade publications 82, 88, 99–100, 161,
    192, 196
traditional journalism 50, 56
training 9, 25, 92, 104, 162, 165–66, 169,
    184, 196; on the job 3, 5, 15, 22, 28,
    69, 75, 77, 86, 93
translation of jargon 147, 158
transparency 33, 46
travel journalism 171–80
trends 88, 129–30
TripAdvisor.co.uk 102–3
trivialisation 36
True, Everett 110, 112–14
Trump, Donald 57
trust 7, 27, 35, 111, 143, 188
truth 8–9, 113, 135, 178–79
Tuchman, G. 144
Tumblr 84
Tungate, M. 85, 87, 91
TV Hits 86
TV news 12, 21, 30–32, 46–47, 51, 66
Twitter 11, 14–15, 18, 51, 53–55, 76, 79,
    84–85, 114–15, 119, 126–27, 130–32,
    162

Ugille, P. 102
uncertainty, elimination of 141–42
unions 22
universities 19, 22, 35, 65, 69–70, 77, 85,
    92, 117, 147
updating 55, 82, 133, 138
UPI 50
USA 7, 15, 22; and UK journalism 40,
    50–58
user-generated content 51–52, 121

Valentine, G. 97
value questions 117
veracity 51, 53–55, 57, 138, 144,
    164
Vernon, Polly 90

Versace 80
vertical media 51–52, 56
Vidal, John 59, 96
video 72
Vinexpo 198
Vinitaly 198–99
violence news value 43
vocational courses 86
Vogue 80, 83, 85, 89, 91, 101
Vox 110
voyeurism 43

Waitrose Food Illustrated 100
Wall Street crash, 1929 20–21
Wall Street Journal 21, 24, 154
The Wall Street Journal 127
Wallpaper 83
Wanderlust 172
Waples, John 28
war reporting 181–91
Washington Post 53, 154
watchdog reporting 8, 40, 149
Watson, Tom 36
Watt, Holly 5
Weapons of Mass Destruction 182,
    188
Weaver, D. 51, 53
Web 2.0 52, 116
websites 27, 81–83, 87, 102–3,
    197
Weigold, M. F. 134–36, 140–42
Weingarten, Christopher R. 114–16
Wells, Steven 113
Wenger, Arsene 13
West (Fred and Rosemary) case 47
Westminster briefing system 31–35, 37
WGSN 88
What Car? 71
Wheels Magazine 77
White, Michael 33, 36
White, Victoria 86
WikiLeaks 52, 56
wikis 52–53
Wilkins, Sasha 83
Williams, Raymond 111
Williamson, David 101
Wilson, E. 84
Wilson, James 21
Wine 200
Winner, Michael 101
Winnett, Robert 5
Wintour, Anna 85
wire-copy 137, 142
Wiseman, E. 108

Witherow, John 28
Woloshin, S. 142
women's press 99
wonder drugs stories 150,
    153–55
Wood, Lucy 85–86, 88
Wood, Roy 101–2
Woolf Reforms 161
Word of Mouth blog 103
working conditions 184, 186
World Student Games 13
World War I 33
World War II 182

writing skills 12–14, 24, 70–71, 85–87, 93,
    109, 111–13, 115, 119–20, 194, 196
WSJ.com 22, 24

Yahoo News 27
Yes Minister 6
Yorkshire Post 27, 60
You 82
YouTube 14, 51, 79, 116

Zajecka, John 154
Zappa, Frank 108
Zeitgeist 84